Praise for *The Towering World of Jimmy Choo*

"In my tenure as the CEO of Gucci, I had dealings with literally hundreds of journalists. Lauren Goldstein Crowe was, without a doubt, the one who was best able to convey the crazy world of luxury goods at a crazy time . . . Sagra Maceira de Rosen equally stood out as the only luxury goods analyst who understood that it takes more to make this business tick than a good spreadsheet."—Domenico De Sole, chairman of Tom Ford International and former CEO of Gucci Group

"A most insightful and entertaining look at the luxury goods world from the most qualified authors!"—Jacques-Franck Dossin, CEO of JF Dossin Brand Advisory and former head of Luxury Goods Equity Research at Goldman Sachs International

"Unputdownable! An intoxicating combination of a great business book and a juicy novel."—Sahar Hashemi, author of *Anyone Can Do It*

"Few emerging brands make it to the pinnacle of luxury and there are a million reasons for this. *The Towering World of Jimmy Choo* is a painstakingly researched, insightful, and easy-to-read primer on the science of spotting, building, nourishing, and selling luxury brands. At last, here is a practical must-read (for everyone) on what it takes to create value in the luxury goods sector."—Antoine Colonna, managing director and head of Luxury Goods Research, Merrill Lynch

"The behind-the-scenes inner workings of the fascinating worlds of private equity and luxury goods finally unveiled. A great distraction from the credit crunch for both financiers and fashion addicts."—Nick O'Donohoe, managing director and head of Global Research at J.P. Morgan

"Lauren Goldstein Crowe and Sagra Maceira de Rosen have artfully woven the intriguing business story of the 'perfect storm' that is Jimmy Choo's unprecedented rise within the luxury industry. They have skillfully captured the unique blend of personalities involved, creating a page-turner for the business-minded as well as fashion-conscious reader."—Marty Wikstrom, founding partner of Atelier Management LLC and non-executive director of Compagnie Financière Richemont SA

THE TOWERING WORLD
OF JIMMY CHOO

THE TOWERING WORLD OF
JIMMY CHOO

*A Glamorous Story of Power, Profits,
and the Pursuit of the Perfect Shoe*

LAUREN GOLDSTEIN CROWE

and

SAGRA MACEIRA DE ROSEN

B L O O M S B U R Y

NEW YORK · BERLIN · LONDON

Published by Bloomsbury USA, New York

All papers used by Bloomsbury USA are natural, recyclable products made from wood grown in well-managed forests. The manufacturing processes conform to the environmental regulations of the country of origin.

LIBRARY OF CONGRESS CATALOGING-IN-PUBLICATION DATA

Crowe, Lauren Goldstein.
The towering world of Jimmy Choo : a glamorous story of power, profits, and the pursuit of the perfect shoe / Lauren Goldstein Crowe and Sagra Maceira de Rosen.—1st U.S. ed.
p. cm.
Includes index.
ISBN-13: 978-1-59691-391-2 (hardcover)
ISBN-10: 1-59691-391-6 (hardcover)
1. Choo, Jimmy, 1961– 2. Women's shoes—Design—20th century. 3. Fashion design—History—20th century. 4. Mellon, Tamara, 1967– 5. Fashion. I. Rosen, Sagra Maceira de. II. Title.
GT2130.D6613 2007
391.4'13082—dc22
2008044378

First U.S. Edition 2009

1 3 5 7 9 10 8 6 4 2

Typeset by Hewer Text UK Ltd, Edinburgh
Printed in the USA by Quebecor World Fairfield

To Zoë and Zachary Crowe and their
great-grandfather Harold Goldstein

To Ian Rosen

CONTENTS

One

GLAMORAMA =
BUSINESS BONANZA

ON THE EVENING OF May 25, 2005, a photograph of a naked
Tamara Mellon, lying on her stomach wearing a diamond ring
and balancing jewel-studded Jimmy Choo sandals on the inverted
soles of her feet, was placed at the front of Christie's auction hall in
London. In front of the photo stood the real Tamara, the president
of the luxury brand Jimmy Choo. In a low-cut black chiffon dress
that showed off her cleavage and in stiletto shoes—as always, by
Jimmy Choo—Tamara looked calm. Especially calm given that in
front of her, ogling her photo, were hundreds of her closest friends
and colleagues armed with cards holding three-digit numbers. Every
seat was taken—the best reserved for those most likely to bid—
and the aisles and back of the sweltering room were packed full of
beautiful women in expensive dresses accompanied by their men,
dressed as if law decreed it, in blue suits with perfectly pressed white
shirts.

"One hundred thousand pounds," the auctioneer said. "Do we
have one hundred thousand pounds?"

Tamara wrinkled her nose, rolled her eyes, and then looked
pointedly at the man in the front row with the gray hair. In response,
he raised his card. Again.

"We have one hundred thousand pounds," said the auctioneer. "Do we have one hundred ten thousand pounds?"

A wave of a card on the other side of the aisle gave him his answer: "We have one hundred ten thousand pounds."

Tamara turned again to the man in the front row and arched a perfectly plucked eyebrow. His hand went up. And then so did a hand on the other side of the room. The exchange continued until Walid Juffali, a Saudi Arabian billionaire, had spent £220,000 (or $396,000) for the naked Tamara. He beat out Flavio Briatore, the Formula One car racing boss and one of Tamara's old flames, who was seated in the front row next to Elton John. It was shy of the £270,000 ($486,000) that Juffali had spent on the naked Kate Moss moments before, but Tamara knew Kate would fetch a prettier price. After all, a photo taken by Sam Taylor-Wood, like Kate's, was considered art. But someone had to follow Kate on auction night, so Tamara sacrificed herself. What choice did she have? She was the reason everyone was at the "4 Inches" auction and book launch. Although the proceeds from the photos of famous women in Cartier jewels and Jimmy Choo shoes would go to support the Elton John AIDS Foundation and not Jimmy Choo, Tamara knew she had an obligation to make the evening as pleasant as possible for all the lesser-than-Kate celebrities she had convinced to disrobe. And thanks in a small way to Briatore, and in a very large way to Juffali (who later said he planned to open a museum to show the huge number of photos he bought that night), the *completely* naked Tamara ("I didn't wear a G-string, to save on retouching," she later said) did not do too badly. By the end of the auction, she would outearn the naked Victoria Beckham (£180,000/$324,000), the naked Elle Macpherson (£160,000/$288,000), and the naked Paris Hilton (£25,000/$45,000) to be the second-highest earner of the night. (All currencies are converted at rate of period referred to.)

The presence of so many financiers like Juffali was unusual for a Jimmy Choo party. Usually it was the wives who came to the launches and various store openings, leaving their husbands at home—or, more likely, at work. But an auction requires a bigger checkbook than a store opening, and since it was all in the name of charity, the husbands were on show. "There were some serious people out there tonight," Tamara said. "I never expected to raise that kind of money."[1] Maybe not on photos anyway. By now Tamara was getting used to mingling with the high-finance crowd—not just as a pretty face, but as a part of their world.

Six months earlier Tamara had fared even better at an altogether different sort of auction. It did not take place at Christie's (where it was so hot that the auctioneer had to warn the audience not to fan themselves with their numbers lest they find themselves owners of a naked Macy Gray). Its control center was the somber offices of the prestigious investment bank N M Rothschild & Sons. Instead of a wisecracking auctioneer, the posh accent of banker Akeel Sachak ensured that the proceedings were conducted with a degree of decorum. And instead of photos of naked women, on the block was the company that Tamara had spent the last eight years building— Jimmy Choo Ltd. The company sold for a price nearly five hundred times greater than her photograph—£101 million (or $182 million). And less than two years after the night of the "4 Inches" auction, the company would be sold again, this time for an astounding £185 million ($340 million), giving her a net worth of upward of £50 million ($73 million).

The transactions caught the attention of investment bankers everywhere. Not only were they a bright spot in what had been a relatively quiet time in mergers and acquisitions in the luxury goods sector, but they also demonstrated that a luxury brand need not be hundreds of years old to be successful. Until Jimmy Choo, the big luxury success stories came from brands like Prada and Gucci that had been part of the cultural or shopping landscape for generations. These two Jimmy Choo deals meant it was possible to build a brand from scratch and make an enormous amount of money in the process. In subsequent years, all of the key protagonists in the launch and buildup of Jimmy Choo would try to duplicate the success of the brand. Tamara would convince movie mogul Harvey Weinstein to buy the iconic U.S. fashion brand Halston in 2007, with the financial backing of a private equity partner, and she would join the company's board of directors. Phoenix Equity Partners, the first private equity owner of Jimmy Choo, would later buy (and sell) the British handbags and accessories brand Radley. Robert Bensoussan, CEO of Jimmy Choo from 2001 to 2007, launched Sirius Equity, his own investment fund to buy and sell luxury brands. In 2008, with Phoenix, he purchased a majority stake in LK Bennett, another fast-growing British shoe brand. Lion Capital, the private equity firm that purchased Jimmy Choo from Phoenix, would in 2008 explore the possibility of an investment in Italian designer brand Roberto Cavalli, bidding against another large buyout fund, Candover (which was being advised by Bensoussan) before Cavalli changed his mind about selling the company.

But even as they plowed optimistically on, the question remained: Was the success of Jimmy Choo a model for a new age of luxury brands or merely just a case of a brand being in the right place at the right time?

Two

THE HARD TIMES OF A VOGUETTE

VOGUE HOUSE, THE LONDON office of the Condé Nast publishing company on Hanover Square, is not usually regarded as an incubator for eager entrepreneurs. The young women—and they are mostly women—who take the low-paying but high-glamour jobs at the various Condé Nast magazines such as *Vogue*, *Tatler*, and *Condé Nast Traveler* tend to behave like young ladies from another era. Posh, polite, and politically conservative, they view their future earning potential more in terms of husbands than careers. Very rarely do they become the founders of multimillion-dollar businesses.

Tamara Yeardye, a one-time *Vogue* girl, would eventually break the mold due in large part to the influence of her father, Tom Yeardye. "He always had a career path in mind for her," said Phyllis Walters, a publicist who employed Tamara when she was still in her teens. Tamara's brother Gregory says that Tamara was always very driven. She was bound for success, whatever her career path. "She always wanted to be independently wealthy," he said. "Every once in a while Dad wouldn't buy her something that she wanted, and I think she thought, 'If I get rich myself, I can have whatever I want and I won't have to ask anyone.'" Tamara credits her ambitious nature to her years in the United States. Tamara and her younger brothers, Daniel and Gregory, moved to California in 1976 when their father moved the family to be closer to hairdresser Vidal Sassoon, with whom he was working. The budding shoe mogul lived with her family in a spacious house with a pool on North Whittier Drive in Beverly Hills, ironically next door to Nancy Sinatra, who sang "These Boots Are Made for Walkin'." The suburban American houses couldn't have been more different from the low ceilings in the Tudor Berkshire cottage in which Tamara had spent her early life. Although she had attended Catholic school in the United Kingdom, in the United States the eight-year-old Tamara was sent to the local public elementary school, El Rodeo, at the bottom of their road. "Vidal told us we were crazy to consider sending the kids to private school in the U.S.," said her mother, Ann Yeardye. "He said, 'El Rodeo is a good school—everyone sends their kids there.'" Built in 1927, the El Rodeo building was as grand as most British private schools—with sprawling grass and the feel of a Mediterranean estate—and it had the reputation for being just as good. But in true Beverly Hills fashion, the school's students had a natural fascination with clothes. Without uniforms, the students from well-off families were enormously competitive in their dress. "I used to go shopping with all the other mothers," said Ann. "When the bills started coming in, Tom said, 'These are for *Tamara's* clothes?'" Ann was buying what the other mothers bought for their children—designer clothes from brands like Gucci and Fiorucci. The bills were one thing, but then began the early-morning phone calls. Tamara said, "I'd call my school friends every morning to find out what they were wearing." After just a few months, Ann and Tom put Tamara into a private Catholic school, Marymount, in nearby Brentwood. When it was time for high school, Tom and Ann wanted her to continue at Marymount, but a willful Tamara was insistent that she should go to Beverly Hills High with her old El Rodeo crowd. As a compromise, Tom suggested boarding school in the UK and, to his surprise, Tamara said okay.

In 1981 Tom moved the family back to the UK and Tamara went off to Heathfield School—an all-girls boarding school in Ascot. One of the oldest girls' schools in England, Heathfield was founded in

1899. It is now officially known as Heathfield St. Mary's after a 2006 merger with another school. Unofficially it is frequently referred to as the sister school to Eton, England's oldest and most prestigious boys' school. At the time of the merger one alum wrote, "Heathfield had a ferociously snobbish culture, in which it really mattered who your family was, where you lived and what kind of husky and gumboots you wore," she said referring to the jackets and boots that are a staple of British country life. "The weekly table plan for the dining room listed girls by their formal titles, so everyone knew whether they were passing the salt to Lady Louisa, the Hon. Henrietta or little Miss Nobody-in-Particular."[2]

Fresh from Los Angeles, Tamara, with a wardrobe filled with bright designer clothes, was looked at by the English ladies-in-training of Heathfield as if she were an alien—not just from another country, but from another planet. Away from her parents, Tamara's inherent rebellious nature could flourish more fully. She was called in to see the headmistress not only for cutting class but for disappearing entirely for days on end. She finished at Heathfield when she was sixteen years old, and knowing university held little interest for her, Tom and Ann sent her to do a stint at the Institut Alpin Videmanette, a prestigious finishing school near the jet-set ski resort of Gstaad, Switzerland. Her parents wanted her to focus on things like polishing her skiing skills and learning French, but she also became friendly with the ne'er-do-well aristocrats and through them mastered the art of serious partying on an international scale. One evening she and her girlfriends escaped from the school by climbing out a small window in the boiler room. From there they jumped off a garage roof into the snow and were picked up by a group of boys and taken to a club in Gstaad for a night of dancing.

After finishing school, Tamara spent six months in Paris. "Tom said he'd support her as long as she came back fluent in French," Ann said. To ensure that it happened, he called his friends in Paris and told them that if they invited her to dinner, they should not allow her to speak any English.

While the kids were in boarding school, Tom and Ann moved to Port Grimault in the South of France. They also bought a house on London's Chester Row for Daniel and Tamara to live in. Back from Paris and still only seventeen, Tamara found that the house was a convenient place for other hip youngsters like Nick Thorp, founder of the popular band Curiosity Killed the Cat, to gather, drink, and hang out. One of her set remembers Tamara's unique way of asking for spending money. "She'd phone her father and say, 'Remember that twenty pounds you gave me yesterday? I spent it on records. Could I have some more?'" Tom began to reply that he would match whatever money she made. "He [Tom] had a very tough childhood, growing up in Mill Hill in London during the war," Tamara said. "He couldn't bear that spoilt brat sort of thing at all, so I was brought up very differently."[3]

Tamara took a stall at the Portobello Market and began selling the designer clothes that her father had bought her. Tom realized there was no separating Tamara and fashion. Keen to see her in a job that did not involve manning an outdoor market stall, Tom put in a phone call to one of his old friends, Sidney Burstein, whom he had met through Vidal Sassoon. Sidney's wife, Joan, was a close friend of Vidal's—he was her hairdresser—and she was also the founder of one of London's most chic shops, Browns on South Molton Street. In the wake of the Swinging Sixties, Mrs. B, as Joan is affectionately known in London's fashion circles, had become famous for bringing foreign designers to London. "Tommy—he was such a good-looking guy—rang Sidney and said, 'I think you'd look after her well,'" Joan remembers. "I think he wanted her trained." Tamara made an immediate impression on the boss. "She always looked great," Joan says. "She always had an eye and a great spirit." Tamara was given a job on the selling floor of Shop 24—the Browns empire now controls several storefronts on South Molton—selling clothes by Azzedine Alaia. There she held her own, despite being far younger than most of the other sales assistants working on the floor. "She was very industrious," Joan remembers. "She always wanted to know about things. She was very bright—you can just tell with people. You could tell by the way she walked."

Tamara also took full advantage of the new job to indulge her passion for designer clothes. "When I left, I owed them more money than I'd earned," she said.[4] Another Browns employee from the day remembers Tamara coming to work dressed in tight black Alaia bike shorts—not that Tamara biked in. Every morning she made the commute from Belgravia to Mayfair in the Fiat Tom had bought her to keep her from driving his car. ("Tom thought she was a terrible driver," said Ann. "He once insisted on getting out of the car when she was driving and hailed himself a taxi.") She would park directly in front of the store on the pedestrian street. "The tickets would just pile up," another former Browns' staffer, the publicist Mandi Lennard, remembers. "But she never cared."

Tamara's next job also came through her father's intervention. Tom got in touch with Michael Collis, the son-in-law of Browns' Joan Burstein, married to her daughter Caroline, who worked as a buyer at Browns. When she married Michael, a hairdresser who knew Tom from his days at Vidal Sassoon, her parents gave them a unique wedding present—a hair salon. Located on South Molton Street, within spitting distance of Browns, the couple decided to name it Molton Brown. Tom asked Michael if he had any ideas about what Tamara could do next. Michael put in a call on her behalf to an old friend, Phyllis Walters, the owner of a public relations firm on nearby Bruton Street.

"I always had need for a good assistant," said Walters, who had about a dozen working for her at the time. So Tamara left the sales floor at Browns, and Walters put her to work doing all of the entry-level things a PR assistant would do—running samples of clothing from the hot designers of the day like Catherine Walker and Versace over to Vogue House and keeping track of press clippings. "Tamara was very willing and a very nice person to have around," remembers Walters. "At nineteen if they can manage to get in on time and dock clothes in and out, that's pretty much it." She also remembers Tamara's making an effort to wear the latest fashions—

oversized camp shirts by Equipment and skintight dresses by Alaia. "I hired quite a few boys, too. It was very entertaining to watch them try to deal with this girl who wouldn't necessarily be wearing the underwear she should have with her low-cut tops."

Following her stint in PR, Tamara took a job working as the assistant to Charlotte Pilcher, the fashion director at the UK edition of *Mirabella* magazine. Former U.S. *Vogue* editor Grace Mirabella had launched the magazine with Rupert Murdoch in the U.S. in 1989. The UK edition was launched in September 1990 and closed in May 1991. When she heard the news Tamara called her dad and asked him to buy the magazine. "She said, 'Dad, it's all set up. Everything is in place,'" remembers Ann. Tom replied, "If Rupert Murdoch can't make money on it, I sure can't make money on it."[5]

But another magazine job awaited Tamara—one at *Vogue*. Liz Tilberis, then editor of *Vogue*, called her friend and Tamara's former boss, Phyllis Walters, to say they were in need of an assistant. Phyllis promptly recommended Tamara. "The ideal girls for *Vogue* care about how they present themselves. They commit to wanting to be in the industry. They also have to be quite cool. They can't be fazed by celebrity. Tamara grew up surrounded by drama and celebrity. She knew these people."

In December 1991, at twenty-four, Tamara began her career at *Vogue* as an assistant to fashion director Sarajane Hoare. Hoare told *Vanity Fair* that it was clear from the beginning that Tamara had a special affinity for shoes and an attention to detail that meant she would not settle until she found the perfect shoe—even if it didn't exist. And that's where Jimmy Choo would come in. He was more than happy to work with her on custom designs to suit her photo shoots.

The routine at *Vogue* was less demanding than that of a small PR agency or a start-up company, and the invitations were even more frequent—invitations that enabled Tamara to partake with gusto in a wild nightlife scene. She and her fabulous friends spent night after night dancing at clubs, drinking glass after glass of champagne, and snorting the not-so-occasional line of cocaine. Tamara said, "Those were the days when we were all single—we wanted to go out every night, to every party, club and restaurant, to be everywhere." Her friend Tamara Beckwith, a famous London party girl in her own right, said, "There is never a dull moment with T on board. She is always having fun and she is always really wild." Beckwith said that although Tamara was well known for her glamorous Alaia wardrobe, she was also down to earth. "One time we went to this club opening, at which no jeans were allowed. I warned everyone, except T, as she never wore jeans anyway. On this night, however, she did, and upon arrival was forced to borrow a pleated puff skirt with an elasticized waist—it wasn't even gross enough to be cool—it was horrendous. But T didn't complain, which sums her up."[6]

Despite the nighttime antics, Tamara was, for a while, able to keep her nose to the *Vogue* grindstone. After a year she was promoted to fashion assistant, the title she held until she left. But by 1995 the partying was getting to be too much for her. Tamara was more often than not walking into Vogue House with a hangover. In May 1995 she resigned her position at *Vogue* and packed herself off to a rehab facility. She said, "It was an emotional rock bottom for me, and I got scared ... [of being] broke, with no children and no husband, and having achieved nothing. Fear motivated me to get better," she said.[7] She went to her mother asking for help. "I'm sick and I want to get better," she said to Ann. Ann's first thought was that Tamara's hypochondriac tendencies were getting the best of her. "We were always in and out of doctors' offices," she said. "Every office on Harley Street knows us." But then Tamara said she had booked herself at Farm Place, one of the Priory Group's hospitals. Farm Place specializes in addiction and has treated some of the UK's most famous names. Ann went to Tom, broke the news to him, and asked for a check for Tamara's rehab fees.

Six weeks later Tamara was back in London, drug and alcohol free. She was also committed to a new business idea she had devised. One of the first calls she made when she returned was to her favorite shoemaker—Jimmy Choo.

Three

A Choo Is Born

In penang, malaysia, in 1969, a small, skinny boy achieved the first real milestone of his young life. He had made, from scratch, a pair of shoes. They were a pair of classic black slingbacks with a diamanté buckle, and they were for his mother. The boy's father, Choo Kee Yin, was an immigrant from China and went through the traditional route of apprenticeship, which meant before he was taught to make shoes, he cooked meals for the shoemakers and was often sent out to run errands, like buying cigarettes for them. With time, Choo Kee became one of the best-known shoemakers in Penang. When his son turned nine he started to pass on his trade to Jimmy. For the years of his training, young Jimmy was only allowed to study and assist his father (and mother, who also worked as a shoemaker). The years as an apprentice did not discourage him— they taught him to love shoes as he loved his parents. "My parents were shoemakers and I have followed my father's lead. He inspired me," said Jimmy.[8]

In 1973, when he was just a teenager, Jimmy was sent to London to visit some members of his extended Chinese family. At that time Penang was in the middle of an economic crisis, which had been brought about by the revoking of the city's free port status. The few job opportunities that existed in Penang were to be found in manufacturing electronics, not in making shoes. When Jimmy got to London, he spoke to his relatives of his love of shoes. They told him about a local school that specialized in the craft of shoemaking: the Leather Trades School, better and more recently known as Cordwainers College.

Cordwainers—the word comes from the Spanish city of Córdoba, famed for its leather—has an illustrious past and can trace its history back to the earliest days of the shoe trade in England. In the twelfth century shoemakers in England were using the elegant Spanish leather and had begun calling themselves cordwainers. That became the name of the first guild of shoemakers in the UK, founded in Oxford in 1131. The London shoemakers followed suit, and their guild became the Worshipful Company of Cordwainers in 1272. Until the sixteenth century, a cordwainer was a shoemaker who used only new leather. This placed the cordwainer craftsman above a cobbler, who would work with used leather. In the Victorian age the traditional apprentice system in England gave way to the rise of the technical college, and in 1887 many of the disparate guilds of shoemakers throughout the country came together to found the Leather Trades School in Bethnal Green, East London. In 1989 the Leather Trades School was given its current name, Cordwainers College, and in 2000 it became part of the London College of Fashion, a one-hundred-year-old UK institution. Cordwainers' current promotional materials boast of its illustrious graduates—not just Jimmy Choo, but Patrick Cox, Emma Hope, and Linda Bennett, founder of LK Bennett. It portrays itself as the shoe design equivalent of Central Saint Martins, the famous London fashion school that has spawned such talents as John Galliano and Alexander McQueen.

But Jimmy's most notable impressions of London were not of Cordwainers. "I came to London, and my first impression was that everybody looked the same," he said. "You think all Chinese people look the same, and I found that with the English. All the buildings seemed very uniform, too. I can see now that they are very varied, but at the time they all seemed to be of a standard British type, which was nothing like the Asian style of building. I also found the weather very cold, and the food … well, not what I was used to! But I stayed."[9]

Jimmy enrolled at Cordwainers twice. The first time was soon after his arrival in London in 1973. He received a diploma, with distinction, from the school in 1974. He then returned to Penang to work with his father. After several years, however, he returned to Cordwainers for additional courses. The school had not changed much, but it was about to. Cordwainers typically had places for thirty students a year, but it rarely attracted that many. It was a school that had become focused on training workers sent from foreign factories and then shipping them back home. Indeed, a key source of students was Bata, the Toronto-based family-owned shoe company, which had been the largest shoemaker in the world since the 1930s. In 1939 Bata was making more than fifty million pairs of shoes a year, which were sold in sixty countries around the globe. Bata would send its best and brightest from places as distant as India and China to learn the trade. Most of the students spoke little English, and few considered themselves to be part of the fashion world. "On our first day we were taken out on the street and shown which way to look when crossing," said Patrick Cox, the Canadian-born London-based shoe designer whose fame began with Wannabe loafers, which he designed shortly after graduating in the 1980s. "We were given tests on the Dewey decimal system. We were taught how to answer the phone: 'Hello, 97342.'" Students at Cordwainers were there to learn how to make shoes—not how to design them.

Jimmy was just another in a long history of downtrodden foreign students. He told the *Financial Times*, "I learned my English in this country … People laughed at me, and at college one teacher said: 'You can't speak English, speak properly.' So I was quiet, no interviews for me. When I first started [my business] in 1988 I didn't give interviews. I was very quiet, because I remembered he'd said: 'You don't speak English very well.'"

Jimmy graduated from Cordwainers for the second time in

1983, but by now the school was at the dawn of a major shake-up. The post-punk, fashion-mad generation of students who had been revolutionizing London's design institutions had also begun to infiltrate the halls of Cordwainers and were telling the teachers what they wanted to learn, not the other way around. Students like Patrick Cox, Emma Hope, and John Moore had visions of what they wanted shoes to look like—visions that were influenced more by people like Vivienne Westwood, the fashion designer who brought punk style to a designer clientele, than by the shoemaking tradition. What they wanted was to learn the skills they needed to realize their designs.

But that wasn't so easy. Not only was access to the tools at the college strictly controlled, but the construction aids and materials available for crafting shoes were strictly run of the mill. Furthermore, the professors who had taught there for decades were not about to start changing their methods for a bunch of odd-looking, curiously dressed Brits with little respect for the institution. "They didn't know what to do with us," said one former student. "They would show us something and we would say, 'We're not going to do that.'" When showing visitors the school, one teacher would point to the new, fashionably dressed students and with a certain degree of disdain say, "Note the garb." So uncomfortable was the relationship of the school with its early trendy students that when Patrick Cox decided to take time off to design the runway shoes for a Vivienne Westwood show, school officials threatened to dismiss him. In the end, fashion won. "Within a few years of graduating, there were lines of Japanese students waiting to enroll because they wanted to be me or John Moore," said Patrick. But after graduation, and in order to produce the shoes they envisioned, Cordwainers graduates needed help, like a place to set up a workshop and the raw materials and components of the shoes. And they found it in the most unlikely of places: the deepest bowels of London's East End neighborhood of Hackney.

On Kingsland Road, right in the midst of Hackney, there was a very large, very ugly building with a very grand name—the Metropolitan. This was short for the Metropolitan Hospital, which is what the building had housed for close to one hundred years, from 1885 to 1977. Slowly the empty hospital rooms began to fill with all sorts of businesses in need of cheap space—from printers to designers, including a shoemaker named Jimmy Choo. But the new tenants did not make the building any more appealing or grand. It soon started to be known as the Hospital, rather than the Metropolitan. To get inside the building, one had to go through a chain-link fence, into a small dark and dank brick shed covered with weeds. The door was often left unlocked, and once inside the premises there were no signs and no directions to lead visitors through the maze of hallways and rooms. Even in this low-end venue, Jimmy's workshop stood out as being minimally equipped. He lived with his wife and baby in a tidy and comfortable first-floor flat not far from his workplace, but he spent most of his waking hours at his workshop at the Hospital, a room with little more than a sewing machine and a worktable. Jimmy branded the shoes he made as Lucky Shoes, a reference to his Buddhist faith. The only distribution outlet was a stall at the local market, which he manned himself.

Another Cordwainers graduate, Elizabeth Stuart-Smith, worked out of the studio next to Jimmy's at the Hospital. Elizabeth was part of the trendy circle that was starting to achieve some recognition in the fashion world, but she recognized that the hardworking Malaysian next door was a far more talented craftsman than she was. She asked him if in addition to his own label he would help her make the shoes for her blossoming label. He readily agreed.

Making high-end shoes in the UK at this time was no easy task, even for Jimmy. The construction of a shoe takes a number of components—uppers, heels, and insoles. They are all made separately and assembled together to make the finished product. For high-end shoes, most of these components come from Italy, as do the best leathers and skins. But Italian suppliers had little interest in selling to someone like Jimmy or Elizabeth, as they were only making a handful of pairs. Hidden in London's East End was another rare resource—the last remaining British factory for high-end shoes.

In the 1950s a man of Turkish descent, Mehmet Kurdash, had the dream to create handmade glamorous footwear in the UK and established Gina Shoes on Old Street in East London. Kurdash had a love of beautiful things and an appreciation for beautiful women: His company was named after his favorite actress, the Italian beauty Gina Lollobrigida. In 1952, according to company lore, he was the first to introduce the stiletto, already a fashion phenomenon in Italy, to the UK. The Gina factory moved to Abbot Street, within close proximity to Cordwainers and the Hospital (which was then still a hospital) in the 1960s. At that time Gina was just one of many shoe factories in the area. In the 1980s the sons of Mehmet, Attila, Aydin, and Altan Kurdash, were running the business and Gina was well known in the shoe world. It didn't take long for Jimmy, like dozens of designers before him, to find them. The Gina factory was furnished with all the machines, tools, and supplies one would find in a top-notch Italian factory, from those used to make the lasts and heels to special machines for cutting leather. The place had a comfortable homey atmosphere to boot—the boys' mother would regularly drop in with a roast chicken and lay out lunch on a linen tablecloth, and the sons were more than happy to help out fellow designers by selling them supplies in the small quantities in which the Italians refused to deal. Jimmy would frequently pop in to buy small lots of leather or molds for a new toe.

The new generation of fashion-mad students like Elizabeth Stuart-Smith had another trait that their predecessors at Cordwainers lacked. They were friendly with the fashion-mad assistants at glossy magazines like *Vogue* and continually shared gossip and information. It didn't take long for word to get back to Vogue House on Hanover Square that there was a shoemaker in the Hospital that could create beautifully made, one-off pairs of shoes on short notice. Jimmy was a dream come true for any fashion magazine's market editor. If one of the magazine's stylists wanted a pair of silver knee-high boots for a shoot on short notice, a junior market editor would contact the usual suspects—or, rather, suspect. In London in the early 1990s the supply of sexy high-heeled shoes was almost monopolistically controlled by the already legendary Manolo Blahnik. But if Manolo had only produced knee-high boots in gold that season, an editor was pretty much stuck. With no cost-effective Federal Express or DHL to express-deliver to London, products from foreign designers such as Sergio Rossi or Charles Jourdan would take too long to arrive. At the time Gina was more focused on what the brothers called "mother-of-the-bride" shoes, not high fashion.

Now a new modus operandi emerged: The market editors charged with calling in the items to be used in the shoots could borrow the gold boot from Manolo's showroom in Chelsea, have it delivered to Jimmy's workshop in the East End, and ask him to re-create it in silver. Jimmy would get the credit in the magazine since the boot was technically his, not Manolo's. Before long, the eagle-eyed readers of these magazines began to wonder who this Jimmy Choo was, and slowly they began to trickle into his workshop.

The unlikely sight of a chauffeured Mercedes parked outside the chain-link fence of the Hospital had, by the late 1980s and early 1990s, become more commonplace. There is no one quite as driven as a fashionable woman looking to stand out from her friends. And in a world where money no longer matters, the best way to do so is to get a hold of something fabulous—and fabulously hard to find. And so, one by one, the chauffeur-driven cars would make their way through London's financial district, the City, past the office buildings where many of these ladies' husbands worked, through the squalor and grime of London's East End. A steady stream of high-fashion devotees arrived daily at Jimmy's door in order to have him make custom shoes to match their gowns. In his humble space they would sit on a chair and he would trace their feet on pieces of paper.

When Jimmy wasn't making shoes for the magazines or for his

blossoming private clientele, he still had his hands full making shoes for Elizabeth Stuart-Smith, whose career was taking off, giving Jimmy a solid and steady income stream. Together they invested in some basic machinery and furniture: a sewing machine, a press, a table for cutting patterns, and racks and racks for drying shoes. It was, said one visitor, "very gluey." "It got smarter," said another visitor, "but it was never smart." The walls were adorned with Jimmy's pages from *Vogue*. Elizabeth and Jimmy would stay up all night working on Elizabeth's orders, Jimmy making the shoes and Elizabeth making the coffee. But in 1988 when she started to sell to U.S. department stores, everything changed. These larger and new, more demanding customers urged her to move her production to Italy and to increase the number of pairs she made in order to bring the manufacturing costs down. Excited at the prospect of joining the big leagues, she made the move. Jimmy was not pleased to see a vast part of his livelihood disappear overnight.

Jimmy's "atelier" became a more feminine, pleasant affair after the arrival of his niece, Sandra Choi. Born on the Isle of Wight, where her father, Ming, and mother, Lai Sing, ran a Chinese restaurant, Sandra grew up in Hong Kong, raised by her grandparents for the first thirteen years of her life. As she told *People* magazine, "My parents wanted us to be educated with a Chinese background."

It did not seem to work. At thirteen she came back home to the Isle of Wight with a look that shocked her parents. She had a half-shaved head, smoked cigarettes, and was wearing baggy men's trousers. They decided to send her to a convent school. At seventeen she made her break for London—she had asked her parents to send her to fashion school, but they refused—so she went off to live with her mother's sister, Rebecca, who was married to Jimmy Choo.

Eventually, in 1991 she enrolled at Central Saint Martins College of Art & Design in the fashion design program, but after a year she left to help her uncle Jimmy full-time. "I met and attended to titled and rich clients who appeared in the social pages wearing Jimmy

Choo shoes. Then came the celebrities and stars from the movie and entertainment world."[10]

Some early clients of Jimmy Choo believe the workshop smartened up a bit when Sandra joined Jimmy in 1989. Initially Sandra's job was to fetch tea and help the customers make their choices. During the first fitting, the ladies would select which toe, which heel, what kind of material (satin or leather), what kind of buckle (plain or with crystals) they wanted. Then they would make the trip again for another fitting. And then they would return yet again, for a final fitting. After a minimum of two or three weeks their shoes would be ready and they would make yet another trip to collect them. Sandra's introduction of a chair for the ladies to sit on is remembered as a major improvement to Jimmy's studio.

However, others, like fashion and interior designer Anouska Hempel, requested that Jimmy come to them. "He was making shoes for a couple of princesses of mine," said Hempel, who is married to one of London's richest men, financier Sir Mark Weinberg. She soon asked him to make the shoes for her couture label. "We worked together for over ten years," she said. "We did extremely well together. I'm a dominating old so-and-so. I'd say I want exactly XYZ. I want the heel from Calvin, the backside from someone else, the toe thinner."

In the days when he was selling shoes from a stall, this would have been satisfying enough to Jimmy. It was a major accomplishment just to have all these rich and famous ladies beating a path to his door. However, seeing Elizabeth Stuart-Smith's and Anouska Hempel's lines take off made Jimmy want more. He began to work a bit harder at promoting himself. His designs made to coordinate with beachwear by Maxxam had their debut at the London Design Show in 1987, and he began selling to Japan, Italy, and Germany. In February 1988, the year that he and Stuart-Smith split, Jimmy complained to the trade paper *Shoe and Leather News* that the magazine credits and the sampling he was doing for other designers were not getting him any recognition. Nonetheless, later that year he won an award at the London Design Show and a feature in *Vogue*. One particular style, the Rosette, was mentioned in all the major fashion magazines. He briefly sold his shoes to a handful of stores, including Harvey Nichols, which at the time sold shoes through a concession run by shoemaker H & M Rayne.

The press was finally noticing Jimmy and the accolades were trickling in, but the business side was still a struggle. Then he got the phone call that would change his life. It was from Kensington Palace. Diana, the Princess of Wales, wanted to know if Jimmy would visit her at her home. "I was so excited I could not sleep the whole night," Jimmy said. "In fact, I was so scared of oversleeping that I practically stayed awake."[11] Princess Diana had heard of Jimmy through her well-to-do friends. As the style icon for the nation, she felt it was essential that she wear mostly British labels. And Jimmy was only too happy to turn out custom pairs in short order to match her various clothes. The two quickly became friends. Jimmy would sit cross-legged on her floor, and they would look through magazines and talk Buddhism and feng shui. "I could never design open-toed shoes for her because it seems baring toes wasn't the royal thing to do," he said.[12] She in turn would well up with tears when he told his stories of twenty-hour working days and how far he had come from Penang. "I didn't realize," she said.

Working with Diana gave Jimmy confidence to branch out. When the Kurdash brothers at Gina came to him with a proposal for a line of ready-to-wear shoes, Jimmy was ready to listen. In September 1992 Gina decided to open its first freestanding store, on London's second most expensive and exclusive shopping street—Sloane Street in Knightsbridge, at number 42. In order to make sure that the new store had the proper product assortment and something for everyone—their own designs were still directed toward an older customer—the brothers approached a couple of the better-known designers they had helped over the years and asked if they would be interested in having their shoes stocked in the new Gina boutique. Emma Hope was one. Jimmy Choo was the other. "We told him we could mass-produce some of his styles and sell them," Aydin recalls. Jimmy didn't jump at the chance. The idea made him nervous. But he knew the brothers well, and with Elizabeth Stuart-Smith's success in mind, he agreed. In 1992 the first ready-to-wear Jimmy Choo shoes appeared, not in a Jimmy Choo store, but in a Gina store. Princess Diana came, his other customers came, but the collaboration did not last long. "Jimmy didn't say anything, but you could tell from his body language that it made him uncomfortable," Aydin remarked. After they stopped producing for him, Aydin saw less of Jimmy. "He went a bit quiet then," he said.

After the Gina experiment, Jimmy began courting potential backers for his business. "He was desperate," said someone who knew him at the time. He had seen more and more examples of how his business could be, and although he was not a businessman by nature, Jimmy had seen enough to know that his current plan of making beautiful shoes by hand was simply not enough and that no matter how many twenty-hour days he worked, no matter how many family members he employed (his wife, Rebecca, a nurse when they met, went to Cordwainers so that she, too, could help out), he would never have the same success as the designers whose shoes were made in factories and not by hand. Now, more than ever before, he wanted that success. He had been to Kensington Palace. He had seen the beautiful Gina store on Sloane Street. He had seen rack after rack of Elizabeth Stuart-Smith shoes go from his workshop to Bergdorf Goodman's shelves. If only he could get the right backing, he could be every bit as successful as they were. He approached some manufacturers in Italy, but in the end he chose a pretty girl he knew from *Vogue* and her charismatic father as his backers.

To the people who had known Jimmy for years, it was quite a shock. "The next thing we knew, Tamara was on the scene," Aydin said. "I do remember telling him to be careful and to always protect his name." Never mind. In 1996, just thirteen years after he received his final degree from Cordwainers, the son of a shoemaker from Penang was on his way to becoming a household name.

But Diana would not be there to see just how big the brand bearing Jimmy's name would become. In 1997 Jimmy Choo was the only shoemaker at Princess Diana's funeral. "The last time I met her was before she left for New York for the auction of her clothes," he said. Although she wore Jimmy Choo shoes to the party before the auction, there were none in the sale. "She showed me all of the clothes for the auction but told me that she'd never auction any of my shoes," Jimmy said.[13] Princess Diana's collection of Jimmy Choos began with a pair of pink pumps. It ended with the pink ballerina flats that were meant to be delivered the day after she died. They are now one of Jimmy's most treasured possessions.

Four

LIKE FATHER, LIKE DAUGHTER

"N<small>O ONE COULD HAVE</small> built Jimmy Choo in the way Tamara has without a lot of grit and determination," said Zoe Appleyard, the venture capitalist and London socialite. "It was there in her upbringing, but it's also in her genes."[14] Indeed. Although Tom Yeardye, Tamara's father, didn't give her the cachet of the old, aristocratic British names that distinguished some of her friends, he gave her something better—killer business instincts.

In 1954 a tall, dark-haired, and ruggedly handsome twenty-four-year-old man was working in County Louth, in the village of Clogherhead, on the set of *Captain Lightfoot*. His job was to stand in for the biggest movie star of the age, the also tall, dark-haired, and handsome Rock Hudson, who was filming with Barbara Rush and Jeff Morrow. *Captain Lightfoot* was a period piece set in 1815 and featured a pair of Irish rebels who engage in various illegal activities—the usual highway robberies and dividing of spoils among the peasant folk—all in the name of the Republican cause. Morrow, the supporting man, had to take sword-fighting lessons from Basil Rathbone, the British actor known for his sword-fighting prowess in films like *The Mask of Zorro*. Hudson, who had only recently learned to ride a horse, needed more than coaching. He needed to have someone else do the riding. Fortunately, the six-foot four-inch Tom Yeardye knew how to ride. He'd been given the job of stunt double after a talent scout spotted the athletic young man in a London nightclub. It was, Tom said years later, his "accidental introduction to the pictures." It was a very lucky accident. Tom's stint in the pictures didn't get him a career, but it did get him an introduction to London's movers and shakers.

Tom had grown up in Mill Hill, a working-class neighborhood in the north of London. The son of an Irish nurse and with an English stepfather, who also worked in film, Tom found early on he had a fondness for work. While still at school he did a variety of odd jobs, from delivering newspapers to painting homes. Although he was accepted into a university, he could not afford to go. At eighteen he did a two-year stint in the service aboard the *Queen Mary*, and when he returned he began a successful career as a body double. He appeared in many films, including *Richard III*, and on the television series *The Adventures of Robin Hood*. But his big break came in March 1957 when he was being tortured as the double for Victor Mature on the set of *The Long Haul*. During a break in filming, Mature introduced him to the blonde bombshell costar of the film, Diana Dors. Diana was already developing a reputation as the British Marilyn Monroe, and her every move was being closely followed by the British tabloids.

When Tom met Diana she was in the midst of separating from her husband and manager, Dennis Hamilton. Dennis had been concerned that Diana would fall for Victor Mature, the good-looking American actor who had already gone through a string of wives. But it was his double who caught her eye. According to Damon Wise's biography of Diana, *Behind Closed Dors*, Dennis learned of Diana's crush when he went out one night, leaving her at home with a girlfriend and with a hidden tape recorder running. When he returned and played the tape, Diana's descriptions of Tom, since lost to history, sent him into a rage. It was clear that Diana and Tom's was not a platonic relationship. Dennis had a fit and threw the two women out of the house. After a few days, Dennis forgave Diana—she was, after all, his only client. But the peace did not last long. On the last Sunday in April 1957, Diana went for a drive in the country with Tom and two other friends. When she returned home, Dennis was in the house. Accounts of what happened vary, but Diana was persuaded to go into the house to talk to Dennis alone. Tom realized something was wrong and after following her inside he found Diana bleeding. Dennis was there holding a gun. Tom overpowered Dennis, knocked him unconscious, and took Diana to the doctor. Then he took her to stay with his mother in Mill Hill. The tabloids covered the incident and branded Tom "Mr. Muscles." Dennis referred to him publicly as "The Film Extra."

Diana was keen to show off her well-built new man. In January 1958 after taking note of Tom's measurements: chest, forty-seven inches; biceps, seventeen inches; thigh, twenty-four inches ("the same as my waist," Diana noted), Donald Zec, a tabloid writer from the *Daily Mirror,* asked what Tom's intentions were. Tom said acting didn't interest him anymore—he wanted to raise pigs, he joked. When Diana sold the penthouse she had shared with Dennis and purchased a fifteenth-century farmhouse with a fifteen-acre farm in Billingshurst, Sussex, called Palmers, Tom took on the job of managing the farm, where he raised horses, not pigs. In order to make the running of the operations easier, they formed a company together, Juliet Holdings, to "carry on the business of farmers and stock breeders and to conduct all kinds of entertainment business." Later Diana decided to do a variety show to boost her career, and Tom recommended she hire the comedian Richard "Dicky" Dawson to appear with her. The move improved her show but ended their relationship—Diana took up with and later married Dicky.

When his relationship with Diana ended, Tom returned to London and got into a different sort of entertainment business. In February 1959 he put all the money he had, plus some that he had raised, six thousand pounds in all, into opening a restaurant. The Paint Box was not just any restaurant. Tom had hired "ten of London's most beautiful artists' models" to pose in the nude so that customers could sketch while they ate. "I want to bring art to the average man's life," he said. The restaurant opened in March and was a success—such a success that Tom quickly expanded. In August of the same year he took over Le Condor, a club on Wardour Street, in London's West End. His plan was to turn what was once an established private member's club—which boasted the Duke of Kent as a member—into a cabaret. In an interview with the *Daily Mail*'s Robert Muller, Tom explained the secret to his success: "When Tommy Yeardye opens a place, it's a personality business. When you make your business into a personality business you've got psychology. I've been associated with Diana Dors, so people like to say they're a friend of Tommy Yeardye's. That's psychology as well."

But by the end of the first month, things turned out to be more difficult than he anticipated. Tom got a phone call offering him "insurance" for fifty pounds a week. When he insisted that he didn't need insurance, the caller said that the insurance he was offering was "different," Tom told a reporter. "That it covered a great deal of things like personal accidents and breakages." The insurance salesman called again a few days later. "It was just like a film script," said Tom. "He spoke as if he were genuinely selling insurance. He said the fifty-pounds-a-week policy was the one that had found favor with all the other clubs in the area."

In the days that followed there were a series of incidents at the club: a waiter was held up with a gun; a man driving a Jaguar tried to run Tom over one night as he left the club; and his manager was attacked by a customer wielding an iron bar, breaking his jaw in two places. A few days later Tom got another call from the mysterious insurance broker saying, "You were lucky, Mr. Yeardye. Next time you might be minus an arm or a leg." Eventually Tom decided to sell the club and his days as a restaurateur were over. At the suggestion of a friend, he moved into real estate and told a reporter, "Now I meet a different class of people entirely."

In that class was another beautiful woman, and this one gave him his next big break. Ann Davis was just eighteen when she first met her future husband. Her boyfriend at the time, a model like herself, introduced her to Tom when they bumped into him the night before Le Condor opened. "I thought, 'Who is that gorgeous man?'" Ann remembers. Tom invited the couple to the opening of the club, but they didn't attend. "I thought he was only interested in dating famous women," said Ann. At the time Tom was dating a string of glamorous women like actresses Shirley Anne Field and Sabrina Sykes. But for years Ann and Tom kept running into each other around town. Tom owned a redbrick building on Horton Street in Kensington where a lot of the models Ann worked with lived and where he himself had a flat. "We'd always pop over to his place for tea," Ann remembers. "He had this shiny black bathtub. When I saw it, I said, 'Who cleans that?' Tom replied with a wink, 'Don't worry, I have a lot of help.'"

When Ann and her boyfriend finally broke up, Tom was quick off the mark. "He phoned me that evening and said, 'Don't get sad over a broken romance, come out to dinner with me.'" On January 14, 1964, they went to London's most happening restaurant, the White Elephant, had dinner, and shared a bottle of the then fabulously chic wine Mateus Rosé. They started to date and a year after their first real date, on January 15, 1965, they married at Caxton Hall, in the registrar's office in the midst of Westminster. The London papers ran a story about the wedding under the headline "Tommy Yeardye Marries," with a list of his famous ex-girlfriends, including, of course, Diana. "He always said that dating her was the biggest mistake of his life," said Ann. "He was forever trying to live it down."

The newly married couple moved into a big house in the heart of Holland Park at 105 Ladbroke Road. Its position across from the local police station didn't prevent Ann's red Jaguar from being stolen. The couple was comfortably well off. Ann was working steadily as a model, in ads for everything from electric ranges to whiskey, though it was her television commercials for Chanel for which she would become best known. Tom had a steady income from the apartments he rented. But from the beginning Ann and Tom debated various business opportunities. "Ann and Tommy were very much in love," said Philip Rogers, who would later work with Tom at Vidal Sassoon. "They were like one person. Tom would discuss everything with her."

During one of her modeling shoots, a hairdresser asked Ann if she had ever seen Carmen rollers. She had not even heard of them. The hairdresser arrived at her house the next day with a set of electric hair rollers. "I thought they were brilliant," said Ann. "In those days we models had to do our own hair and makeup for shoots. I thought, 'No more sleeping in curlers.'" The device was deceptively simple: It was a metal rod surrounded by wax, which was encased in a curler. When plugged in, the rods would heat up, warming the wax and heating the curlers. Even if the product was expensive, Ann considered it money well spent and bought a set. When Tom's sister, a transatlantic stewardess, came to visit, she, too, fell in love with the device. Tom was looking to diversify from property (Labour Party prime minister Harold Wilson was making it much harder for landlords, explained Ann), so he gave his younger sister an assignment—check whether there was anything like the Carmen rollers on the American market. She did, and reported back that there was not. Tom and Ann then approached the man who held the UK license for the curlers and asked if he was interested in working with them to expand into America. He said no, as he couldn't afford the risk. But he invited the inventor, a Danish electrician named Arne Bybjerg Pederson, who had designed the rollers for his wife and patented them in 1963, to come to London to meet Tom and Ann. Pederson agreed to grant them the license to market them in the U.S., but insisted that they buy a minimum of five hundred machines. "They were going to retail for fifty dollars a machine. It was a huge commitment," said Ann. She remembers that they spent an additional five thousand pounds on the move to New York. Tom left his youngest sister, Kathleen, in charge of their Holland Park home and had his mother deposit the rent checks from his tenants.

In the spring of 1965 the couple moved to New York, where they lived in a prewar building at 320 East Fifty-third Street.

Coincidentally, Vidal Sassoon was also in New York, running hair shows for the cosmetics brand Charles of the Ritz. When Vidal saw the curlers, he was also fascinated. "He said, 'I'd like to go into business with you; we'll call it the Sassoon Set,'" Ann remembers. But at Charles of the Ritz they did not think they could sell electrical products alongside cosmetics. Tom then approached Glemby, at the time one of America's largest hair salon chains. Founded by the Glemby brothers in 1883, the company's first business had been selling handmade hairnets, but it later diversified into distributing all sorts of supplies for hair salons and then into running the salons. The company was split in 1942, and one of the men who worked with the brothers, Morris Finkelstein, took over the salon business, which by then consisted of 105 salons, mainly in the U.S. In 1949 Morris's sons, Nathan and Seymour, joined the business. Tom called on the two at Glemby to see if they were interested in the curlers. They didn't see the potential either. Tom's next move was approaching each of the department stores individually, a time-consuming strategy that involved lots of travel.

When a modeling scout saw Ann at a party and suggested she do some modeling in the U.S., Tom urged her to do it. "I wasn't keen," she said. "We were supposed to be working together. But he said I'd be bored going to Chicago in the dead of winter and thought it would be a good way for me to make friends." It was also a good way to make money. She could make three hundred dollars a day, while in London models were only getting thirty-five guineas a day. Tom set out on his own and signed deals with both Saks Fifth Avenue, which displayed Carmen rollers alongside their cosmetics, and Bonwit Teller. The business was a success, but Tom was getting concerned that even protected with a patent, cheap knockoffs of the simple device were inevitable, and he decided to sell the company. Ann says that Clairol bought it for three million dollars in August 1966. In November 1966 Tom and Ann decided it was time to return to England. Ann wanted to start a family and was concerned about being so far from her own family. It was a decision they would always question. "Tom loved America," said Ann. "He first went there after the war on the *Queen Mary* and went to all the jazz clubs. He was eating filet steak while there was food rationing in London. He was besotted with the U.S."

Back in the UK, Ann was reading an issue of *Country Life* magazine when she came across an ad featuring what she considered to be the perfect family home—a Tudor-style house in Winkfield, near Windsor. Tom called an estate agent in the area, who told him the house had just received an offer. Weeks later he and Ann went for a drive in the country and decided to go past it. "It was like a picture postcard," said Ann. The property had manicured grounds, a tennis court, and a separate barn. On the way back to town they stopped by the agent's office. He told them the initial offer had fallen through. The house was theirs, and before long Ann was pregnant with Tamara.

One of the early visitors to their new home in Winkfield was Seymour Finkelstein. Glemby was looking to expand into the UK market, and Tom Yeardye seemed just the man to help them. Seymour's son Paul was working in the Glemby business when Tom first met his father and uncle. "We liked each other immediately," said Paul. Shortly after Tamara's birth in July 1967, Tom agreed to help them. Since it was a family business, there was no opportunity for Tom to own a part of it, so instead the newly minted millionaire was paid a generous salary.

Tom opened the first Glemby salon at JJ Allen, the Bournemouth, Dorset, department store. "We had zero salons in the UK," said Paul. "He [Tom] built the business. He was always very deal oriented, but he was very, very good with people."

It was a talent others recognized as well. One day Tom ran into his old friend Vidal Sassoon. According to Ann, Vidal said, "What are you doing in hair? Would you think of doing it for me? I have a big name, but I'm not making any money." It was perfect timing for both parties. After three years at Glemby, Tom was ready for a move. "It was a privately held, family-run company," said Paul.

"Tom left because of limitations on his personal growth." And although he hated the thought of leaving the Finkelsteins, who were now his close friends, he was intrigued by the opportunity to build something with Vidal.

Neither Vidal Sassoon nor any of the people who worked for him can remember how he first met Tom. Vidal says, "I met him socially." Joshua Galvin, who worked with Vidal Sassoon at the time, remembers Tom and Vidal lifting weights at the Universal Gym on New Oxford Street with him. By 1970 Vidal's salon was the center of London's social universe. Everyone who was anyone was there having their hair done and sharing in the gossip.

It was a place in society Vidal Sassoon never dreamed he would occupy. He was born in London's East End in 1928. When his father left his mother, she had to put both her sons into an orphanage because she could not afford to feed them. From age five to age eleven, Vidal saw his mother only once a month. Eager for him to have a profession, she took him to see an East End hairdresser and asked if Vidal could be his apprentice. The hairdresser responded that he could, if she would pay him to train the young boy. She explained that she could not. As they turned to leave, the fourteen-year-old Vidal helped his mother with her coat and held the door for her. The hairdresser was impressed by his manners and agreed to take him on for free. In his early twenties, Vidal joined the Israeli army and fought in the Arab-Israeli war. When he came back, he went to London's poshest neighborhood, Mayfair, looking for work. "They [the salon owners] told me to learn to speak properly and then come back," he remembers. He spent two years in voice elocution lessons to shed his East End accent.

In 1954, when he was twenty-six, Vidal Sassoon was ready to start his own salon. It was on the third floor of a nondescript building at 173 New Bond Street, the wrong end of the famous street. But slowly he built a steady clientele. In 1958 Vidal opened his ground-floor salon on the posh part of Old Bond Street—across from what is now Cartier—with a thirty-thousand-pound investment from a farmer. Although it is often said that Tom Yeardye launched Vidal

Sassoon, that farmer was not Tom Yeardye. It was a New Zealand sheep farmer whose wife, Suna Prevost, was a client. And although the sign over the Bond Street Sassoon salon read "London, New York, Paris," there were no other Sassoon salons, merely affiliated hairdressers who would exchange clients. Tom told Vidal that the only way he would join the company was if he had part of the equity. He borrowed $700,000 (£250,000) and bought out the Prevosts.

When Tom joined Sassoon, the operation in London was, as one staffer at the time said, "a big Yiddisha number." In other words, it was a family affair run by Sassoon's brother, Ivor, and his best friend, Joshua Galvin, a hairdresser who met Vidal in New York on Sassoon's first trip there in 1960 and "the only hairdresser ever hired without a test." At the time, moving from New York to London "was like leaving a racy blonde and arriving back with a little old gray-hair lady," Galvin recalls. "We didn't know that London was about to explode. And we were right at the front of it with Vidal." Vidal was sharing a flat in Maida Vale with Terence Stamp and Michael Caine, who would come in to have their hair done to suit their roles. Roman Polanski filmed Catherine Deneuve from the balcony of the salon. Peter O'Toole had to sit in the basement to have his hair done, lest the crowds that gathered outside the windows to watch the avant-garde hairdressers caught sight of him. In 1967 they opened the first Vidal Sassoon school in a small ground-floor space. "People wanted to watch all day," said Joshua.

Vidal had been commuting back and forth between London, where he had his chic clientele, and New York, where he was doing the hair of more and more celebrities, like Mia Farrow in *Rosemary's Baby*. Finally he decided to open an office in New York. The managing director in London, Gerald Austin, went with him. Vidal wanted to bring in someone who could run the salons in the UK and work on expansion. Still, insiders were shocked when Tom arrived. For one thing, the Glemby business was not what anyone would call hip. And for another, it was rare that an outsider would get such a top job at Sassoon. Vidal neglected to tell his team that

Tom wasn't just a manager—he was also a partner in the business. Joshua Galvin was the general manager of the UK operation at the time. "Before we know it, he's shadowing Gerald, and then Gerald moves to New York and Tommy is the new managing director," Galvin says. "I said, I need someone who can run the salons and who has ambition," Vidal recalls. "He doubled the profits in two years." With Vidal spending much of his time in America, the ambitious Tom had plenty of room to maneuver.

The staff in London was perplexed by the largesse of Tom's lifestyle: the fancy house, the Frank Foster custom-made shirts— when Tom flew, he flew first-class. He told Vidal that all of these steps were important to maintain the company image. In 1973 Tom asked the man who took care of him when he flew on TWA, Lou Rodwell, the head of special services, to come and work as his executive assistant. "I said, 'Tom, I don't know anything about hair,'" Lou recalls. Tom replied, "You're a people person and we want people persons."

Tom may not have gotten along with some of the old-time Vidal staffers, but he did get along with some of the newer employees. "Tom made Vidal," said Philip Rogers. "When he came it was a very small business. He was very entrepreneurial." Caroline Hayes Walker, another Sassoon alumnus, met Tom in 1969, when she was working in the first of the Vidal Sassoon schools. "He came in with Joshua to find out why they were suddenly making so much money," she remembers. "He came in and asked another teacher, 'Who is responsible for all these deposits?' He pointed at me and said, 'She is.'"

Tom came back the next day and asked the nineteen-year-old Caroline what she needed to get the place really cooking. She said, "More space." Three weeks later he took her to look at a mews house on Davies Street nearby Claridge's Hotel. She said she told him, "'Not big enough.' He laughed and told me I could start there." Tom began to call on Caroline to help him understand the artistic personalities in the business. "He couldn't understand why they wouldn't do certain things. I'd tell him, 'Look. It's just not cool.' He found he could talk to me." In addition to her straight-talking style, she had another appealing asset. "Everything I touched turned to money," she said. The school grew into the basement of Davies Street then onto the upper floors and into neighboring houses.

In addition to growing the schools, Vidal credits Tom for building up the salon business. No one else at Vidal had experience in running more than one salon at a time. At Glemby, Tom had run dozens. He began pushing Sassoon into new areas: Leeds and Manchester in the UK and, surprisingly for the mostly Jewish firm, four in Germany: Hamburg, Berlin, Frankfurt, and Munich. And he pushed the company into new, profitable businesses, including a line of wigs that were made in Asia and sold in department stores all over the UK, including Selfridges, the famous London department store that sits in the middle of Oxford Street.

Vidal meanwhile had moved his U.S. headquarters from New York to L.A., in order to please his wife, Beverly, who was a born-and-bred Californian. For Tom, the move made working with Vidal from London nearly impossible. "Vidal was always ringing at four A.M.," Ann remembers. Vidal says, "He wanted to come to L.A. and I made it easy for him."

One of Vidal's hairdressers in New York, Joseph Solomon, was very keen on starting a line of haircare products. After all, the products that Tom had launched in the UK had never enjoyed much success. "No one really wanted to do it at the time," said a consultant who worked with the company then. "He [Joe] annoyed them so much they finally gave him fifty thousand dollars and said, 'Go do it.'"

Originally the product line was meant to sell only to salons—Joe would take it to the hair shows in jugs. They toyed for a while with the idea of selling to high-end department stores, but recognized that the real business was always going to come from the mass-market drugstores and supermarkets. Eugene Howe, a friend of Vidal's in London, designed the iconic brown cylindrical bottles, and a scientist named Don Sullivan invented the formulas and the almond scent. Tom, who arrived that same year, would be in charge of the U.S. salons and schools. He told Caroline that she should come to California, too, and when she agreed, Tom put her in charge of the only school in the U.S., in San Francisco.

"I left England and woke up in a dream," said Caroline. "I was picked up at the airport in a limo. Tom gave me tons of cash to get myself set up. I'd never had more than fifty pounds on me at one time before." And Tom wrote ahead to the U.S. school to tell them in no uncertain terms that the twenty-something woman with the purple hair was now their boss. "They rolled out the red carpet for me," Caroline said. One day Tom called her and said, "I want you to open in Hong Kong." Caroline replied. "Where's that?" She had left school at fifteen. "I had no formal education," she said. "But there I was opening schools in China. Tom guided me. He gave me scope and then he'd say, 'What's next?'" What was next was a bit of trouble in Hong Kong when the girlfriend of a Sassoon associate began hitting on her. "I rang Tom and said there's trouble. He said, 'Is Bernie hitting on you?' I said, 'No, his girlfriend!' Tom couldn't stop laughing, but then he said, 'Don't worry, I'm coming out.' And he got on a plane from L.A. the next day. He never made you feel bad when these things happened, he just dealt with it."

Things were not going as smoothly in London. After eighteen months, Joseph Solomon came to the UK and suggested to Philip Rogers (who having started at Vidal Sassoon in 1964 was now running the UK salon and school business) and Annie Humphries (who was Sassoon's top colorist) that they do a staged management buyout of the Vidal Sassoon salons and schools. They were joined by Christopher Brooker, the creative director of the company, although Philip and Annie bought him out shortly after the deal was done— he had wanted to change the name from Vidal Sassoon, and they did not think that was a good idea.

Back in Los Angeles, Tom's master plan was to franchise the Vidal Sassoon salon concept. "He said there was a fortune to be made," Vidal said. "We could charge each franchisee fifty thousand dollars plus royalties. We could send our own teachers in. Tom was all for it." But the Vidal Sassoon board didn't agree. The company was putting a lot of its money and energy behind products, and the board thought that franchised salons would dilute the Sassoon name. "There was a big argument," Vidal remembers. Ann said, "He told Vidal that he'd done all he could. They decided to sell the company so that Tom could be cashed out."

Tom remained in L.A. and took on some small projects, like buying a newspaper called *Beverly Hills People*, which covered all the local parties, and launching Micro Cool, a water-misting system that would cool people outdoors without actually getting them wet. Tom also started to work with Pamela Mason, the former wife of film star James Mason and the new owner of Britain's biggest wool company, Illingworth Morris. Pamela had inherited the majority share of the company from her father and had initiated a major management upheaval. She fired the company's auditors, insisted that her son be reinstated to the board, and appointed Tom executive director and "world salesman," arguing that Tom would open up the market in the United States. "There will have to be some changes," she told the board in September 1979. "Get off your butts." At Illingworth Morris, Tom initiated several undertakings: he made a deal with Leon Block, a New York designer favored by Nancy Reagan, for a line of ready-to-wear items made from Illingworth's wool; he got a license from the All England Lawn Tennis and Croquet Club for a line of Wimbledon-branded clothing to be made in Hong Kong; and he said he wanted the U.S. to account for 50 percent of the company's foreign sales. But industry analysts didn't think Tom was the right choice for the job. One told the *New York Times* in June 1981, "Yeardye is off paddling his own canoe, while the other directors have to deal with the real problems." And a London stockbroker added, "They [Tom and Pamela] are concentrating in the U.S. because they live there." Pamela defended Tom to the *Times*, saying, "Selling is selling." But the next month she called for his removal from the board along with two other board members. In August, Tom resigned.

In April 1983 Vidal called Tom with some good news. The Sassoon business had been sold to Richardson-Vicks, a pharmaceutical company. By this time the Vidal Sassoon empire was generating revenues of $110 million (£72 million) a year, and 80 percent of that was in the U.S. "Vidal always gave shares," Annie Humphries said. "He was quite good about that." And each share in Vidal Sassoon was now worth twenty-seven dollars (eighteen pounds). "Everyone did well," said Joshua. "And Tommy did very, very well." "He had a chunk of shares," confirmed Vidal. "I said to him, 'There's a hell of a lot of money coming your way.'" Caroline Hayes, like all the noncore shareholders, had to sell her shares, too—she got $120,000. At the same time Vidal called Philip Rogers and told him that he would have to take over the U.S. Vidal Sassoon salons and schools. It was primarily a paper transaction.

The U.S. salons and schools had been separated from the product division and they had a debt of $1.25 million (£824,000), for which Philip and Annie were now responsible. But they knew that the existence of the salons was crucial to the image of the products, so they negotiated a twenty-five hundred dollar per person per day rate for any consulting work that would enhance the product line. "It would have taken ten years to pay down the debt," Philip said. "But then the Olympics happened." An enterprising public relations woman, Jackie Applebaum, had secured the rights of Vidal Sassoon to be the official sponsor of the Olympic Games in 1984. In addition to providing products, they also had a salon set up in the Olympic Village that had to be staffed by the salons Philip and Annie now owned. They in turn charged Richardson-Vicks $2,500 (£1,600) per person per day for the six-week run. At the end of it, the debt was entirely cleared.

In 1985, in order to fend off a hostile takeover from Unilever, Richardson-Vicks was sold to Procter & Gamble and Vidal Sassoon along with it. It was a move that deeply upset Vidal. Years later he would sue Procter & Gamble for mismanaging his brand. "Had I had to do it all over again, I would have kept the company and would have kept Tom," he said. Instead Tom went back to buying properties and investing in small businesses. He would remain an investor in various ventures until his daughter came up with an idea that would change the fortunes of the entire family.

Five

High Heels Are Hard Work

T HANKS TO TOM, AN essential part of the Yeardye family life had always been discussing possible business ventures. Long before she had left *Vogue*, Tamara had been contributing to the family discussion with a concept for a new shoe brand, built around the custom business of her shoemaker friend in Hackney. Why not, she thought, develop a luxury, ready-to-wear line of shoes to be broadly distributed under the Jimmy Choo name? "Jimmy Choo was just a great name for shoes,"[15] Tamara said. "It rhymes, it sticks in your head." Tom didn't think it was a bad idea. "I spent a fortune buying shoes for Tamara and her mother," he said later. "I would say, 'We've got to get into this business someday.'"[16] But he wasn't completely convinced either. The biggest question mark for him was not the validity of the concept, it was that the fact that he was now sixty-five years old, ready to retire, and eager to move back to Los Angeles with his wife, Ann.

But Tamara was resolute—and relentless. Finally Tom told Tamara to go out and try to raise the money herself. "You have a lot of rich friends—why don't you ask them for the money?" he said. And he told Ann, "I don't want her to think it is easy to raise money."

Tamara did as she was told and went out and spoke to the most likely of the candidates in her affluent circle, including Dodi Al Fayed, the son of Muhammad Al Fayed, the owner of Harrods. (Dodi would later die in the car crash that killed Princess Diana.) Every one of them said no. But some were willing to offer advice and make crucial introductions. Yasmin Mills, a former model and a London socialite, took Tamara to lunch at San Lorenzo and introduced her to Natalie Lewis and Tracy Brower, two young women of Tamara's age who had recently set up their own PR firm in London, Brower Lewis. Tamara knew good PR was key to a fashion launch and, despite not having any sketches, materials, or even a commitment from Jimmy, she won them over with her enthusiasm. They agreed to do the PR should the deal come through. But that was still far from certain. She had been as relentless with Jimmy as she had with her father, but so far he remained unconvinced by her charm offensive. Finally he responded by telling her to come work with him in his studio—so she could actually learn what she was getting into, he said. And so he could learn a bit more about her, he thought.

Tamara's 1995 began in the comfortable confines of Vogue House on Mayfair's Hanover Square and ended in a dirty, glue-filled workshop in Hackney, where she worked every day for three months. But instead of becoming discouraged by the surroundings and the messy work she focused her attention on the never-ending stream of rich ladies who made the trek across London to visit Jimmy's cold, dreary workshop for a pair of custom-made Jimmy Choos, and she became even more convinced she could turn the high-class cobbler into a mega brand. She kept pushing Jimmy to move ahead with the original idea that had brought her there: to let her take a stake in his company and launch a ready-to-wear line of shoes.

Tom and Ann were sounding out the idea with their friends in far more salubrious locations. At a lunch at the Hotel de Paris in Monte Carlo with the multibillionaire Barclay twins, David and Frederick, two old friends from Tom's property days, Tom told them of her plan. He said, "This daughter of mine wants to open a shoe company. At my age, do you take those chances? We want to take life easier." The brothers said, "Why not have a go? Give her a chance; we'll both back her."

Ann took the idea to one of her friends in London, Liz Ward, who owned a designer consignment shop on Kensington Church Street called Designer Bargains. It sold the cast-off clothes of the wealthy women who lived in the area. Liz told her that all the women who provided her with stock went to Hackney to have shoes made by Jimmy. She thought a line of ready-to-wear shoes bearing his name would be a huge success. Ann began to take care to point out to Tom every mention of Jimmy's name in the fashion press: "Look, Tom, shoes by Jimmy Choo," while reading *Vogue*. "All the rich West End ladies are wearing them," while reading the *Evening Standard*; "Diana is wearing them," while reading *Hello*.

It took a few months, but finally he was convinced. Tom and Ann decided they would fund the start-up themselves. "It could be over in five minutes, but I don't want to bother if it is just going to be for one or two shops," Tom said to Ann. "If we're going to do it, it will have to be a success." He politely declined the Barclay brothers' offer of funding.

On his side Jimmy was finally ready for the next step. Tamara set up a meeting with her parents and Jimmy at the house on Chester Row. Jimmy was as cautious as he had been with the brothers from Gina. "Things moved at a very slow pace," said Ann. Nine months later, in May 1996, they were finally ready to sign contracts. On the day of signing, Jimmy balked and tried to walk away. His lawyer convinced him to stay, saying that the deal was a good one. He signed. Tamara's family became the first outside shareholder of the company.

The transaction was structured as a typical capital increase. Jimmy would not receive any money from the sale of half of the company. Rather, the money from the Yeardyes would fund the launch of a ready-to-wear collection as well as the opening of Jimmy Choo boutiques in exchange for a 50 percent stake in the new company, Jimmy Choo Ltd. This included the Jimmy Choo name. Not included in the deal, however, was Jimmy's couture business. He could continue to make shoes for his wealthy clients and keep that income for himself.

In the company structure, Jimmy's role was to design the collection of shoes every season. Tom became the managing director and the chairman of the board, taking over the business and administrative aspects of the company, and Tamara became the president, in charge of manufacturing, promoting, and marketing the ready-to-wear collection of shoes.

As the deal was being structured, at the end of February 1996, Tom took care of some family business. He instructed David Morgan, a lawyer based in Jersey, an offshore tax-free jurisdiction, to set up a trust to hold the shares of Thistledown International Ltd., the British Virgin Islands company he had set up to conduct the investment in Jimmy Choo. Even though Tom considered this a "family investment," he, as the head of the family, was the principal beneficiary of the trust and therefore the principal owner of the 50 percent stake in Jimmy Choo.

In an interview with the *Sunday Times* a few years later, Jimmy explained why his forays into ready-to-wear had not worked out with anyone else. "I had not yet found a partner with the perfect combination of youth, style and intelligence, or someone who, most of all, was willing to work as hard as me." He added that he was impressed by Tamara's "innate style and worker-bee attention to detail."[17]

The Yeardye's initial investment was £150,000 ($230,000), and the money was already allocated by the time the ink on the contracts was dry. The first move was to secure the storefront they had found on Motcomb Street in Belgravia. The shop was small—about fifty square meters (540 square feet)—but cozy, with a large purple velvet sofa for customers to sit on and with a very girly feel. At the back there was a small kitchen, and in the basement there was a storage room filled with stock for the store, a small showroom, and an office with two desks, where Ann and Tom could often be found working. What it lacked in size it made up for in charm and location.

Motcomb Street is a stylish cobblestone street at the heart of Belgravia, an easy walking distance from Harvey Nichols, the most fashionable of London's department stores, which sits at the top of Sloane Street. Harvey Nics, as it is affectionately known by London's fashionistas, is the equivalent of New York's Barneys. Not just a place to shop, but a place to be seen. Motcomb Street is also close to Knightsbridge—a major shopping center—and convenient to Mayfair, where many London financiers work. It was, in all these aspects, the exact opposite of the boutique of their chief competitor—Manolo Blahnik.

To this day, the only place to buy Manolos in London is at Manolo's own shop on Old Church Street, a side street in deepest Chelsea. It's a mostly residential area, and a twenty-minute walk from the nearest underground station. It is not convenient to Mayfair's Bond Street or Knightsbridge's Sloane Street, where most of the world's top luxury labels can be found. Nor is it convenient to Knightsbridge's Beauchamp Place, home of San Lorenzo, or Mayfair's Mount Street near Harry's Bar, two of the most popular lunching stops for the ladies who shop. If one wants to visit the store, one must be prompt. Linger too long at lunch and there will be no time left for the torturous taxi ride down the traffic-saturated King's Road. The boutique closes promptly at five thirty during the week and at four forty-five on Saturdays. And one must be fast. Manolo has been in business since the 1970s, and the shop on Old Church Street is his original one. It is bigger than the one on Motcomb Street, but not by much. A popular shoe will come in only a few pairs per size. None of London's other stores are allowed to carry the brand, lest they cannabalize sales from the Old Church Street boutique. For women with a day job, it is nearly impossible to buy a pair of Manolo Blahniks in London. In fact, many of London's serious dressers buy their Manolos in New York, where, thanks to an enterprising franchise partner, George Malkemus, they are available at Neiman Marcus, Bergdorf Goodman, Barneys, and even online, in addition to the Manolo Blahnik boutique, just off Fifth Avenue.

A key part of Tom and Tamara's business plan for Jimmy Choo was to sell shoes to top-tier multibrand boutiques and department stores like Harvey Nichols. Far from worrying about the famous store potentially taking sales from them, they were eager to expose the brand and its new products to the thousands of well-heeled women who each day herded into the hippest retail emporiums in town—women who might not know to make the special trip to Motcomb Street.

But there was a lot of work to be done before that could happen. Despite the long courtship, tensions between the Yeardyes and Jimmy soon emerged. They were working under very tight deadlines, and Jimmy needed to design two collections at once—one to sell at the Jimmy Choo store when it opened in August 1996 and another wholesale collection to be shown to retailers and the fashion press at the Fashion Footwear Association of New York trade show in early June. To get the samples to the trade show on time they needed the designs to be in the factories by March or April at the latest. And, of course, they still had to find the factories. Tamara immediately started pressing Jimmy for designs for the ready-to-wear collection so that they could head to Italy and meet with potential manufacturers. Not enough sketches were forthcoming. Sketching shoes was not Jimmy's forte—making them was. To make matters worse, Jimmy was as busy as ever. He still had to produce shoes for his private clients in order to support his family. He was none too pleased to find that he was being asked to do this extra work when no extra money was going into his pockets. Tamara and Ann began go to Hackney daily to try to get Jimmy to focus on the needs of the new company.

It was Jimmy's wife's niece, Sandra Choi, who stepped into the void. Tamara would come into the workshop in Hackney, describe the shoes she wanted, and Sandra would sketch them while Jimmy would walk in and out from the workshop and make comments, usually negative ones. "Tamara was pushing to go higher and higher on the heels," said Ann. "Jimmy would say, 'No higher!

You're destroying the balance.'" Tamara would counter, "Look, Jimmy, there are high-heeled shoes all over the place. We have to have them."

When they finally had a collection of sketches together, Tamara, Sandra, and Jimmy flew to Italy in search of factories to manufacture them. Tamara said, "I had to go out to shoe factories in Italy with no shops, no track record, only a handful of designs and persuade men to do business with me, a young woman. It wasn't easy."[18]

"Not easy" was a major understatement. In June they packed their bags to go to the Fashion Footwear Association of New York trade show, as planned. But the samples from Italy, which were to be shipped directly to New York, did not arrive on time. Tamara resorted to trying to sell the collection to the retailers by showing them Sandra's sketches. Although people were intrigued, no one was going to place an order for expensive shoes they had never seen. The reason soon became clear when the prototypes finally arrived in New York and the quality was so poor that they could not be shown to the potential customers. An entire season's worth of shoe samples was paid for and discarded.

After New York they returned again to Italy to try to find another factory. Tamara thought she had struck gold when they found one that was willing not only to make the shoes, but also to market and sell them. Tamara phoned Tom and said, "They can do it all!" Tom said, "Hold it, Tamara. That's what we do. They're going to take seventy-five percent of the money. When you come home I'll explain it." Tom would explain it to Sandra also, and she would translate into Chinese for Jimmy. On their next trip, Tamara decided it would be best if she, Sandra, and Jimmy could learn Italian so to better negotiate with the factory owners. She asked Tom for money for lessons. "Could someone please teach Jimmy English first?" Tom joked. "You don't need to speak Italian. Stay focused on what you're doing."

When Tamara came back from Italy she brought along with her cases of shoes for the Motcomb Street store. They were generic shoes, bought from the stock of a manufacturer, not the shoes she and Sandra had designed. But that was a detail best ignored. With the Motcomb Street store opening in days, they were in desperate need of something, anything, to sell. Jimmy Choo labels were sewn into the shoes and added to the small assortment that Jimmy himself was able to provide.

Months later they had the good fortune to meet a production agent who would solve their problems. Anna Suppig-Conti, joined later by her brother, Mossimo, would not only find the factories to make the shoes, but also supervise the whole production process so that there would be no more surprises like the one in New York. Anna and Mossimo were based in Florence, the heart of the shoe-producing region of Italy, fluent in the language of lasts and heels, and on good terms with the multitude of factory owners who populate the region. With Jimmy Choo as the first client, Anna and Mossimo formed a company called If,srl. Because as Anna once explained, "If it works, it works—if it doesn't, it doesn't." It did, and both are still part of the Jimmy Choo team.

Back in London, there were cultural issues of another sort. Before the Motcomb Street store could open, Jimmy insisted it be checked over by his feng shui master. He was flown in from Malaysia at the expense of the Yeardyes. "Because he was very high ranking, we had to put him in a first-class hotel," said Ann. After he finished rearranging the store—moving the cash register so that money wouldn't fly out the door and such—he moved on to rearranging Tamara's flat, and then on to the homes of Jimmy's clients. "They all started hiring him," laughed Ann. "He was making a fortune, but we were paying his bills."

The Motcomb Street store opening in the fall of 1996 was celebrated with a party at the members-only Wellington Club. All of Tamara's years of partying paid off, as London's most well-heeled and most talked-about socialites were in attendance.

The store's first saleswoman was Hannah Colman, the girlfriend of Tamara's youngest brother, Daniel. Hannah was then eighteen

years old, finished with school, and thinking about taking an extra
course the following year. Tom said to her, "Why are you studying if
what you are passionate about is fashion? You don't need a course—
you need to work on the shop floor. That's where you learn." Ann
thought, "Oh, Tom, her parents are going to be so upset with you."
Tom told Jimmy that now that the store was open, Sandra also
needed to be at Motcomb Street full-time. She, Hannah, and Tamara
were, after all, the company's only salaried employees. Jimmy was
not pleased. Sandra was his best assistant and over the years he had
become increasingly fond and possessive of her. "That was a wild,
creative and happy time for Jimmy and me," Sandra later said of
her years with Jimmy.[19] Although he had no choice but to relent, he
insisted that a friend of his who drove a minicab pick her up every
day precisely at six P.M., and bring her back to Hackney to continue
to help him produce his private clients' orders.

Sandra's main job was design, but everyone, including Sandra,
Tamara, and even Ann, was expected to take their turn on the
selling floor. Although the company was small, it was not without
its share of politics. Sandra was particularly prickly because of the
personal relationships within the staff. Ann remembers that when
Sandra minded the store she would play little tricks, like mixing
up the shoes in the stockroom so that when the next person took
over, there would be a black stiletto and a pink slingback in a box
instead of a matched pair, causing no small degree of embarrassment
in front of a customer. In later years the antics became an in-joke
among all of them.

Despite the petty jealousies, Sandra found the excitement of
working with Tamara and her family and the challenge of designing
a whole collection was far preferable to making just one pair of
shoes at a time in a cramped workshop with Jimmy. She and Tamara
worked so well together that they stopped seeking Jimmy's approval
and just designed the collection by themselves. "Being girls gives
us such an advantage in designing," said Tamara. "We know what
it's like to wear these shoes."[20] And the differences between them

helped give the collection a wide range of styles. Sandra said, "We are opposites. I like things that are cool and hip. And she [Tamara] will put a whole look together and it's more refined."[21]

Sure, some thought that some of their early designs seemed to have more than a passing resemblance to Manolo Blahnik's, but despite this waspish gossip, no legal blows were ever exchanged over the matter. Others in the shoe trade say the manager of Blahnik's London store had his own way of dealing with the issue. He banned Tamara and Sandra from crossing its doors, greeting them with the finger rather than unlocking the door when they rang the bell. Sandra later said that she would look at Manolos just to make sure her designs were different. Accusations aside, at least they had shoes to sell—and they were very pretty shoes.

As Sandra and Tamara grew closer and closer, Jimmy became more and more concerned. Once when a customer gave Sandra concert tickets, meaning she would not be back at the Hackney workshop by six that evening, Jimmy went ballistic. He came into the store and began shouting. Tamara ran around the corner to the Lowndes Hotel, where Tom and Ann were having lunch, and said, "Jimmy is raging." Tom stood up from his lunch and walked back to the shop with Tamara. He said, "Now see here, Jimmy, we will not have this. Don't ever do it again," remembers Ann.

Despite the fact that he owned half of the company, Jimmy did not always appear to act in its best interests. He came by the store nearly every day and drank his special blend of coffee and tea. ("We'd ask him what he wanted, coffee or tea, and he would say, 'Yes,'" said Ann.) But when the PR girls from Brower Lewis would organize interviews with the press, Jimmy would tell journalists that he was not the one designing the shoes, not the image they wanted to convey. When he came to the monthly board meetings, he would bring his attorney along and contribute little. But worst of all, he began complaining to his clients, saying that the Yeardyes had done him a disservice. Since the circle of ladies in London who buy shoes that cost several hundred pounds was relatively small, left unchecked this soul-searching might prove disastrous to the nascent Jimmy Choo ready-to-wear brand.

By the end of 1996 it was abundantly clear that Jimmy was unlikely to fulfill the role the Yeardyes expected of him. Tom offered to pay him £1,000 ($1,500) for each sketch he produced, yet still none were forthcoming. In December, Tom asked Sandra if she would like to officially become the creative director of Jimmy Choo. Sandra later said, "I was looking for bigger things to do. Jimmy is a beautiful shoemaker who makes the most gorgeous shoes. But … we were committed to producing regular collections. When it came to creating a collection consistently, he was not quite there … So out of desperation, I did the collections as time went on."[22] She added, "Jimmy and I were physically exhausted from work and I could see what was coming if I remained."[23] She accepted the post in early December. But a seismic change had also taken place in Sandra's personal life. She had fallen in love with the man Jimmy had hired to drive her to and from Hackney. When Jimmy found out, he began raging again. Sandra turned up on Tamara's doorstep with no place to stay. If she had been conflicted in her loyalties before, she no longer was. In early 1997 she moved into the Chester Row house. She lived there with Tamara and Daniel for a year, dated the minicab driver for several, and cut off all contact with Jimmy for many more.

Six

THE AMERICAN INVASION

WITH SANDRA AND TAMARA working on the product, Tom took charge of an area he knew well—real estate. In addition to the Knightsbridge store, he had found offices for the company on Pont Street, above the venerable London wine shop Jeroboams. Tom's next priority was to find a way to open Jimmy Choo stores in the United States. He had been approached by the developers of the Venetian Resort Hotel Casino with their plans for the five-hundred-thousand-square-foot Grand Canal Shops that was to be set in the new $1.4 billion (approximately £1 billion) mega-resort. The plans included spaces for all the big luxury brands: Louis Vuitton, Chanel, Dior, Burberry. It seemed an honor and Tom signed on the spot. He also wanted to make sure he had stores where *he* chose, starting with New York. To do this he invested another £600,000 ($900,000) and looked up an old friend from his Sassoon days, Philip Rogers. Philip and Annie Humphries now owned all the Vidal Sassoon salons and schools in the U.S. and had moved the U.S. head office from Los Angeles to Boston to be nearer to London, their home base.

Over the years since Tom's departure from Vidal Sassoon, he and Philip had spoken frequently. Philip would regularly ask his old boss for advice. Now it was Tom's turn to ask Philip for help. Over lunch at the restaurant in the Carlton Tower hotel in Knightsbridge, Tom explained to Philip that although he had started to talk with a few

U.S. companies about partnering in the States, he didn't want to get into business with any of them. Philip interrupted him and said, "I know where you're going with this, Tom. You want to do it with me."

Rather than going through the expense and aggravation of setting up Jimmy Choo's own U.S. subsidiary or share a chunk of the profits with an established American partner, Tom asked Philip if he could use the Vidal Sassoon administrative structure to run Jimmy Choo's retail operations in the U.S. In exchange, Philip and Annie would be given a 50 percent stake in the company that would own Jimmy Choo's U.S. stores. The Yeardyes would own the other half. Philip agreed. After some consideration, he decided it would be best if his company, rather than Annie and himself personally, owned the stake; after all, the Sassoon employees would be expected to also do work for Jimmy Choo. This U.S. deal was done, but without the consent of Jimmy, who refused to sign off on it but did not have enough weight on the board to veto it. "I think he was afraid," said Ann. Tom asked Philip if he had any leads on affordable retail space in Manhattan. Philip did, and with his help Jimmy Choo found a boutique in the Olympic Tower just off Fifth Avenue, which made it far less expensive than a store that opened directly onto the famous shopping street.

Philip also had another idea: Why not open in New York and Los Angeles at about the same time? The Los Angeles Vidal Sassoon salon was leaving Rodeo Drive after almost thirty years. Philip had found another space on the corner of North Canon and Little Santa Monica Boulevard. The new space was near Rodeo but much less expensive, and it was larger than they needed. What if they divided it and turned part of it into a Jimmy Choo store? Tom thought it was a great idea. And although Tamara was thrilled at the prospect of having not just two, but three stores in the U.S., she had her reservations about the Los Angeles location. She absolutely wanted a store in L.A. but she wanted it to be on the top shopping avenue of the city, Rodeo Drive, "with the right neighbors," she said. Tom looked at the space Philip had found and convinced her it was the right way forward. The Jimmy Choo portion was indeed small, smaller even than Motcomb Street, but as Philip said, "it was very imposing for what it was." Philip had given Jimmy Choo the highly visible corner on North Canon and Little Santa Monica Boulevard and a great deal on the rent. Jimmy Choo would only pay $6,000 (£3,500) a month of the total $15,000 (£9,000) due. And since Jimmy Choo was a new company with no track record, Philip would use the link with his company, Vidal Sassoon, to guarantee the lease. "I doubt that anyone else would have done what I did for that brand and for the Yeardyes," Philip said. They began planning for a fall 1998 joint opening.

With Tom shouldering much of the administrative work, the stress of launching a new company did not hurt Tamara's social life. Even without the champagne and the drugs she was a regular on the London scene. She was declared "exotically beautiful" at the *Tatler* magazine "hot dates" party in November 1997. Going out and talking up Jimmy Choo shoes to her well-shod friends was now part of her job. While Tom was working with Philip on ways into the American market, an American man was working his way into Tamara's heart.

In May 1998 Tamara attended the wedding of the man she had been dating when she was wooing Jimmy Choo. Henry Dent-Brocklehurst, the godson of Camilla Parker Bowles, who would become the wife of Prince Charles, was married at his home, the fifteenth-century Sudeley Castle. Henry married a beautiful Hawaiian model named Lili Maltese and *OK!* magazine had given them $1.2 million (£730,000) for the rights to photograph the wedding. After the event an exhibition about the wedding was set up in the castle for the ticket-buying public. The carefully posed pictures of the bride and groom in *OK!* were somewhat upstaged by the sight of Liz Hurley's underpants. Liz wore a red Versace dress slit so high up her leg that her sequined leopard-print underwear was clearly visible. Liz later said she had not intended to upstage the bride. "I had no idea that it was so revealing," she said.

The guests were the usual London party-going set: the Rolling Stones' Mick Jagger and his then-wife, the former model Jerry Hall; actor Hugh Grant; interior designer Nicky Haslam; socialite Tara Palmer-Tomkinson; singers Simon LeBon, Nick Rhodes, and Bryan Adams; writer AA Gill, and a newcomer, a California import that Henry knew from his days in Los Angeles, Matthew Mellon. Tamara had briefly met Matthew earlier at a Narcotics Anonymous meeting, but he had failed to make an impression. This time was different. For one thing, he jumped into her car as she was driving back to London. It was love at second sight—at least for him. "I had two hours to close the deal," he later said. "I knew that car journey would be the most important trip of my life." She said he was "one of the funniest men I'd met in my life. He would have me on the floor in stitches. I also thought he was one of the most good-looking men I'd ever seen."

Matthew, one of the heirs to the Mellon Bank fortune, had already spent the first of his thirteen trust funds by the time he met Tamara. He had lived a notoriously sordid life in Los Angeles, surrounded by drugs and Heidi Fleiss's call girls. Tamara was not put off by his past. "It's not a big deal," she said. "If you live in L.A. and you haven't been to rehab, you're just not cool." One of Tamara's best friends, *Tatler* columnist Vassi Chamberlain, said, "She [Tamara] saw a wounded bird that she wanted to love because she had been one herself." The romantic pairing of Tamara and Matthew turned out to be the perfect mix of brains and beauty, but in this instance Matthew was the beauty and Tamara had the brains.

Matthew's early life had veered frequently between the tragic and the comic but came out heavily weighted on the side of the tragic. He was the great-great-grandnephew of Andrew W. Mellon, the tycoon who founded Union Trust Company and was one of the heads of the Mellon Bank. His aunt Bunny was one of the world's great fashion icons; she even had her gardening clothes and table linen made at Givenchy's haute couture atelier in Paris. On his mother's side he hails from the old American dynasties of the Drexels and Biddles, but though his mother's family was more prestigious, the Mellons were more controlling of the progeny.

Matthew's toddler years, from age two to four, were spent with his two brothers on his father's eighty-foot yacht, the *Caribou*, which was usually harbored either in Maine or in the Caribbean. Aside from being a keen sailor, fisherman, and pianist, Matthew's father, Karl, was also suffering from bipolar disorder. He abandoned the family when Matthew was five, and his mother later remarried. Karl came back to make amends when Matthew was sixteen. "I hadn't seen him for eleven years," Matthew said. "He pretended nothing had happened. He had long hair and a beard. He was sitting in his car and he said, 'My apologies for not being in touch. I hope you forgive me, and I hope we will be in touch from now on.'"[24] They would be, but not for long. In 1983 Karl committed suicide shortly before Matthew graduated from high school. "No matter how abundant my life has been, nothing has been able to fill the hole left by my father's death," he said.[25]

At the time of his father's death, Matthew was unaware that he was in line to receive a substantial inheritance. His mother had kept the knowledge of the thirteen trust funds from him, thinking it would save him from becoming spoiled. Although he summered in exclusive locales like Mount Desert Island, Maine, and Palm Beach, Florida, he would take jobs digging ditches or working as a chef at Danny's Seafood Connection restaurant in Boca Raton, Florida. From the age of sixteen to twenty-one his allowance was just one hundred dollars (sixty-one pounds) a month. But even without the money, his name was enough to get him into the tabloids. At nineteen, he briefly dated Melissa Rivers, the daughter of comedienne Joan Rivers, until Joan put an end to the relationship.

It was not until his twenty-first birthday that Matthew learned the truth about his fortune. On that birthday his uncle Jay, the head of the Mellon family, threw a party for him in Pittsburgh, the family seat. He took him into the top-floor boardroom of Mellon Bank to tell him that he would be getting, that very day, $25 million

(£14 million), just the first of the trust funds to come. "It was a rather overwhelming figure," Matthew later said. "My life changed dramatically. I knew then that I was faced with a whole new set of challenges. I immediately started subscribing to the *Wall Street Journal*."[26] Unprepared for such a windfall and still recovering from the death of his father, he also embarked on a hedonistic spending spree. Rather than merely join St. Anthony Hall, the University of Pennsylvania fraternity his family members had pledged for years, he also bought a ten-bedroom house up the road for after-parties. "It was like *Animal House*, only worse," he said.[27] He also bought the first BMW M5 in America and a speedboat (for nude waterskiing) and began to demonstrate signs of having inherited his aunt Bunny's fashion instincts. "I would go to Brooks Brothers or Ralph Lauren and buy 20, 30 pairs of shoes, 100 shirts," he said.

Upon graduation in 1989, Matthew was offered a modeling contract in New York, but the stuffy blue-blooded Mellons would not allow it. Instead Matthew worked for Rudolph Giuliani as a speechwriter. "My job description was opposition writer," he said. "Basically, you'd go out and dig up dirt on the opponents, write about it, then fax it to twenty-eight different publications in New York. Within a day or two, you saw the difference in the polls." His job took him to strange and foreign lands, like Brooklyn. "I had never even been to Brooklyn. Can you imagine, me, a New Yorker, never being there?" he said.[28] After work Matthew continued his antics. "I used to love to go dancing by myself in New York," he said.[29] "Believe it or not I used to win those crazy dance contests downtown. I was getting bored with the whole Upper East Side scene, so I would get in my Bentley and cruise down to these really seedy nightclubs and break out dancing. I didn't know anyone there and they didn't know me. It was kind of a release."

Before long even the dancing wasn't enough. In 1993 he moved to California to become a rap music producer at the label Grindstone. "I went out to L.A. for sex, drugs and rock'n'roll," he said.[30] He found them. He bought several Ferraris, leased an eight-thousand-dollar-a-month house in Beverly Hills with his cousin, the philanthropist Ginger Grace, and got another place in Malibu. "Eventually it got rough," Matthew said. "People were showing up with handguns and drug stuff and it was just total madness."[31] One Sunday morning in 1994, after an overdose in L.A., the *Vanity Fair* columnist Dominic Dunne and the son of an unnamed famous actor took Matthew to his first 12-step meeting at Cedars-Sinai hospital. He then checked into the Promises rehab clinic in L.A.

"The problem with Los Angeles is that the drug culture out there is so strong. This movie star and that big director are doing it, so you feel like it's okay to partake," he said.[32] When he got out of rehab, he moved in with Henry Dent-Brocklehurst, a recovered addict living in L.A. William Cash, a friend of theirs who was in L.A. at the time, later wrote that "they spent much of their time floating around the swimming-pool on a pair of Day-Glo plastic crocodile floating armchairs." Matthew said, "I soon realized that WASPs have more in common with upper-class Brits than with other Americans."[33]

The driven, vivacious, British Tamara was just what Matthew was looking for. "He has two rules in life: He says he would never date an actress or a singer," Tamara later said. That September he sold his Los Angeles home and moved to London to be with her. Tamara's brother Greg found the couple a home in Belgravia by dropping letters into every house in the area asking if anyone wanted to sell. Finally he found them a twenty-five-hundred-square-foot, ground-floor and basement duplex apartment on Eaton Place, not far from Tamara and Daniel's house on Chester Row. The Mellons paid for the flat, but Tom took charge of the negotiations and paid for its renovation and furnishing. Eight months and £400,000 ($625,000) later—a bit of which went to outbid Damien Hirst on an early twentieth-century bench covered in pink silk—it was ready to make its debut in the interior-decorating press. One writer found it surprising that most of the closet space was Matthew's. But even that wasn't enough to make him happy. "Matthew hated London at first," said Tamara. "The weather really got him down, and English people take a lot longer to know, whereas in Los Angeles they are much warmer and more gregarious."

As luck would have it, the inhabitants of Los Angeles were about to play a big part in the development of Jimmy Choo. That summer the shoes were to make their first appearance on the biggest fashion stage the world had ever seen. On July 5, 1998, on episode five ("The Power of Female Sex") of its first season, Jimmy Choo shoes debuted on HBO's *Sex and the City*. By the time the show had run its course, Manolo Blahnik had racked up more credits—fifty-six to Jimmy Choo's thirty-four—but Jimmy Choo had the distinction of being the first shoe brand mentioned on the show.

It is hard to overestimate the effect the show had on many fashion brands, including Jimmy Choo. The four female protagonists living in New York City became instant sartorial role models for women all over the world. But for the Jimmy Choo brand, in its nascent stages, the effect was greatly magnified. Suddenly women in Middle America were exposed to a brand whose product they had never seen. And the fact that it was mentioned in the same breath as labels like Gucci, Prada, and Manolo Blahnik meant that despite its short history women who had never heard of Jimmy Choo before assumed it was a brand of equal stature.

The debut on *Sex and the City* made it all the more essential that Jimmy Choo open its own boutiques in the U.S. as soon as possible, to capitalize on the exposure. To manage that feat in Los Angeles, they hired Michael Stachowski, one of the most popular salesmen on Rodeo Drive.

Michael had previously worked for the legendary L.A. store Fred Hayman, and had heard about Jimmy Choo from Jane Ross, a Los Angeles–based celebrity stylist. She had been flipping through the pages of a British fashion magazine when she saw a picture of a shoe. "I don't remember which magazine it was," said Jane, "or if it was part of the advertising or the editorial, but I still remember the shoe. It was a pink pastel sandal. It was glittering. It was for evening." She took the magazine to Michael. Fred Hayman was then the most famous retailer of designer labels in town and the only store in Los Angeles dedicated to dressing stars for the Academy Awards. Celebrities would go there—sometimes with stylists, sometimes with their friends or partners—to select and *buy* the gowns they wanted to wear on the big night. Fred Hayman stocked brands like Giorgio Armani, Escada, and Valentino, but for shoes there was pretty much only one choice—Manolo Blahnik. Yes, there were a lot of Manolos, but, said Jane, "everyone likes a choice." "You have to look them up," she told Michael. He did and Fred Hayman became the first Los Angeles retailer to stock the Jimmy Choo shoes. Tom and Philip thought Michael was a natural to shepherd Jimmy Choo through the murky celebrity-infested waters of Los Angeles.

But the celebrity world was changing fast. Tamara knew that if she wanted to make the brand really sizzle in L.A., she had to win over those celebrities, and it would take more than just hiring their favorite salesman to do it. By 1998 the cult of the celebrity was well under way and growing exponentially. *InStyle*, a new magazine that focused on the minute details of celebrity dressing, launched in 1993 and had quickly become one of the most successful magazine launches ever, with a readership of more than one million. Suddenly it seemed as though people needed a celebrity endorsement to buy something as mundane as toothpaste. Fashion designers, led by Giorgio Armani, had realized the importance of the tacit celebrity endorsement and were falling all over themselves to get their gowns onto the red carpet, particularly the grandest red carpet of all—the one leading into the Academy Awards. Forget about selling them— they were giving them away and also giving large gifts to the stylists, who had become critical to the dressing process. Jewelry designers were also lining up to loan expensive baubles to actresses, and even paying them directly for the privilege. Tamara was certain that if it was working for fashion and gems, it could also work for shoes. But to get the L.A. celebrities, even free shoes were not going to be enough. They needed a local personage whom the celebrities knew and would trust.

Marilyn Heston is married to Charlton Heston's son and had worked in the celebrity PR game in Los Angeles for years before signing Jimmy Choo. She had left BWR Public Relations in 1991 when she had her son, and, like many women, she was not particularly eager to return to full-time employment while he was still young. In 1997, when her son started preschool, she began to think about what she would do next. She ran into her former assistant, who had also left BWR. The woman told Marilyn that she was now doing PR for fashion companies and asked Marilyn if she would be interested in working together. Marilyn pointed out that she knew nothing about fashion. "It's still PR," her friend said. "It's not that difficult. It is just clothes instead of people." They set up a company called GGI, or Get Good Ink.

Philip Rogers got in touch with Marilyn via a contact in New York and asked her to put together a proposal for the dual Vidal Sassoon/ Jimmy Choo store launch in November 1998. "I'd never even heard of Jimmy Choo," said Marilyn. But hers was a new company and she needed every client she could get. Once the deal was signed, she jumped into action. "I immediately rang Lisa Love at *Vogue* and asked her to meet me," Marilyn said. Because there were no single-brand shoe stores in Beverly Hills, Marilyn knew *Vogue* wouldn't have a conflict of interest when it came to lending its name for a party. To heighten interest and to save on expenses, Marilyn proposed that the launch party should be a charity event. Proceeds from sales done on the evening would sponsor the Children's Action Network. That way, the luminaries who were invited to shop could justify any expense as doing their part for a good cause. Some celebrities, such as actresses Rosanna Arquette and Rita Wilson, were invited to come by, pose on the red carpet, and pick out a pair of shoes for free. To keep costs down, Tamara's brother Daniel was the DJ and Marilyn got Dudley Moore's Maple Drive restaurant to donate the food. "I had a dozen girls in the shoes and they were all really excited about the brand," Marilyn said, speaking of her high-profile guests. "Everyone was comparing feet and shoes." Philip invited the

Sassoon crowd, and Tom Yeardye saw his old colleague Caroline Hayes, who was now working with Philip and Annie on the U.S. Vidal Sassoon schools. Tom had an issue with his former protégée. She remembers that he marched right up to her and said, "Why didn't you tell me there was so much money in women's shoes?" Caroline burst out laughing, "I don't know, Tom; we were in hair!"

After the store launch, Tamara and Marilyn decided the best way to continue the momentum in L.A. was to make a very large showing at the Academy Awards the following March. The week before the 1999 Oscars, Sandra and Tamara (with Matthew in tow) flew to Los Angeles with sixty pairs of shoes in seven different styles, but in only one color—white. They took a suite at L'Ermitage Hotel and planned an all-out attack for the Academy Awards on March 21. They had seen how many times Kate Winslet had mentioned her Jimmy Choo shoes when she won the Oscar for *Titanic* the year before. Until then, only dress designers had been mentioned by name on the red carpet. Marilyn and Tamara wanted to push the trend. Marilyn would escort a wide range of actresses and stylists through the suite, and Tamara and Sandra would promise that the shoes could be dyed to match the celebrities' dresses as late as the night before the event. "They effectively set up a boutique," said Cameron Silver, the owner of the best-known L.A. vintage store, Decades, who dressed many actresses for the awards. "They would accommodate you on a different level. They weren't just sending out loaners in sample size. Dyeing shoes to match the dress? No one else was doing it."

It was a significant investment for the small company, but one Tom never questioned. When he looked at the amount of press generated by the Academy Awards, it was easy to see that placing shoes on a few of the right feet would easily bring in more in free publicity than the money it cost to get them there. So much the better if they thought they had a sure thing. At the end of 1998 Tamara had met the actress Cate Blanchett at a party. Cate, an Australian, is one of the most sought-after celebrities in fashion. She has a unique personal style and is willing to take the odd fashion risk—something many of the cookie-cutter celebrities of Los Angeles are not willing to do. Tamara told Cate about Jimmy Choo and they concocted the ultimate PR stunt: What if Jimmy Choo made a pair of shoes for Cate with diamonds? Real diamonds. Tamara contacted Craig Drake, a Philadelphia jeweler whom Matthew knew well, and asked if he would make something special—a diamond bracelet that could double as the ankle strap of a shoe. Cate was sure to be nominated for an Oscar for her starring role in *Elizabeth*. When Tamara told Craig who the shoes were for and where they would be worn, the small local jeweler leaped at the chance for a bit of big-time PR. The story of the eggplant-hued shoes with the forty-carat diamond bracelet was covered by major press outlets from the Xinhua News Agency in China to the *New York Times*. They had been writing about those shoes since February, quoting the price at $110,000 (£67,000). Of course, Cate did not buy the shoes and would not be keeping them. Her dress and shoes were auctioned for charity before she ever wore them (and before anyone ever saw the shoes), bringing in $15,000 (£9,000) for the American Foundation for AIDS Research. Why so little? It was always planned that after the event the shoe would be dismantled and the diamonds returned to Craig Drake.

Tamara and Marilyn also had preshow promises by Geena Davis and first-time nominee Rachel Griffiths to wear the shoes. "In the beginning Jimmy Choo would give shoes to anyone," remembers Silver. But not all went according to plan. They managed to give out all the shoes (other stars wearing them that year included Kim Basinger, Jennifer Lopez, and Minnie Driver), but the night before the awards Cate Blanchett's stylist, Jessica Pasteur, called Marilyn Heston to tell her that the diamond shoes they had made weeks ago were a size too small. They were not comfortable, and Cate would not be wearing them.

In fashion terms, this was a disaster. Everyone had already written that Cate would be wearing Jimmy Choos, and now all the shoes they had brought to give to celebrities were gone. The shelves of the L.A. Jimmy Choo boutique were also bare. In a panic, Marilyn began phoning the Los Angeles department stores that stocked Jimmy Choo. The Saks Fifth Avenue in West Hollywood had a pair, but it, too, was half a size too small and it was black, not the eggplant color of Cate's dress. Marilyn jumped in her car and drove over to Saks and bought the shoes. Then she called Jack Zatikian, the only man in town who could help her in such a shoe-crisis moment.

Jack had come from Armenia with his father in 1980, when Jack was twelve. His father had been a shoemaker working from his garage since he was twenty years old. But, unlike Jimmy, Jack did not find this appealing. "I didn't want to do it," Jack said. "I wanted to be a jeweler." In 1982 his father set up a shoe repair shop in Beverly Hills on the corner of Sunset Boulevard and Rodeo Drive. Jack would work for him after school. "I went to Hollywood High," Jack says. "At the time they called it Armenian High." Much of their business came through Luda, a saleswoman at Fred Hayman who would recommend Progressive Shoe Repair to her wealthy clients. Jack's father became known as an expert in fixing expensive shoes. In 1984, when he had finished high school, Jack bought the business from his father. "Now he works for me," Jack said. The night before the 1999 Oscars, Jack got a call from Luda, who told him that a woman named Marilyn was going to be calling—and that it was urgent. "We've got a big problem," Marilyn told Jack when she phoned. "Cate's shoes are too small." She got his address and then, with Matthew by her side, drove from Saks Fifth Avenue in Beverly Hills to Jack's house in Los Feliz, East L.A.

"She showed me the shoes and told me that after I fix the size, I had to make them purple. I called my employee and we met at the shop at midnight," Jack said. They worked all night to extend the base of the shoe, reattach the upper, cover the whole thing in white satin, and then dye it to match the swatch Marilyn had given him. "It came out great," Jack said. "No one could tell." He phoned Marilyn at seven A.M. to tell her they were ready. Two hours later she came by with $100,000 (£60,000) worth of pearls and told Jack, "They're real, they're from Mikimoto, and they have to go on the shoes."

Despite the acres of press, the diamond shoes stayed home from the ball. Craig Drake was convinced that Cate did not wear them because they were getting more attention in the press than she was. Nevertheless, both Jimmy Choo and Craig Drake got what they really wanted—thousands of pages of free publicity, including the cover of *Vogue*. "Her PR was upset because all anyone was talking about was Cate's feet," Marilyn said.

Others in the shoe business quickly noticed the new attention on celebrity feet and the reason why. In subsequent years L'Ermitage Hotel would also host suites for Stuart Weitzman, Tod's, and Hush Puppies, each trying to catch the eyes of celebrity stylists. Manolo Blahnik was the one designer who refused to succumb to the Oscar madness. His in-store boutique at Neiman Marcus in Beverly Hills agreed to loan sample pairs of shoes to celebrities, but Blahnik refused to give them away free of charge. They must pay for the shoes, he said; otherwise it would be a compromise of his artistic integrity.

Despite the ever-increasing number of shoe brands that had no such qualms, Tamara and Sandra were always able to stay ahead of the competition. The following year Tamara and Nadja Swarovski, heiress of the Austrian crystal empire and a friend of Matthew's, teamed up to do a special collection for the millennium Oscars— seven one-of-a-kind styles all embellished with Swarovski crystals. "It was a big investment but it kept them on top," said Marilyn Heston. The suite at L'Ermitage Hotel contained a specially made range of crystal-studded bags, jewelry, and shoes and an on-site "tailor" to customize the shoes—Jack. They hosted a tea party to promote the event, and, again, actresses and stylists came streaming through. One of the most famous stylists, Philip Bloch, asked that a box of shoes and bags be delivered to Salma Hayek immediately. L'Wren Scott, the fashion director for the awards, ordered dozens of pairs for various hosts and performers. When one stylist known for her love of food would not return their calls, they ordered a huge Chinese buffet knowing that such a feast would entice her. There was a small men's collection, designed by Tamara's brother Daniel and Sandra that drew interest from Jude Law and one of Tom's old acquaintances, Michael Caine. Tamara and Sandra signed a confidentiality agreement so that they could be told the details of Hilary Swank's dress, and they offered to make a crystal-studded cane for Best Actress nominee Janet McTeer when they saw that her broken foot was going to prevent her from wearing Jimmy Choos. Angelina Jolie came by and tried to buy a pair. Sandra was alone at the suite and told her she could have them. But Angelina does not like freebies. It took Sandra twenty minutes to convince her that there was no way for her to even take money at the suite. There were no receipts, no cash register, and no credit card machine. In the end, Sandra won.

At a pre-Oscar party the night before the awards ceremony, Marilyn Heston was still not resting on her laurels: She saw Julianne Moore and pounced. "I went up to her and told her I was working with Jimmy Choo, just in case she wanted anything. She said, 'Thanks, but I'm all good,'" Marilyn said. Julianne was wearing Chanel and was supposed to also wear Chanel shoes to the ceremony. "The next day she came in looking for a pair of size sevens in black, three hours before she was leaving to get ready. We didn't have any; we had just let the last pair go." It was Jack to the rescue again. "He had to dye them," Marilyn said. "She left for the awards barefoot with her wet shoes in her hand." Tamara later said, "We were working twenty-four hours a day. We'd get calls at four A.M., people screaming and crying because they didn't want to wear the dress they'd originally chosen and they needed new shoes." When all was said and done, the net haul was more than fifty actresses, including Hilary Swank, Uma Thurman, Catherine Keener, Salma Hayek, Samantha Morton, Cate Blanchett, and Julianne Moore. *WWD* (*Women's Wear Daily*) did a small item on Marilyn called "The Player." To maximize the impact and minimize the investment in lasts, the most expensive part of a shoe, the final "one-of-a-kind" styles in the Oscar suite turned out to be the precursors of the autumn collection. The same styles were sold months later to the general public, sans crystals, for between $600 and $900 (£350–£500).

Endorsements for the brand were not coming just from the entertainment world. The following year, in January 2001, the twin daughters of George W. Bush wore Jimmy Choo shoes to their father's inauguration as president of the United States. The designer of their dresses, Lela Rose, told the press that the girls "didn't want to look like their mother."[34]

But politician's daughters, even those of a president of the United States, do not a brand make. Every year Sandra and Tamara had to come up with a new twist that would keep them ahead of the competition at the Oscars, be it hand-painting designs on the shoes by an imported British artist or adorning the shoes with fresh flowers—roses, orchids, and tuberoses—by acclaimed florist Eric Buterbaugh, who had come up with a way to make them last for twenty-four hours.

Over the years, as the brand grew increasingly popular, the question became one of quality over quantity. Tamara and Sandra were no longer interested in dressing everyone, just the A-list. In 2007 the producers of *Good Morning America*, with help from Christina Cuomo, wife of the cohost Chris Cuomo and a friend of Tamara's, arranged to bring their so-called Oscar Princess to the Jimmy Choo Oscar suite. The Oscar Princess is a young American girl who has had a life of hardship. Diane Sawyer and Chris Cuomo take her to Los Angeles and get her decked out for the Academy Awards. It is one of the show's most popular segments. But when the camera crew arrived to film some background material in the Jimmy Choo suite, Tamara sent them away, saying she wasn't "camera ready." A decade of catering to the movie star class had taken its toll, and Tamara now considered herself one of them. The producer of the segment was not amused. He went straight to the Stuart Weitzman suite, where

Stuart was more than happy to welcome one of the most popular TV programs in the United States and dress its princess.

In addition to loaning shoes for the awards ceremonies, Jimmy Choo was also happy to loan them for the movies themselves. While brands like Manolo Blahnik would only lend shoes if the characters were sympathetic and the entire production appealed to the taste of Manolo, Jimmy Choo seemed less concerned. For example, in the film *In Her Shoes* Cameron Diaz plays a deceiving drunk who sleeps with her older sister's fiancé. Which shoes does she steal from her sister's closet? Jimmy Choos. However, in other films the product placement of Jimmy Choo was superb. In *Legally Blonde 2* the protagonist, played by Reese Witherspoon, looked stunning in a plethora of Jimmy Choos, none made from leather to suit her character's pro-animal stance.

The New York store launch, held just days before the Los Angeles opening, was slightly more fraught than the West Coast one. At Matthew's urging Tamara suggested hiring his friend Lara Shriftman's firm, Harrison & Shriftman, to do the PR of the opening, and Tamara's London team approved the choice. But negotiating the New York social waters was still not easy.

Lara and her partner, Liz Cohen, had spent the last year pulling off their greatest PR coup: making a nobody from England into the It girl of the season. They had been inviting Alice Larkin (a former Betsey Johnson salesgirl) to all the right parties, making sure she was photographed with the right people and wearing the right clothes. It turned out that creating an It girl was fantastically easy. Within a few months Alice was on the cover of *Manhattan File*, the New York society magazine, and *Vogue* did a story on where she had her hair highlighted. But when the news broke that the husband of one of the city's most famous socialites, Samantha Kluge, had also fallen for her, Alice instantly became an outcast in Manhattan's society circles. Unfortunately, she had already been invited to come to the party for the Jimmy Choo store opening. The night of the launch party Tamara began getting calls from irate socialites, friends of Kluge, threatening to boycott. The opening of the shop itself went off smoothly—the famous British girls-about-town sisters Plum and Lucy Sykes cohosted the party, and Lara later bragged, "All the Brits are here tonight." All except for Alice Larkin, who had been told plainly not to attend.

The following year, Tamara would launch a major wholesale client of her own, one that would sell Jimmy Choo shoes both in London and in New York and eventually around the globe. One day Tamara had a meeting in her office above the store in London with a friend of a friend, Natalie Massenet. Natalie had met Tamara once before, when she was invited to attend a prelaunch luncheon for Jimmy Choo. Natalie now came to see Tamara on official business of her own. She was there to sell Tamara on the merits of a new retail venture—an Internet store that she hoped would sell the same labels as Harvey Nichols and have the look of a glossy fashion magazine like *Vogue*. It would be called Net-à-Porter, a play on *prêt-à-porter*, the French word for "ready-to-wear." At the time, the debris of mediocre but expensive apparel and luxury sites was littering cyberspace, with ill-conceived concepts such as luxlook.com and Boo.com. Most luxury-brand leaders believed that their customers would never shop online. After all, the Internet was pretty narrowly perceived as a male domain. And it was a pretty geeky male territory at that.

Natalie, a former staffer at *Women's Wear Daily* and *Tatler*, knew better. "Women will go to the moon if they have to, to get the things they want," she said. She went to Tamara and explained her concept: same-day deliveries for orders placed before noon, free returns collected at your home or office, amazing packaging, and an editorial written around each product that explained not just what it was, but also showed you how to wear it. "Our whole idea is that we are fashion editors choosing the next hot items for fashion addicts worldwide," she said.

"It took Tamara about eight seconds to decide," recalled Natalie. "She said, 'Yes, that sounds like the way I like to shop.'" Inspired by her decisiveness, Natalie decided to take it a step further and asked if she could have the shoes on consignment and pay for them only after they sold them. To her surprise, Tamara agreed.

At the time of their meeting, Natalie had not officially begun fund-raising. She had kept the site going with a couple of thousand-pound loans from her friends, because she knew that without a strong list of committed labels her chance at raising the £800,000 ($1.3 million) she needed to stage a full-scale launch was nil. Now that she had Jimmy Choo on board, Natalie was able to lure other British brands like Anya Hindmarch, Orla Kiely, and Earl Jeans, although the last pulled out just before the launch.

The brand-enhanced business plan of Net-à-Porter found its way to a beach in the Bahamas. There a pretty Venezuelan entrepreneur named Carmen Busquets was sunning herself with her boyfriend, a venture capitalist. Carmen had spent the last two years looking at business plans for Internet-based luxury companies and dismissing them. "They were all so greedy," she said. "They were all hundred-million-dollar businesses. I lost hope." But when her boyfriend handed her the Net-à-Porter business plan to read on the beach, she could barely contain her excitement. "I took it and marked all down the sides, 'Yes! Yes! Yes!'" For years, Carmen had been running a fashion boutique in Caracas. She would go to the European collections with her camera and then mail to her best clients the photos from the catwalks. They would place their orders and, helpfully, pay in advance. She found that when customers can choose what they want from an entire collection, they are much more likely to keep the items. Carmen was achieving 90 percent sell-through rates. (A department store is doing well when it sells 50 percent of its stock at full price.) So Carmen knew that women would happily buy a $10,000 (£6,000) dress from only a photo. She also knew that because of her own experience as a retailer, she could help Natalie bring in more labels. "I knew the Italian side," Carmen recalled.

"But we had to find a solution to get into France." She convinced Yves Carcelle, the head of the fashion and leather goods division at the French group Louis Vuitton Moët Hennessy (LVMH) to test Net-à-Porter with Pucci, the colorful Italian brand they had just acquired. When the Web site launched, Tamara's enthusiasm paid off. Jimmy Choo became the number one seller on the site.

When Natalie returned to Jimmy Choo's showroom to do the buying for the second season, Tamara asked if the shoes were selling well. Natalie assured her that they were. "Good," Tamara said. "So this time, you pay us in advance."

Later Tamara and Tom did a deal with Net-à-Porter to build the Jimmy Choo Web site and e-commerce business as a joint venture. It is the only such partnership Net-à-Porter has ever done. "They're our biggest brand," Natalie said. "We think it's a shoe moment; we think shoes are the new handbags."

To crown a nearly perfect year for Tamara, in December 1998 Matthew took Tamara to Pittsburgh for an annual Mellon family charity dinner fund-raiser. While there he picked her up in a limousine strewn with rose petals, blindfolded her, and took her to a waiting helicopter. Once on board he recited a poem he had written and then proposed to her. They then circled the Mellon Bank building so that Tamara could have a bird's-eye view of the family seat. She later said she remembered thinking at the time: "This is typical Matthew. Everything done to extreme." Extreme or not, the romantic moves had the desired effect. Tamara said yes.

Seven

A Good Man Is Hard to Lose

W HILE THINGS WERE HEATING up with Matthew and Jimmy Choo, the company, they were cooling off considerably with Jimmy Choo, the man. In 1998 Tom urged Jimmy to move from his workshop in Hackney into more respectable surroundings. Ann remembers, "He told him it wouldn't do to have him in Hackney anymore." Tom told Jimmy, "Your name is on doors around the world. You have to move." Jimmy found a townhouse on Connaught Street in Bayswater, just north of Hyde Park and just west of Marble Arch. Although it was not as posh as the location of the Yeardyes' store in Belgravia, it was a big improvement on the studio in Hackney. It had space for a workshop in the basement, a showroom for his couture shoes on the ground floor, and room for his family to live on the floors upstairs.

There was no fanfare surrounding the opening. When Jimmy finally did an interview, it was in February 1999, some ten months after the couture store had opened. He explained, "I didn't have any publicity because I am superstitious. Last year was the year of the Tiger. This year is the year of the Rabbit. I'm going to have good publicity this year. The rabbit is soft and lovely and has special chi. So, it's a good year for me."[35] His feng shui master came to give the store and workshop a clean bill of health before Jimmy moved in. The master also weighed in on other matters, predicting that

Jimmy would win Best Accessory Designer, the prestigious award of the British Fashion Council (BFC). The chi must have been strong. Jimmy Choo got his eighth BFC award nomination—but this time he won. The headlines the following day were all about the avant-garde Turkish designer Hussein Chalayan, who won Designer of the Year for the second year running, but the industry chatter was about the feud between Tamara and Jimmy. She had lobbied hard with the BFC to collect the award. Jimmy argued that at most brands design is done by teams, and his argument won. Rumors of a rift were beginning to trickle out of the fashion world. When asked about it in an interview, Jimmy said, "I love the idea of couture and its emphasis on creation. There's where I made my name—in design—and there's where I'd like to stay. After all, it's very important for any big-name designer to have a couture range. I leave the ready-to-wear to my partner and team."[36]

But privately, Jimmy was beginning to speak more and more frequently about his frustrations with Tamara and the Yeardyes. Rightly or wrongly, he felt he had been taken advantage of and that his name was being exploited without his consent. "I think he was sad," said Anouska Hempel. "He felt betrayed and let down that he'd allowed his name to be circulated around the world on good faith. He is a charming little chappie. He's very old-fashioned. He trusts people."

On April 23, 2000, the *Mail on Sunday* wrote a feature all about the two Jimmy Choos, making public for the first time Jimmy's disquiet at Tamara and Tom's moves. It quoted Jimmy as saying, "Anyone can sketch a shoe." To which the fashion world responded … ho hum. There were far more important things to worry about—like Tamara's wedding.

The May 2000 wedding was Tamara's first chance to show the world that she was more than just an average It girl. Her Blenheim Palace wedding was cast as carefully as one of her shoots in *Vogue*.

The night before the wedding there was a not-so-intimate

rehearsal dinner for 170 people in the gardens of Sudeley Castle, where guests enjoyed a buffet dinner and the performance of a group of ballerinas under a glass marquee that had been imported from Paris and protected guests from the spring rains. Robert Kass, one of Tamara's old chums from Los Angeles, joked to *Tatler*, "I thought we were meant to be in a castle. But we're in somebody's backyard. I wanna ballroom."[37]

The next day was better. There were two couture gowns, one by Valentino for the main event (for months Tamara had phoned in her measurements every week to the atelier in Rome) and another, on standby, by London designer Maria Grachvogel, who made Tamara's rehearsal dinner dress; forty-one carats of Harry Winston diamonds; four hundred guests, and dozens of doves. Tamara said of Valentino, "He has 40 years' experience of making women look beautiful and when I got married I wanted a dress that would make me look beautiful in a timeless way. If I want to be trendy, I'll buy Galliano. If it's a special occasion when I want to look elegant and wonderful it's always Valentino."[38]

The ceremony was held at a small church near the estate. Tamara had borrowed racks of Ellie Saab dresses from Marilyn Heston for her friends to wear. Young boys in morning coats led the guests to their seats, and the Rolling Stones' keyboard player, Matthew Clifford, had composed a special processional march for the event. Although the British made a strong showing—Liz Hurley stole the headlines the next day, this time for showing up twenty minutes late in a white floor-length Versace fur coat with Hugh Grant, the week after they announced their separation—the crowd was heavily weighted on the Mellon side. The side that was decidedly less chic.

After the ceremony the guests gathered outside the church, as is traditional, to cheer the bride and groom. But when they arrived at the top of the church steps, they were hurried out of the way. "It was all about 'stay clear of the doves,'" said one guest about the birds they had arranged to set free after the event. "The whole thing was just orchestrated for the photo shoot."

Things did not improve much at the Blenheim Palace party afterward. The food was not the problem; the Admirable Crichton, an expensive catering firm used by Sting's wife, Trudie Styler, and companies like Gucci, Bulgari, and the Royal Academy of Arts, did its usual stellar job. Nor was the decor; gorgeous flowers by Ken Turner covered nearly every surface. The guests were dressed to the nines. *Tatler* noted, "There wasn't a little black dress in sight. Not one. That's called fashion history," although the photos that accompanied the article proved the point wrong. But even worse than a cultural faux pas such as friends wearing black dresses to a wedding, people who barely knew the couple were surprised to find themselves at the head table. During the speeches, no one thanked the Yeardyes, despite the fact that Tom had footed the entire bill. Tom had given the couple a budget that, according to friends, they quickly blew through. "He vowed he wouldn't give her a penny more," one friend recalled. "But I am pretty sure he did." Family friends of the Yeardyes felt that the whole thing was upsetting to Tom and Ann. "They were made to feel subordinate—it was all about the Mellons," said another. Indeed it was Jay Mellon, Matthew's uncle, who served as the evening's master of ceremonies, not Tom, although he made a touching speech. Friends of Tamara and Matthew found it equally awkward. Matthew flew a band in from America called Boogie Knights that was far too loud, making conversation impossible. A five-foot cake made of profiteroles almost crashed to the ground. After the meal, people rushed to leave. Outside there was torrential rain, making a quick exit impossible. Mobile phones did not work (making it hard to reach chauffeurs), and there was no landline available in the house. Those who stayed watched fireworks through torrential rain.

The pictures of the wedding that appeared in the respectable pages of *Tatler* and *Vogue* made it all look fairy-tale perfect. *Vogue* called Tamara the icon of a new wedding movement—the "modern traditionalists." The gushing *Tatler* article written by one of Tamara's oldest friends, Vassi Chamberlain, was comically saccharine: "Mellon cousins played with Sloane squares; Palm Beach beauties caroused with English boys."[39] On a more practical note, Tamara later told a journalist, "We had record sales that week. I would say 90 per cent of the girls [at the wedding] were wearing Jimmy Choos."[40]

After their honeymoon at the Amanresorts in Bali, Tamara and Matthew retreated to the Hamptons for the summer. From there Tamara saw Jimmy Choo get its best-ever mention on *Sex and the City*. Running to catch the Staten Island Ferry, Carrie Bradshaw, the lead character, loses a shoe. "Wait! I lost my Choo!" she cries out as the boat pulls away from the pier.

Jimmy knew just how Carrie felt. He took the opportunity of Tamara's absence from London to boost his own image. With a PR firm of his own guiding him, he began going to parties, doing interviews, and contributing to small but high-profile design projects, like creating special boots for the British luxury brand Daks, and starting a line of feng shui shoes that had powerful crystals sewn into the straps. On his annual trip to Malaysia—where, thanks to Tamara, the shoes were being sold by the department store Isetan—he was knighted by the Sultan of Pahang. He was now officially Dato' Jimmy Choo.

According to the Yeardyes, Jimmy began to become increasingly difficult when it came to their business. He was talking so openly, so regularly, about his dissatisfaction with the partnership that, according to Ann, Tom had to take steps to protect the Yeardyes' interests and had his attorney write a cease-and-desist letter. Jimmy, Ann recalls, responded with a letter from his lawyer saying Tamara was no longer allowed to speak to the press. He then began taking advice from the husband of one of his customers who was a senior executive at a U.S. film company. He was pushing Jimmy to find a solution to the situation, and the one he favored meant suing the Yeardyes. Tom took the film executive to lunch in an attempt to head off a fight. Tom offered to buy Jimmy out of his half of the company. Jimmy refused to sell.

*   *   *

Meanwhile, from her U.S. summer base in the Hamptons, Tamara was settling into her life as a future billionaire's wife. Photos of Tamara in the early days of Jimmy Choo show a pretty but down-to-earth girl. Even on photo shoots she was loathe to pile on the makeup. Ann said, "I was always telling the PRs that she should get dressed up for the photos. This is fashion, you should glam her up." Surrounded by the Park Avenue princesses in the Hamptons, Tamara was learning a lifetime of lessons on primping—fast. An article in the British press explained the rigorous regime involved in keeping up with the top ring of the New York social set:

> She hires couture dresses at £100 [$150] a time, with matching jewellery, bags and pashminas every week from Bodie & Gibbs (despite the fact she could afford to buy them). "If you hire them, he'll never see you in the same dress twice," she says. But that's the least of her beauty regime, which costs about £600 [$900] a month (excluding clothes). "I have reflexology and do kick-boxing and aerobics three times a week with personal trainers," she says. "It's all discipline—I get up at 7.30 am to do exercise and then fit in grooming appointments between nine and 10. I've had Botox three times."[41]

And at least one of those was a "his-and-hers" session done with Matthew. But despite appearances, it was the Yeardyes and the Jimmy Choo company that were footing the bill for the majority of Tamara's upkeep. A friend remembers one notable outfit given to Tamara by Matthew—a white leather dress from Joseph to match the interior of his new Maserati.

That winter, while on holiday in the Bahamas, Matthew rented a boat for a group of Tamara's friends. Tamara packed ten pairs of shoes for the ten-day trip. Why so few? Well, she was on a boat most of the time, she explained to her assistant. In port at Harbor Island after having to navigate some rough seas, Matthew went clubbing with the boys—and he relapsed. When he returned to the boat, he locked himself in the guest bathroom for two hours. Tamara realized that Jimmy was not the only discontented man she had in her life. It was the beginning of a downward spiral. Tamara and her friends would years later describe to *Vanity Fair* how, after that fateful trip to the Bahamas, the only thing predictable about life with Matthew was that it was unpredictable. The magazine reported, "Her mornings at work were frequently spent placing calls to his family members, hotels, and various car services trying to track him down ... Hotels would call her, saying that her husband had left without paying the bill and she'd pick up the tab. It seems Matthew had run out of money."[42] At least until he came into his next trust fund.

When Matthew wasn't on drug benders, he was making his presence felt in her company. He would come into the office after hours to use the phones and computers (until Tom told Tamara to set up an office for him at home), and he insisted on making his opinions known on the Jimmy Choo men's line, despite the fact that it had been launched by Tamara's brother Daniel. Behind the scenes, he was also urging Tamara to get tougher with just about everyone—from the owners of the stores that stocked Jimmy Choo shoes, to Jimmy, and, shockingly, even with her beloved father, Tom.

Back on the scene in London in January 2001, the first thing Tamara did was to give a big interview to one of the city's favorite tabloids, the *Evening Standard*. In it she described brown crocodile slingbacks as "a great basic." She then went on to note, pointedly, that when she got involved with Jimmy Choo, the brand wasn't even on the map. "Manolo Blahnik was the only competition," she said. "That was it. Jimmy was making two pairs of shoes a day, by hand, from a workshop in the East End." She hammered home the strides she made in celebrity dressing: "No accessory company has ever done what we did at the Oscars," she said. "Angelina Jolie, Sadie Frost, Minnie Driver, Cate Blanchett ... it would be easier to name the people we don't dress. I've always worked and I am quite ambitious."[43]

The confident façade masked all hints of the chaos that was unfolding at home, as did the news that Tamara was now pregnant.

Tom, meanwhile, was making new additions to the staff at Jimmy Choo headquarters on Pont Street. Despite the growing profile of the brand, it was still a tiny company. In 1999 he got back in touch with his old executive assistant from Vidal Sassoon, Lou Rodwell. After Philip and Annie had taken over the salons and schools, Lou's career had taken him to the petrochemical industry, where he had worked as a finance director for sixteen years. Tom phoned him and said, "Come join me." Lou told his bosses he was taking early retirement and left the company on May 31, 1999. On June 1 he started at Jimmy Choo. "Tom and I had maturity and knowledge of finance," said Lou. "But the youngsters had the ideas and the energy. To work with young people at the end of my career was a shot of adrenaline in the arm. They had the charisma. Tom and I were the engine."

Tom was not the only one in need of backup in the office. Between the Oscars, the wholesale appointments, and the factory visits, the workload began to be too much for even the hardworking Sandra. And now that Tamara was pregnant, it was even more apparent that help was needed on the design team. That summer Jimmy Choo hired its first outside designer. Jonathan Kelsey was a recent graduate of the prestigious Central Saint Martins fashion school. Although Kelsey had been accepted into the Royal Academy of Arts program to work on a master's degree, he did not have any actual experience as a shoe designer. But Tamara and Sandra liked his sketches of shoes and other products he dreamed up while at school, like sunglasses, and they gave him the job. The fact that Kelsey came from the inner circle of British hipsters did not hurt either. His cousin Stuart Vevers was a close friend of Katie Grand, the influential stylist and editor of *Pop* magazine. Vevers would go on to take the top design post at Mulberry, the British shoe and accessories company, and later at Loewe, the Spanish luxury leather brand. Kelsey would later be hired to launch a shoe collection for Mulberry and launch a collection of his own. The Jimmy Choo design studio was also the launchpad for Beatrix Ong, another Chinese, British-trained shoe designer.

With the business growing fast, in October 2001, Jimmy Choo moved the store from its original location on Motcomb Street to a one-thousand-square-foot space at 169 Draycott Avenue. The turnover of the company by 2001 was on its way to reach almost £12 million ($16.3 million), although the bulk of it, 90 percent or so, was still in wholesale sales. It was nonetheless generating high levels of operating profits, close to £2 million ($2.8 million). To celebrate the new store Tamara held a ladies' lunch—tea and sandwiches— and the proceeds of sales went to the Twin Towers Fund. Tamara lunched on cucumber sandwiches while quietly giving thanks that some of the friction in her life would soon be gone. "I don't want to be just a rich man's wife," she had said shortly after getting married. "I want my independence."[44] Within a month she would have it—at least from one man.

Tom was convinced that making peace with Jimmy was out of the question. If Jimmy was not going to sell to him, they were in a stalemate. Tom decided the only way out of the awkward situation was to find an outside investor who could buy the company, or at least buy Jimmy out of it. He spoke to Merrill Lynch in New York about quietly investigating a possible sale of Jimmy Choo. "Tamara was okay with that; she considered herself of an ilk that she knew she'd do something else," Philip recalled. "She knew she had her father behind her." As they began to talk to potential buyers, Tom learned that Jimmy Choo was also making the rounds, hoping to find someone to buy out the Yeardyes. It seemed as though a new game had begun. One called "who can find a buyer first?"

Eight

THE BUSINESS OF LUXURY

ALTHOUGH TAMARA AND TOM may not have realized it at the time, the Jimmy Choo story is inextricably intertwined with the onset of the modern luxury goods industry and its phenomenal growth over the last few years. Jimmy Choo is indeed one of the greatest success tales in modern luxury goods and, to date, the only true luxury brand of the twenty-first century.

Other contemporary brands with the same status in our collective consciousness are decades old. Almost without exception, every well-established luxury brand with which Jimmy Choo boutiques rub shoulders on the main fashion avenues of the world was founded in the nineteenth or early twentieth century. Among the oldest are Hermès, founded in 1837; Burberry in 1856; Bulgari in 1884; and Louis Vuitton in 1854. Others, dating from the early years of the twentieth century, include names such as Chanel, founded in 1909; Prada in 1913; Gucci in 1921; and Fendi in 1925. Even the brands founded during the advent of the designer-driven, ready-to-wear years are decades old. Dior was founded in 1946, Valentino in 1959, Yves Saint Laurent in 1961, Armani in 1975, and Versace in 1978. Some of them are still deemed successes because at some point in the not-so-distant past they remade themselves with forward-looking new designers, revamped their advertising campaigns, and, as often as not, acquired new owners.

Many of the brands that Jimmy Choo might consider peers in age are not pure luxury brands. They have found success by establishing second, cheaper lines or via brand extensions. Take Marc Jacobs. His company was founded in 1984, but it did not begin to make real headlines until Louis Vuitton Moët Hennessy (LVMH) acquired a stake in it in 1996 and began injecting serious capital into the business to open stores, advertise, and develop a wider product assortment. Its cash cow, a moneymaking, affordable collection called Marc by Marc Jacobs, was launched in early 2001. This line plus successful ventures into many other product categories (leather accessories, perfumes, and shoes, to name a few) drove Marc Jacobs brand revenues to more than $200 million (£100 million) in 2007. It is still too soon to say if other, more recent launches or relaunches, such as Peter Som or Halston, will be able to achieve success on a Jimmy Choo scale.

Even if luxury goods have been part of our Western society for centuries, the modern luxury goods sector as we currently know it started to take shape less than three decades ago. At the birth of this modern industry were two key men who made enormous contributions toward shaping the face of the business of luxury: Bernard Arnault and Nemir Kirdar. Many people are likely to be acquainted with the former, the sharp and savvy chairman of the leading luxury goods conglomerate LVMH and the wealthiest man in France. But most people have probably never heard of Nemir Kirdar, the discreet chairman of the Bahrain-based investment company Investcorp, the first private equity firm to ever invest in luxury brands.

Both men were visionaries in understanding where the markets for luxury goods were headed. Kirdar entered and left the game early (Investcorp had exited all of its luxury investments by 2000). Arnault, on the other hand, remained a player in the industry and is now the world's undisputed luxury leader.

Arnault came from a modestly wealthy French family that owned a construction business. In his early career days, after graduating

from the elite École Polytechnique, one of the world's most
renowned schools, Arnault joined the family business, which was
one of the top vacation home developers in France. It later expanded
into the United States to do the same in Florida. But Arnault's heart
was not in vacation homes. He began to think about the untapped
possibilities of luxury brands. In 1984 he managed to gain control
of a huge bankrupt French holding company, Société Foncière et
Financière Agache-Willot, which was being auctioned off by the
French government. Among its many, mostly worthless assets was
one of the leading French textile groups, Boussac, and within it the
legendary brand Christian Dior. Over the following four or five years
Arnault sold off most of the manufacturing assets of Agache and
undertook a restructuring of the business that pocketed him roughly
$500 million (£375 million) and left eight thousand employees out
of work, shocking the socially conscious French establishment with
his business tactics. He kept, however, the jewel of the empire,
Christian Dior. Dior would be the base of his own luxury goods
group, one he thought would mimic the leading luxury group of
the time, LVMH. At the time it owned the luggage maker Louis
Vuitton, champagne brand Moët & Chandon, Hennessy cognac,
the Guerlain perfume and cosmetics brand, and the rights to Dior
fragrances.

After acquiring Christian Dior, Arnault's next move was to create
a new brand from scratch. In 1987 he hired Paris's most talked-about
designer, Christian Lacroix, away from the couture house Patou and
set him up with his own atelier. (Patou would later successfully sue
Lacroix for breach of contract.) Later in the year, taking advantage
of internal succession issues, Arnault managed to acquire Celine,
the French leather goods and women's wear brand that, created in
1945, was still in the hands of its original founder, Madame Céline
Vipiana.

But LVMH was soon to become more than a role model for
Arnault in the buildup of his luxury empire. It was to become his
prey. Henri Recamier, then president of Louis Vuitton, invited

Arnault to intervene in a feud between him and Alain Chevalier, the CEO of Moët Hennessy. Arnault, again displaying an undeniably aggressive approach to business and deal making, surprised Recamier when he acquired a controlling stake in LVMH in 1988. By 1990, after a bitter two-year battle, he had ousted the group's previous owners and management team, including the man who had asked for his help.

By the time Arnault got control of LVMH, Louis Vuitton, under the leadership of Recamier, had already begun its regeneration process and was one of the largest brands in luxury goods. It was generating revenues of more than $750 million (£420 million) at the time and boasted some 125 stores around the world. But despite the strength of Vuitton, LVMH was still not fully regarded as a luxury group. It was seen mostly as a beverages company, and for a good reason: In 1995 LVMH was deriving just a quarter of its €4.5 billion revenues from its fashion and leather goods brands. The bulk of the group's turnover (close to 40 percent) came from its wine and spirits brands, while perfumes and cosmetics made up another third of its revenues. To further diversify the group toward luxury, Arnault acquired Loewe, the Spanish leather brand; Kenzo, the hottest Japanese label of the time; and the illustrious French brand that Audrey Hepburn made famous, Givenchy.

As Arnault was getting control of Christian Dior, Investcorp, an investment company funded mostly with oil money from the Arabian Gulf states, was already investing in the luxury sector. Its chairman and founder, Nemir Kirdar, recognized early the allure and power of luxury brands, influenced in no small measure by the fascination that its own investor base had with brands. Among Investcorp's first investments in 1984 was the legendary Fifth Avenue jeweler Tiffany & Co., a company in which Investcorp orchestrated a turnaround and then later, in 1987, a listing on the New York Stock Exchange. The fascination with luxury and the success of Tiffany & Co.'s initial public offering (IPO) encouraged the Investcorp team to buy and later sell some ten additional luxury brands over the following twenty years, across a wide spectrum of products: from luxury speedboats (such as Riva, the glamorous Italian company) to luxury department stores (Saks Fifth Avenue, which was held by the firm for almost fifteen years) and luxury watches and jewelry brands (Ebel, the Swiss watchmaker; Breguet, the world's oldest watch brand; and Chaumet, a legendary Place Vendôme jewelry brand).

But without a doubt, the best-known and most successful investment that Investcorp ever made in the luxury sector was Gucci. In 1993 the famous Italian leather goods brand was on the brink of bankruptcy. Internal family disputes and years of poor management had resulted in damaging strategic moves. The brand name had been licensed widely and appeared on everything from lighters to socks and umbrellas. The often questionable quality and design of these products had eroded the Gucci brand's allure and, mixed with severe family strife, had brought the company to its financial knees. Investcorp teamed up with one of the family heirs, Maurizio Gucci, to buy out the rest of the family.

Maurizio had made some key moves to improve the brand—most important, hiring Dawn Mello, the charismatic president of New York luxury emporium Bergdorf Goodman, to be Gucci's creative director. She in turn hired a new design team that included Richard Lambertson and the then little-known Tom Ford. Investcorp soon removed Maurizio, as he had little in the way of practical know-how when it came to running a company. And as it turned out, he also had little time. He was murdered by a hit man hired by his ex-wife in 1995. Richard and Dawn left Gucci shortly after Maurizio.

Investcorp appointed Domenico De Sole, a Harvard-educated Italian lawyer who had long worked with the Guccis, to be CEO of the group in 1994. Prior to this appointment, De Sole had worked as the Gucci family's lawyer and served as the CEO of the company's U.S. operation. When he arrived at Gucci's headquarters in Florence, De Sole found a company in turmoil. Most of the staff had resigned, and the factories were threatening to stop production. De Sole gave the important job of designing the next collection to the only member of the design team left—Tom Ford. Then he went on the road with briefcases full of Investcorp lira to convince the owners of the factories that manufactured Gucci's goods to keep working. After some initial clashes, De Sole and Ford realized they were a strong team and began the long, hard work of restructuring the company and restoring luster to the brand. Ford's first collection in the fall/winter of 1995 was an unexpected and unreserved critical and commercial success. The company tripled its sales almost overnight, and for the following years, under the leadership of "Tom and Dom," the brand went from strength to strength. It was one of the most lauded brand turnarounds ever, creating a model for brand relaunches in the years to come.

In the 1990s another luxury group was also in the making: Richemont, the owner of both Cartier and Dunhill, which was in the hands of the South African Rupert family. The group's origins date back to the 1940s. From its roots in the tobacco business, Rothmans International (to this date the group remains an important shareholder of BAT, British American Tobacco), under its chairman, Johann Rupert, amassed the most coveted collection of top jewelry and watch brands in the world. Richemont group was created in 1988 with the merger of both the tobacco business and its luxury assets Cartier, Dunhill, Montblanc, and Chloé. In 1993 the luxury assets were segregated into a separate unit, Vendôme Luxury Group, which was later listed on the stock exchange and renamed Compagnie Financière Richemont. Rupert was fascinated not by what he regarded as fickle fashion brands, but rather by heritage, staying power, and the traditional values of "true luxury." The heritage and legend of Cartier was obvious; it was the best known and largest jewelry brand in the world, thanks in no small part to the successful development of its watches. Rupert's view was that traditional Swiss watchmaking, with its history and craftsmanship, was a unique and scarce resource that was incredibly difficult to replicate and would become increasingly valuable as the demand for luxury watches increased. Although Johann was not a likely candidate for buying fashion brands, he was clearly a top candidate whenever a small family watchmaker wanted to retire.

The democratization of luxury in the 1990s, or the move to make luxury brands accessible to larger numbers of people, had a predictable result. Investment bankers started targeting companies that had historically been owned and run by close-knit families. After all, where the consumer goes, Wall Street follows. In the early 1990s only the venerable Hermès, Tiffany & Co., and LVMH were publicly traded on the stock market, and LVMH was considered mostly a beverage stock because of its large spirits and champagne division.

The IPO of Italian jeweler Bulgari in early 1995 marked a milestone in the modern history of the business of luxury. Francesco Trapani, another U.S.-educated Italian like De Sole, and the son of one of the Bulgari daughters, had at twenty-seven years old become the CEO of the company. He retained U.S. investment bank Morgan Stanley to raise the funds to finance an ambitious global expansion plan, and in 1995 the company went public and its stock started to trade on the Milan Stock Exchange. On the day of the IPO, the shares opened at 8,600 lira ($5.32) and in less than a year had more than doubled in value. Few in the investment community could have predicted such large returns from such a small company. Morgan Stanley began to push Investcorp for a Gucci IPO.

By the time Investcorp took Gucci public in October 1995, it was the hottest brand in fashion and in the business of fashion. The "Tom and Dom" dream management team, with Tom continuing to design, season after season, the most acclaimed collections of the time and Domenico managing the business in a modern, dynamic way that focused on tightly controlling both the production and the distribution of the brand, coupled with the success of Bulgari's debut on the stock market, enticed investors to take a serious look at the luxury sector. As a result, the IPO of Gucci was a huge success. Investcorp sold 49 percent of the company with a dual listing, not in Milan, but on the New York and Amsterdam stock exchanges.

The price was twenty-two dollars per share at the time of the listing but jumped to forty-eight dollars per share over the next six months, and by March 1996, when Investcorp decided to sell its remaining 51 percent stake, it netted a total of $1.45 billion (almost £1 billion), a nearly sixfold increase on its initial investment.

If Wall Street had been flirting with luxury goods before, it was in love now. And the love deepened with each of the lucrative IPOs that followed over the coming years: Donna Karan, Polo Ralph Lauren, Ittierre, TAG Heuer, Wolford, Burberry, Tod's. Even Versace had an IPO in the making, but it was canceled just after the untimely death of its designer and main shareholder, Gianni, in the summer of 1997. All of these companies made big money for investment banks and managers, if not for the average investors. The luxury goods sector was born.

Suddenly teams of bankers and equity analysts at the top investment banks were busy brokering the deals and analyzing the businesses and the valuation of the shares of the incipient luxury sector. Reports with suggestive names such as "Gucci: In the Lap of Luxury" or "The Luxury Goods Handbook" highlighted the sector's macro dynamics, like the correlation of the share prices of luxury stocks with Japanese yen movements, and micro drivers, like the higher value of a directly owned retail distribution network versus an array of licensing deals. These reports were circulated to and avidly read by investors, bankers, and company executives, fueling the appetite for luxury assets. Articles about luxury goods companies and their management teams began to appear in publications other than the trade title *Women's Wear Daily*. General interest business publications like *Fortune* and the *Wall Street Journal* hired reporters to cover the luxury sector full-time. Newspapers and trade publications such as the *International Herald Tribune, Financial Times, Women's Wear Daily*, and *Luxury Briefing* started to organize well-attended conferences with speakers and guests from the most distinguished companies in the sector. The broader financial community, and the broader public, was finally starting to get to know the ins and outs of the business of luxury.

At the end of 1996, Tom and Tamara Yeardye were forging a partnership with Jimmy Choo, taking a 50 percent stake in the company that would be the seed of one of the most successful launches in luxury goods ever. But this small transaction was just a tiny drop in the avalanche of deals that was still to come in the luxury sector.

The biggest luxury brand shopaholic was Bernard Arnault. LVMH's ambitious chairman kept adding, not just brands, but whole new divisions. In 1997 LVMH purchased Duty Free Shoppers (DFS), the €2 billion duty-free giant of the Asian market, which flourished thanks to the wallets of millions of Japanese tourists. It created the base of a new division of the luxury conglomerate called the selective distribution division. Later, Arnault added Sephora, the innovative chain of perfumeries, and Le Bon Marché, the Parisian Left Bank, ultra-chic department store.

The watches and jewelry division was created just two years later, in 1999, as Arnault embarked on his first foray into the watch business by buying Swiss watch brand TAG Heuer, a company that had gone public in 1996 but never flourished in the stock market. To TAG Heuer he added the Place Vendôme jeweler Fred and two of the watch brands that Investcorp had bought in the late 1980s and early 1990s and now was trying to offload from its portfolio— Ebel and Chaumet. The most recent addition to the LVMH watch portfolio was Hublot, purchased in 2008.

In the midst of this buying frenzy, another luxury goods empire was to emerge out of the French retail conglomerate Pinault-Printemps-Redoute (PPR). PPR was controlled by François Pinault and managed by his charismatic CEO, Serge Weinberg. Pinault would turn his group of midmarket department stores and mail-order catalogs into a luxury group in perhaps the most talked-about entry into the luxury goods market.

Toward the end of 1998, Gucci's share price had been badly hit in the stock market collapse in the aftermath of Asia's emerging markets financial crisis. By year-end the Gucci shares were hitting lows not seen since the IPO two years earlier. Gucci stock was starting to look undervalued, at least in the mind of the CEO and owner of one of Gucci's keenest competitors, Patrizio Bertelli at Prada. To the shock of executives in the still mostly staid world of fashion, Bertelli had amassed a 9.5 percent stake in his competitor. Industry observers began to wonder if a takeover was in the making. It was. In early January 1999, LVMH announced that it had more than 5 percent of the shares of Gucci. Gucci share prices skyrocketed from 50 euros per share to 70 euros per share almost overnight. A takeover now seemed inevitable. However, in a surprise move that provided Bertelli enough cash ($140 million/£85 million in total) for his own brand acquisition spree, he sold his 9.5 percent stake to Bernard Arnault at LVMH, who added the shares to the 5 percent stake he had already acquired. Bertelli later acquired Jil Sander, Helmut Lang, Church, and a stake in Fendi.

Interestingly, the amount that LVMH paid for the 9.5 percent stake in Gucci was higher than the price that Investcorp was asking when it first attempted to sell Gucci in 1994 and that LVMH had found too expensive. But that was then. This time LVMH continued to buy up Gucci stock so that by the end of January 1999 it owned 34 percent of Gucci shares and Arnault started requesting seats on Gucci's board, a move unacceptable to De Sole, as LVMH was one of his chief competitors. By then, De Sole had already called in investment bankers at Morgan Stanley to stage a defense against what he saw as a hostile takeover of the company. If the bankers could not fend off a takeover, he hoped that at least they could get Gucci's shareholders (himself and Ford among them) the lofty price he felt they deserved. The "Handbag Wars" had begun.

The bitter battle lasted throughout 1999. A team of Morgan Stanley bankers headed by Michael Zaoui came up with an innovative but convoluted solution that involved the issuance of new shares into a special trust held for employees. That would effectively dilute LVMH's holdings from 34 percent to 20 percent. Arnault fought it aggressively in the Dutch courts. In the meantime, bankers were able to find a more traditional solution—a white knight. Unbeknownst to most in the industry, François Pinault and Serge Weinberg at PPR had been quietly looking at buying Yves Saint Laurent (YSL). With Alber Elbaz at the creative helm, YSL was owned by the French cosmetics and drugs company Sanofi. When the Morgan Stanley bankers called Pinault about Gucci, he saw his moment. Advised by J.P. Morgan, Pinault eagerly stepped into the white knight role and acquired 40 percent of Gucci's stock, with the blessing of Ford and De Sole. When the deal was announced it came with an added surprise. PPR revealed that it would also acquire YSL and put it under the auspices of Tom and Domenico, thereby creating the Gucci Group. Instead of adding a thriving brand to his portfolio, Bernard Arnault found he had instead created his greatest competitor—a group that would operate in the same sectors as his brands and compete for the same managers, the same real estate, and the same customers.

The war intensified and LVMH continued to battle with Gucci and PPR in courtrooms, boardrooms, and the pages of the financial press throughout 2000. LVMH was now stuck with a 20 percent stake in Gucci, but with no control and no board seat—an unacceptable situation.

As Gucci's management started to restructure YSL, it also began to add new brands to the portfolio, something encouraged by Pinault, its new shareholder, who now found he had the platform to build a luxury group to rival LVMH. Boucheron, Bottega Veneta, Sergio Rossi, and Balenciaga were added within a matter of months. Stella McCartney, daughter of the former Beatle Paul, left her post as designer at Richemont's Chloé to start her own label at the Gucci Group, and designer Alexander McQueen left his post at LVMH's Givenchy to focus on his own brand, also at the Gucci Group. By the time the deals were done, at the end of 2001, Gucci Group's revenues had swelled to well over €2 billion ($2.2 billion/£1.25 billion).

In early September 2001, after years of legal wrangling, LVMH agreed to an exit from Gucci. Arnault would sell part of his 20 percent stake to PPR, and PPR would agree to buy out the remaining stake, as well as any other minority shareholders who so desired, at a pre-agreed minimum price of $101.50 per share by April 2004. That agreement protected Gucci's share price from the collapse in luxury goods stocks that followed the terrorist attacks in New York on September 11, since it effectively guaranteed a minimum price in nearly three years' time, but it was dismal timing for PPR. The stock tumbled by over 50 percent overnight. It was a small source of comfort for Bernard Arnault. After all, if his archrival had waited, they would have been able to get their hands on the remaining Gucci shares for far less.

Through the thick of the Gucci battles, LVMH still continued to collect luxury assets, venturing into Italian brands with the acquisitions of Pucci and Fendi. For the latter, Arnault teamed up with Patrizio Bertelli at Prada to bid head to head against De Sole at Gucci, who was also interested in acquiring the brand. Then came the younger American luxury sportswear brands Marc Jacobs and Michael Kors, and the more established American brand favored by working women, Donna Karan. In what seemed part of the formula, Jacobs and Kors also took on the top creative jobs at two of the other group's more established brands, Louis Vuitton and Celine. By the end of the millennium, with a euphoric luxury market and all those acquisitions to add to the top line, LVMH reached revenues of €11.6 billion in the year 2000 ($12.2 billion/£6.8 billion), almost four times those of the group at the start of the decade. But despite all the headline-grabbing acquisitions, it was still a single brand, Louis Vuitton, which drove the group. Louis Vuitton's sales and profits had continued to skyrocket thanks to its consistent strategy and devoted Asian clientele. It now accounted for more than half of all LVMH's profits.

Richemont was also a strong player in the acquisition frenzy, albeit with a more focused approach. Cartier, Dunhill, Chloé, and Montblanc were joined in 1996 by the legendary Swiss watchmaker

Vacheron Constantin, and later by the Italian watch brand Officine Panerai, the venerable French jewelers Van Cleef & Arpels, Swiss watch company Piaget, and French leather goods house Lancel, all acquired in the late 1990s. In early 2001, at the pitch of the luxury acquisition fever, Richemont bought the luxury watch assets of German industrial and telecom conglomerate Mannesmann (IWC, Jaeger-LeCoultre, and A. Lange & Söhne) for the staggering price of close to one billion euros. By the end of the year 2000, revenues at the group were close to reaching three billion euros. Rupert highlighted his rationale in a humorous presentation to financial analysts and investors in 2001. At the pulpit of a conference room at a swanky hotel in the City of London, he explained the correlation between the profitability of various industries and the price per kilo of its respective core products—all indexed to the price per kilo of gold. He argued that the price per kilogram of a product was highly correlated to the intrinsic profitability of that industry. Cars, being heavy, scored at the very bottom of the spectrum and thereby drove very low levels of profitability for their makers. However, Swiss luxury watches were very close to the top, surpassed only by microchips and certain pharmaceutical pills, such as Viagra. All three—chip makers such as Intel, pharmaceutical companies, and, of course, Swiss watch brand companies—enjoy very high levels of profitability as small objects that capture huge levels of know-how. On that logic, Richemont had been selectively and successfully adding to its portfolio.

With the events of September 11, however, the merger and acquisitions activity in the luxury goods sector came to a screeching halt. The euphoria that had permeated the business evaporated overnight. Luxury business started to see steep declines as Western consumers became increasingly conservative in their spending and Japanese tourists, a key consumer group in luxury, stopped traveling. Share prices of luxury goods stocks declined sharply.

Digesting previous purchases and shying away from new acquisitions was the new order of the day as Arnault, Pinault, and Rupert began to realize that they could no longer run their empires out of the public eye. Shareholders put pressure on them to work on making the recently acquired brands profitable and to sell "nonstrategic" investments instead of making new ones. They brought in new managers with the skills to run multinational brand portfolios from consumer products companies like Procter & Gamble and Unilever, raising eyebrows among the hardened followers of fashion. Aside from their skills, those hires signaled to shareholders and the financial market that, finally, these were businesses that would be run like businesses.

With corporate buyers out of the game (at least on the buying front), investment bankers struggled to put together merger and acquisition deals. They started to groom luxury goods companies and attempted to convince them to go public.

Burberry was one of them. The brand, part of the UK retail conglomerate Great Universal Stores (GUS), had been revived by the charismatic American Rose Marie Bravo, who had moved to London from the U.S. in 1997 to become the company's CEO. Her dynamic American style honed during years at the helm of U.S. luxury department stores such as I. Magnin and Saks Fifth Avenue worked wonders at the staid British brand, until then best known for its raincoats. Rose Marie infused Burberry with new energy, hiring first Roberto Menichetti and then Christopher Bailey as creative director and Mario Testino to shoot the new advertising campaigns starring Kate Moss and Freddie Windsor, cousin of Queen Elizabeth II. Soon enough the iconic Burberry plaid was hip again. With a revamped product and image and a restructured business that involved opening flagship stores around the world, expanding the brand into new products and managing its licenses better, Burberry was, by the summer of 2002, ready to be spun-off from GUS and independently listed on the stock exchange.

Throughout 2003, as the stock markets started to recover and investors started to look more favorably upon the luxury sector, other companies began to follow suit. Aeffe and Valentino, among others, staged successful IPOs between 2003 and 2006.

Other activity in the sector was also starting to heat up. Bankers were pushing for and finding that there were merger and acquisition deals to be made with another group of buyers—private equity funds. Private equity funds are investment vehicles that, rather than buy and sell shares of publicly listed companies on the stock market (like pension funds or hedge funds), buy individual companies, often from private hands. The purchases can be of the entire company or, more often, of a substantial majority stake. Many of the target companies for private equity funds either have strong growth potential and are seeking the capital to grow, or are in need of a turnaround or restructuring, often under new management. These funds always invest in companies with the intention to sell them in the medium term, once the goals set at the time of the purchase are attained (a four- or five-year holding period is typical). The "exit" can be orchestrated as a sale to a corporate buyer or another private equity firm, or, alternatively, as an IPO, listing the shares on the stock market.

Undoubtedly the easiest way to generate great returns on investment for private equity is through financial engineering: use large quantities of debt (rather than equity) to finance the purchase of a company, and then pay back those loans with the profits generated by the companies themselves. This clearly adds risk to the companies, as the margin of maneuver (and error) with a large amount of debt on its balance sheets is much smaller. But higher risk usually implies higher returns. Since the funds are basically financing a substantial part of the purchase price with money from lenders rather than their own, at the time of the exit the potential to generate high returns on the equity invested is vastly increased.

Despite the success that Investcorp had with Gucci and Tiffany, others in private equity thought the sector was still too risky. Yes, the private equity firm Doughty Hanson was able to exit its investment in TAG Heuer in an IPO in 1997, but the troubled experience that Texas Pacific Group was having with Bally was doing nothing to quell those fears. After acquiring Bally for some $200 million

(£125 million) in 1999, the company tried to initiate a Gucci-style turnaround and found that it wasn't as easy as Tom and Dom made it look. They ended up holding the company for almost a decade— far longer than the ideal private equity holding period.

The intangible risks of a creative enterprise put fear into the otherwise rational minds of financiers, but there was hesitancy on the other side of the table as well. Fashion and luxury companies tended to be closely controlled family enterprises that felt uncomfortable with loading their balance sheets with debt. Furthermore, as they increased their networks of boutiques around the world, as was de rigueur in the modern business model of luxury, companies were also increasing their proportion of fixed costs. Rent payments, like debt payments, have to be paid whether a store sells a lot or a little. The last thing companies want is to have to meet more fixed yearly commitments, particularly if economic times turn bad.

It was twenty years after Investcorp's first forays into the luxury industry that other private equity funds became more widely interested in luxury brands. The dynamics of the luxury industry were now much better and more broadly understood, as information had become more publicly available. And just as important, the amount of capital flowing into the coffers of private equity funds was more abundant than ever before. So with plenty of money to invest, private equity started to venture more aggressively into the world of luxury and fashion. And Jimmy Choo was shaping up to become one of the most desirable brands to own.

Nine

THE MAKING OF A MANAGER

ASK ROBERT BENSOUSSAN WHERE he is from and he says, "Fashionland." It is an in-joke of sorts among luxury goods executives. Because when Robert says Fashionland, he does not mean Paris or Milan or New York. He means Morocco. Bensoussan grew up in Casablanca, surprisingly the hometown of many well-respected names in fashion. Ralph Toledano, who has held the reins at Chloé since 1999, and Sidney Toledano (not related to Ralph), the CEO of Christian Dior since 1998, were two of his best friends growing up. Also hailing from Morocco are Alber Elbaz, the current designer at Lanvin; the Marciano brothers, founders of denim brand Guess; and Joseph Ettedgui, the London-based designer and retailer. Ralph, Sidney, and Robert all hailed from middle-class Jewish families who had big ambitions for their sons. They steered them toward serious careers in medicine, law, or engineering. Not that careers in fashion were unheard of in Jewish families. Robert is known to tell a joke about a Jewish boy who goes to Harvard undergrad and then law school. When he graduates, his father, beaming with pride, says, "Okay, son, now you have to settle down and choose. Is it going to be menswear or women's wear?"

Robert's father was born in a small village near Tangiers when it was under Spanish rule. Robert's mother, Rose Torres, was Spanish, Catholic, and Republican, and escaped to Morocco from Valencia as a refugee when dictator Francisco Franco took power in 1939. His parents met at a ball in Casablanca. Marrying a Catholic in the wake of World War II was no small deal for a boy whose family was devoutly Jewish. The couple dated a long time. When they finally married, four years passed before Rose became pregnant. Robert was born on Valentine's Day 1958.

Casablanca in the 1960s was a lively multicultural capital. The Jews mixed well with the Arab Muslims and the French Catholics. And glamour was a key part of the life. "Even though they were not rich people, our parents were partying a lot," said Sidney. "I remember them going out every evening—my father trying on his custom-tailored suits, and my mother in Christian Dior." Despite their glamorous after-hour lives, Robert, Ralph, and Sidney grew up in sensible family homes. The boys studied hard and, like ambitious people from small countries all over the world, dreamed of going someplace more exciting—someplace like Paris.

Robert applied to university as soon as he could. There were three thousand candidates for the two hundred places at the world-renowned ESSEC Business School in Paris, but he still made the cut. Sidney and Ralph Toledano were already in Paris, studying at another prestigious university. "We were all very serious when we were studying in Morocco," Robert says. "There was nothing else to do." Paris was a different story entirely. The boys, together with another friend from Morocco, Edouard Ettedgui (now the CEO of the Mandarin Oriental Hotel Group), would meet each night at midnight and hit all the top Parisian night spots—places like Jimmy'z, the famous nightclub that also has an outpost in Monte Carlo; the disco Élysée Matignon; and 78, located at 78 Champs Élysées. The set of good-looking boys with multicultural backgrounds quickly found themselves in the thick of things. Robert met luminaries such as Serge Gainsbourg and even helped carry a drunk Mick Jagger to his car from Élysée Matignon. In the summer of 1978 the three went to New York to see the city and try their hand at getting into the most exclusive nightspot in the world—Studio 54. "We looked like surfers," Robert remembers. "We got picked every night."

When he graduated from ESSEC in 1980 Robert was addicted to fun. He applied to the best schools to study for an MBA—Harvard, Wharton—and although he was accepted, when push came to shove he just could not commit to more years of expensive schooling. A friend told him that a French textile company was hiring three people to work in Brazil. "He said, 'We'll get two of the three jobs—and all of the girls.'" The company was La Lainière de Roubaix, one of the biggest French industrial groups of the time. Robert was ambivalent about the job but excited about the women he would meet in Brazil and, more important, about the chance to live in a warm climate again. "I went to the final round of interviews and my friend was not there. He was a windsurfer, and when I rang him and asked why he didn't make it, he said, 'The waves are too good. You get the job and I'll come and visit you, and we'll still get all the girls.'"

Robert joined the firm as the number two person in the finance department. It wasn't a bad job straight out of college, but his progress was hindered at first by the fact that he spoke no Portuguese—something he had neglected to mention to his employers during the interview process. Upon arrival he was housed in a cheap hotel in São Paulo, a city that resembles New York more than Rio. The rain fell steadily for days, and Robert considered going home. A cousin of his father took him under his wing and helped him find his way around. On his first day of work the other staff members were pleasantly surprised to meet such an optimistic and agreeable young man. "Everything was 'Good!' or 'Perfect!'" says Robert. "That was all I could say in Portuguese."

There was 30 percent inflation a month at the time in Brazil, and the company was forced to recalculate prices and salaries every three months. The finance office was no place for a shirker. His boss, Dieter Liebert, was a German who had worked at IBM. With Robert he spoke English. He had a sign on his desk: WHEN YOU COME IN,

IF THERE IS ONE PROBLEM, BRING ME TWO SOLUTIONS. Robert knew he was going to have to catch on fast or get out. He spent every night studying Portuguese, not in a classroom, but rather sitting in front of the TV watching soap operas from six to ten P.M. with a dictionary in hand. Every morning he would come in and recount the plot to the company secretaries. They would help him with the language behind his boss's back, and within three months his command of Portuguese was so good that he had secured both his job and a Brazilian girlfriend.

Robert says it was his first boss who taught him everything he knows about cost control. "Thanks to him I can look at a sheet of figures and see where the problems are." But after two years, Robert wanted something more challenging. The company owned the Brazilian rights to Lacoste, the sportswear brand known for its tennis shirts and alligator logo. Robert asked if he could mastermind the brand relaunch in Brazil and his bosses agreed. The brand had suffered the same fate as many once-luxurious brand names that had been careless with their expansion. The product had been cheapened, the allure tarnished. Robert decided to make it the country's most expensive sport shirt again. He asked for regular updates on competitors' prices, and fixed Lacoste's so that they were always higher. And in order to control the tumultuous effect of inflation, he began to sell against a fixed index. Convincing retail customers that they were the ones who should bear the brunt of changes in the currency wasn't easy, but in the end all of his competitors followed.

By 1984 Robert had not only gained invaluable experience managing a brand, but he had also acquired a sexy Brazilian wife, a famous fashion journalist who had written for the hugely popular Brazilian *Playboy* magazine before turning to public relations. Mission accomplished—it was time to return to Europe. When a headhunter called with a job in Brussels at OKE, a brand started by a former Benetton executive, he leaped at the offer. It wasn't Paris, but it was close. Upon arrival he found that the company's problems were beyond control. He did a bit of financial triage, urged the owners to sell, and packed the family bags again.

Back in Paris at the end of 1985, he heard that Charles Jourdan was looking for someone to run its ready-to-wear clothing division, and he landed the job. At the time, the slow, tortuous decline of Jourdan was already under way. Ready-to-wear and accessories, not including shoes, were the company's only profitable divisions. But shoes accounted for 85 percent of the Jourdan business. It was Robert's first job in a shoe company, and although he didn't have anything to do with the shoes, he watched as the fortunes of this famous house got worse and worse.

Charles Jourdan had begun the company in 1919. His youngest son, Roland, joined the company in 1940 and served as its CEO between 1970 and 1981—the brand's years of international growth. In addition to its own brand, it produced shoes for Christian Dior and other respected designers. The company owned all of its factories. While owning factories was once a huge advantage, in this case it was also the company's Achilles heel. The Charles Jourdan factory made high-heel shoes—and only high-heel shoes. Making flats, which were becoming fashionable at the time, was impossible, as was moving to another factory, thanks to the French unions. The long history of the brand meant the factories were dictating the brand's shoe styles, not the sales and marketing and design teams.

In an interview with the *Dallas Morning News* in 1985, the couple who had been designing for Jourdan for over a decade, Bernard and Françoise Didelle, revealed the stubborn attitude that was to bring the company down. Asked to describe the Charles Jourdan look, Françoise said, "Modern. Not retro. It doesn't work. Never. For a long time it's been the attitude of fashion to go back to 1945, or the '50s or the '60s, and the '70s now. But you have to change." As other French shoemakers like Robert Clergerie and Stephane Kélian began to turn out more fashion-forward shapes—no matter how retro in feel—the young hip customers whom fashion lives on turned toward them and away from the brightly colored pumps that Jourdan continued to stubbornly produce. Watching the fortunes of the famous house decline taught Robert a valuable lesson: Product must always come first. Robert stayed at the troubled Jourdan for only a year. And he got out just in time. The next year Jourdan announced it was laying off 3 percent of its workforce. Despite several attempts at resuscitation, including help from the French government, Charles Jourdan finally closed down in 2007.

In 1986 Robert got what he calls his first big job. He was hired to be the commercial director at the French fashion house Sonia Rykiel. Sonia Rykiel was one of the most popular designers of the 1970s and 1980s, and hers was a tightly run family company. Sonia designed with the help of her daughter, Nathalie. Nathalie's husband, Simon Burstein, the son of the founder of the famous London store Browns, was the CEO. Somewhat ironically, it was the husband of Simon's sister, Caroline, who was simultaneously helping a young Tamara Yeardye get her first real job, as a salesgirl at Browns. Simon recalls that one of the freelance salespeople he had on board to help with wholesale sales during the collections recommended Robert. Robert joined at a time when the brand—and the industry at large—was at its peak. The late 1980s were a time of incredible development in fashion. The founding designers were still in charge, but tables were turning on the business side. An ambitious group of executives was coming in and pushing the brands to expand into new markets and products to meet the needs of the growing number of wealthy customers.

Simon remembers that Robert showed entrepreneurial instincts early on. "He tried to get me to do a deal with Lancel for a handbag license. His friend Sidney [Toledano] was running Lancel, and Sonia Rykiel bags didn't exist at that time. He was a very, very smart guy." More of Robert's time was spent building up the international markets. "Robert had connections globally." Simon recalls. One of the first priorities for Rykiel was Japan. The company already had a distribution deal with a Japanese department store chain, Seibu, but when Robert joined he put renewed energy behind the development.

Robert and Simon tripled the business in three years, making it the second-strongest French brand in Japan after agnès b.

But working for a family-run company the size of Rykiel had an obvious drawback: There was only so far an ambitious executive could go. Robert left and went to work with Wolfgang and Margaretha Ley, the founders of Escada, first as the head of Cerruti women's wear and then as the international director of sales for the group.

One of Robert's new fashion friends was Richard Simonin, the number two at Kenzo. Kenzo and Rykiel shared many accounts and the two used to run into each other often. Simonin called Robert one day to say he was considering leaving Kenzo to take the top job at Givenchy. He was hesitant because Kenzo was still an independent brand and Givenchy was part of the LVMH stable of luxury brands. Robert took a different view. "If you don't take this job, you'll never know if you can be a number one or not." Simonin took the job and later passed Robert's name to Concetta Lanciaux, the head of human resources at LVMH and one of Bernard Arnault's closest advisers. "He was very well dressed and you could tell by the way he talked he was cultured and he had a sense of humor," she said. "He was not somebody standard." She suggested that he take over Christian Lacroix, the only brand to have been started, rather than acquired, by LVMH. In the six years since Arnault had poached Lacroix and his partner, Jean-Jacques Picart, from the house of Jean Patou in 1987, the company had been through six CEOs. The company books at the time Robert joined were relatively straightforward—there were 100 million French francs of sales and 100 million French francs of losses ($6 million/£3.5 million). But the company had also racked up a net loss of about $35 million (£21 million) since its inception. "It was a big job for him, but I really liked him so I pushed for him very hard," said Concetta. Now it was Robert's turn to see if he could be a number one. Robert accepted the challenge and began work in February 1993.

One of the key debates within LVMH was what to do with

Christian Lacroix's haute couture. It was, without doubt, one of Lacroix's creative strengths, but with only one hundred dedicated clients it cost far more to put on the pricey shows and keep the full-time atelier than the company was ever going to make from it. Executives within LVMH were split: Cancel it and save millions, but lose the publicity and alienate the designer. Keep it and the rest of the company has to do twice as well to cover those losses. Robert decided to do the latter and keep couture afloat. But even that was not straightforward. One of his predecessors had decided to license out the rights to Christian Lacroix ready-to-wear to Mendes, a French manufacturer that was also producing and distributing the YSL Rive Gauche line. Although Robert worked to bring down prices of the Mendes-produced ready-to-wear, largely by pressing Lacroix to simplify his designs in order to make manufacturing less costly, that was not enough. The U.S. market still was not drawn to Lacroix's exuberant designs. So Robert decided to follow in the footsteps of the Italians and of Kenzo and launch a diffusion line, Bazar de Christian Lacroix. When not done well, a diffusion line tends to be a watered-down version of the main line, with cheaper fabrics and poor construction. But when done well, it could be a line of simpler products that could be worn with the main line and would also appeal to more conservative customers like those in the U.S. Lacroix described Bazar like this: "It is like watering down scotch, but this time we're using bubbly water, not flat." And he told *Women's Wear Daily* that he had been working on several of the pieces for years—there just hadn't been a reason to move them off the drawing board before now.

Convinced not only of what he wanted to do, but how he wanted to do it, Robert left his apartment one evening, crossed the hall, and knocked on the door opposite. It was the flat where his friend Richard Simonin lived. By this time Kenzo was part of the LVMH stable and Simonin was the CEO of both Kenzo and Givenchy. "I want you to manufacture Bazar for me," he said. Simonin agreed, making it one of the easiest manufacturing deals ever done. The line exceeded expectations by 30 percent the first year, bringing in more than $27 million (£17.6 million) and representing 25 percent of the entire turnover. As Robert described it, "Some people like it and some hate it. It has its own signature. It is also a good, well-made product that we are able to ship on time." More partnerships followed: a jeans line with Gilmar, a jewelry line with Monet, a line of household furnishings with Christoffle. One of the first to believe in the potential of brands owning their own stores, Robert started opening boutiques that were both directly owned by the company and in partnership with franchisers. The annual losses were diminishing, but profits were not yet on the horizon.

As the press stepped up the number of "When Will Arnault Pull the Plug?" stories, pressure on Robert grew. Bernard Arnault declared that the house would be profitable in 1996. In July 1995 Arnault installed John Galliano at the house of Givenchy. The message was clear: He had a new favorite designer. By 1996 revenues from Bazar were only $20 million (£12.8 million) as fashion trends continued to move toward minimalism and further away from the colorful Christian Lacroix aesthetic. The growth rate of the company shrunk from 50 percent in 1995 to 20 percent in 1996. In January 1997 predictions of profitability were pushed back to 1999. Robert told Reuters, "Making this house profitable would be the easiest thing in the world. We shut the faucet, stop investments, and in three years we're finished." And indeed that is what some inside LVMH were urging Robert to do, particularly with the drippy faucet that is haute couture. But Robert resisted. Not only because it would upset the designer, Christian Lacroix, but also because he believed in the power of the haute couture to create a brand image, an image that could then be leveraged through the sale of other, less expensive products. Robert told his bosses that if they wanted to cancel the haute couture, they had to do it themselves. On the other side, he was also getting pressure from Lacroix himself. Lacroix is a designer from a generation where fashion, not profits, came first. When Robert joined, Lacroix agreed to some cost-cutting measures, like staff reductions in the atelier and design studio, in the name of turning the house around. But after five years of feeling that pennies were being pinched to no avail, he was no longer inclined to make what he considered to be huge sacrifices. Robert was stuck in the middle, trying to appease a group that demanded results and trying to appease a designer who felt under attack.

In the end it was too much. When the announcement came out that a new CEO for Lacroix had been found, it was said that Robert would be working in LVMH international development. He said later, "I should have quit two years earlier." Concetta was sad to see him go. "I was very upset that he left. If he'd come four years later, he could have sincerely changed the fortunes of Lacroix." In the end he increased the longevity of Lacroix at LVMH, but it only postponed the inevitable. LVMH sold the brand in early 2005 to the Falic Group, a Florida-based family with interests in the duty-free business. In early 2008 the Falic Group was once again looking at ways to unload the still unprofitable house.

In 1997, as tensions between Tamara and Jimmy were intensifying, Robert Bensoussan left LVMH and the last corporate job he would hold. He worked for a time as an adviser to Rose Marie Bravo, who was in the midst of masterminding the turnaround of Burberry— the latest in a string of brands trying to shed its shabby image and return to more glamorous roots. In 1999 he consulted for Joseph Ettedgui, a UK designer and retailer who was exploring funding options and who later sold his company, Joseph, to Belgian financier Albert Frère, and in 2005 to the Japanese textile company Kashiyama.

Simultaneously, Robert had been consulting for Gianfranco Ferré, a large designer with an even larger reputation, who had failed to capture the imagination of the fashion elite in a decade. At the end of 1999 he took the top job at Ferré and made the move to Milan. Once there Robert again found himself stuck between a designer and a financial hard place. Ferré and his business partner, Franco Mattioli, had not spoken to each other in over a year, when

Mattioli had announced that he wanted to sell his 49 percent stake in the company and retire. To make matters worse, the company was losing about $9.5 million (£5.8 million) a year. Robert's first task was to stem the losses and turn the company into one that looked likely to turn a profit by the end of 2001. That was the easy part. However, even with the improved income statements, the two former partners were still stuck with each other. Ferré also owned only 49 percent of the company that bore his name. The remaining 2 percent was held in a trust that would accrue to whichever partner did not sell. This clause made it almost impossible for Mattioli to sell his stake. Few serious investors would consider spending that amount of money without getting control in return. And even when potential investors were found—the Italian textiles companies Marzotto, Fin.part, and Ittierre all expressed interest—Ferré was able to put a stop to talks with the veto power that had been granted to him. In the end Robert managed to sell 90 percent of the company— Mattioli's and some of Gianfranco Ferré's—for a figure reported to be between $150 million and $175 million (£100–115 million) to Ittierre just days before Christmas 2000.

Marzotto and Ittierre were both big Ferré license holders, and Robert told the respective CEOs that the only way they would get the deal was by appealing to Gianfranco's ego. Ferré was promised that that his brand would become the biggest in Europe and, crucially, that he could begin again to design a couture collection—a task he first undertook when he was made the creative director of Christian Dior in 1989. Although couture collections almost always lose money, designing couture had been a big part of his job when he was at Christian Dior, and ever since he had been replaced by John Galliano in 1996, he had missed it terribly. The promise that he could have his own couture collection in Paris within two years convinced him to agree to the sale. But the promised couture collection never materialized. It was announced in 2003 that it would be pushed back to 2004, but soon after, Ferré himself announced that haute couture was "not modern." Did he mean it? Possibly. Couture was having a tough time. But more likely it was a way of saving face. It was not going to be Robert's problem. In the midst of the agonizing deal, Robert had seen his future on the racks of Harvey Nichols, the chicest department store in London. It was a pair of sexy stilettos—part jewelry, part shoe—and it bore the label "Jimmy Choo."

Ten

PHOENIX RISES

E NAMORED WITH THE SHOES and curious about their origin, Robert started to make inquiries: Who was Jimmy Choo? Who owned the brand? And, most important, did they want to sell? Phone calls bounced around Europe until Lori Yedid, a fashion executive with Aeffe in Italy, directed Robert to Tamara. He called her in late April 2001 with his pitch at the ready. As he began to explain his track record at Sonia Rykiel, Cerruti, Lacroix, and Ferré, in order to convince her that he was the one who could take the business to the next level, she interrupted him. "Did Merrill Lynch send you?" she asked.

Although Tom Yeardye had retained the powerful U.S. investment bank Merrill Lynch in the hopes of selling to a buyer in the U.S., where the business was booming, things were not going particularly well. One Gucci Group executive who saw the presentation said, "It was the worst-organized presentation I ever sat through." The company was too small for Gucci anyway.

Bill Susman, a Merrill Lynch banker, was brought in late in the game after another banker on the transaction retired. "My job was basically to make peace between Jimmy and the Yeardyes. It was clear that all Jimmy wanted to do was make shoes. Tom was acting as a father and as a shareholder. He really believed that Tamara epitomized the customer, unlike Jimmy. She was the image and lived the lifestyle of the brand," he said.

Soon after the phone conversation with Tamara, Robert met with her and Tom at Tamara's house to speak in more detail about the situation at Jimmy Choo. Part of the problem from a buyer's standpoint was that the deal was an odd one, reflecting the turmoil within the company. A shareholders' agreement required that any buyer had to purchase 70 percent of the company, but it was made clear that 50 percent had to come from either Jimmy's stake or from the Yeardyes' stake as they could no longer work together. It was up to the new owners to choose with whom they wanted to work. Tom was willing to renegotiate that point as he was keen to retain a large shareholding in the company. Another major issue was that the rights to open Jimmy Choo stores in North America had been granted to Tom's old colleagues Philip Rogers and Annie Humphries, and to Tom himself, as he had retained a substantial stake as well in the U.S. operation. Tom promised that Philip and Annie would sell those rights if asked. And lastly, the price tag: They were asking an astronomical sum—around £50 million ($72 million). It was the height of the luxury goods merger and acquisition bubble, after all.

The lack of a professional structure behind the Jimmy Choo operation may have scared off some potential buyers, but it only served to make the company more attractive to Robert. The more chaotic on the back end, the greater the impact a serious manager, like himself, would be able to make. The choice between the Yeardyes or Jimmy Choo was an easy one. Although Choo's name was the one on the label, everyone he had spoken to—from the retailers to the factories to members of the press—said the same thing: The success of the ready-to-wear line was due to the efforts of Tamara and Sandra, with the support of Tom. And Tom was now ready to take a backseat. He told his wife, Ann, "I need someone with running legs. I need someone to do the work."

But before Robert could do anything, he had to find backers for the deal. Ever since his days at LVMH, Robert's entrepreneurial drive had led him to dedicate some of his free time to looking for deals and the people to help him do them. While working on one of those deals, the UK brand Joseph, Robert worked with a financial advisory group called Phoenix Equity Partners. Founded in London in 1991, Phoenix had developed a successful private equity business that focused in midmarket British deals, those valued between £50 million and £200 million ($70–280 million). The firm had been bought by the U.S. investment bank DLJ in 1997. But in 2000, Credit Suisse First Boston (CSFB) took over DLJ. Since CSFB already owned a larger private equity business in Europe, the partners of Phoenix's private equity arm decided to make their next deal their own and buy themselves out. By 2000 Phoenix had plenty of capital to invest, having just raised a new £430 million ($650 million) fund. The size of the deal with CSFB was not disclosed, but since it was an amicable split, much of the purchase price was deferred and was based on the future performance of the fund. The deal process was used to market Phoenix to other entrepreneurs looking for someone to assist them in a buyout. Phoenix's Web site boasted of its abilities to help entrepreneurs, in much the same way as they had helped themselves. The firm's official motto became: Run by entrepreneurs, for entrepreneurs.

Since the Joseph deal, Robert had kept in touch with the people at Phoenix, in particular with David Burns, the head of the consumer, leisure, and retail practice. Robert had started to discuss with Phoenix the possibility of jointly setting up a separate investment vehicle to hold any luxury acquisitions they could make together. When Robert came to Phoenix with Jimmy Choo, "Jimmy who?" was the reply. Phoenix was, after all, more used to acquiring things like Pirtek, the UK's leading supplier of on-site industrial hydraulic hoses and fittings, and Integrated Dental Holdings, the UK's largest owner of dental practices. Robert told them to go home and ask their wives about Jimmy Choo. They did, and they came back brimming with enthusiasm.

Robert then phoned his Moroccan friend Edouard Ettedgui.

There were two deals to be made—one with Jimmy and the Yeardyes and the other, his own, with Phoenix. He didn't just want to work for Phoenix managing a company in its portfolio. Rather, he wanted to become partners in a new investment vehicle, Equinox Luxury Holdings, which would invest in other UK brands that, like Jimmy Choo, could be developed. He asked Edouard if he knew of anyone who could help him with his own negotiations with Phoenix. Edouard suggested that he contact Stuart Chalfen, Edouard's former colleague from his days at British American Tobacco. Chalfen was the former in-house lawyer. Although Chalfen was retired, he agreed to advise Robert.

Negotiations were also under way in the midst of the Yeardye family. According to informed sources, Tamara had been pushing her father, with Matthew's support, to formally give her her own share of the Jimmy Choo business. She told her father that if she did not get a substantial portion of the Yeardyes' half of the business, she would quit. Tom was not thrilled—it was meant to be a family business—but he had no choice but to agree. Losing Tamara would almost certainly scuttle the sale of the brand and Tom stood to lose millions. It was also a requirement on the part of Equinox that Tamara retain a stake in the business that everyone claimed she had built. In late August 2001, as the prospects of signing a deal with Robert and Phoenix loomed, Tom instructed his trust administrators in Jersey (a tax haven located on a small island off the south coast of England) to take the steps to divide the family holdings in Jimmy Choo and formalize Tamara's direct ownership of the business. One half of the Yeardyes' stake in Thistledown International, the holding company of their stake in Jimmy Choo, would remain in Tom's trust. The other half would be set aside for Tamara. Tom asked his lawyers in Jersey to set up a new trust, with Tamara as principal beneficiary, to hold her now-segregated stake in Thistledown. Effectively, she would own a quarter of the Jimmy Choo business outright.

*   *   *

On September 11, 2001, the Phoenix Equity investment committee met to approve the Jimmy Choo/Equinox transaction. However, when the partners left the meeting they learned of the terrorist attacks on the World Trade Center in New York. Clearly nothing was going to happen soon. As the Phoenix investment committee was meeting, Robert was en route to meeting Raj Patel, the Jimmy Choo accountant, and Lou Rodwell, the company secretary, at Jimmy Choo's Pont Street offices. It was a sunny day and Robert decided to walk the fifteen minutes from his rented flat on Beauchamp Place in Knightsbridge to Belgravia. His cell phone rang as he entered the building. It was his brother in Paris. "Did you hear?" he said. "Planes have crashed into the Twin Towers in New York." Robert assumed it was a small incident. "I can't talk now," he said. "I have a meeting." But when he walked into the small office he found that all the phones were ringing—and all with the same news. The meeting was postponed. Robert's London flat had no television, so he went across Pont Street and checked himself into the Sheraton Belgravia Hotel, so that he could watch what was happening on CNN. After the initial shock wore off, Robert was convinced that the deal was dead. In his mind, he began counting the money he would lose in lawyer fees and then shrugged it off. "There are worse things in life than that," he thought. The next day he checked out and went home. Remembering the images of the crumbling Twin Towers, he comforted himself with the thought, "Business is something you can always rebuild."

The day after the attacks he heard back from his would-be partners at Phoenix. It wasn't good news. David Burns, the Phoenix partner who had been most enthusiastic, said, "The world is changing. The money [for the Choo deal] is in the bank, and it will be there in a month's time. We don't know where the world will be in a month's time," referring to the uncertainty in the global markets that had developed overnight. However, at Phoenix, David Burns was not quite as negative as he had sounded on the phone. He was still excited at the prospect and wanted to get the deal done. A couple of weeks later he asked to see the sales figures from Jimmy Choo in the days after the attack on the World Trade Center. When they came through everyone was astounded. In all of Jimmy Choo's U.S. stores, sales had increased between 30 and 40 percent compared to the same week a year earlier. No one knew why. When faced with a life-and-death situation, could it be that people went *shopping*? Philosophical questions aside, the fact remained that the world was an uncertain place, and that uncertainty was reflected in the share price of the luxury goods companies, which had collapsed in the wake of the attacks.

David called Robert and argued that the plummet in luxury goods company valuations meant that the price they had been discussing should be cut to reflect the current uncertain scenario. All luxury goods stocks were substantially down, almost 40 percent on average. For Robert, a change in price was not ideal, but at least he still had a deal. He now had to convince Jimmy to take it. The whole company was revalued at close to £18 million ($26 million) and Robert managed to convince Jimmy to sell his 50 percent stake to Equinox Luxury Holdings, the investment vehicle he had set up with Phoenix to purchase the brand and now chaired, for £8.8 million ($12.6 million).

Robert had left it up to Tom to convince his old friend Philip Rogers, who owned the U.S. business, to sell his and Annie's shares. This had been a condition of the deal from the outset. "Tom told me that if I insisted on staying on board the deal would go sour." Philip said. He had grown up under the tutelage of Tom Yeardye. It was Tom who had insisted that Philip be given an equity stake in Vidal Sassoon decades earlier. "From a business standpoint selling my stake was mad. It was only out of loyalty to Tom and Ann that I did it. It was my way to repay him." An additional $5 million (£3.5 million) went to buy both the three U.S. stores and the distribution rights to the U.S. market. The European and U.S. operations of Jimmy Choo were then combined under a new holding company, Yearnoxe Ltd. Equinox ended up taking control of 51 percent of the capital of the new holding company. Tamara and her father split the remaining 49 percent equally. Robert was appointed CEO of Jimmy Choo. Tamara was named president, Tom continued in his role as chairman of the Jimmy Choo board, and David Burns from Phoenix also took a seat on the board.

Jimmy was paid the £8.8 million ($12.6 million), although reportedly some of his proceeds went to his adviser, the film executive. He announced that he would embark on educational and charitable projects and would continue with his custom-made business. He tried, and failed, to convince Robert and Phoenix to fund the couture part of the Jimmy Choo business. Robert knew the perils of couture all too well from his days at Christian Lacroix, and he also knew he had more than enough work on his plate just running the main company. Instead Jimmy became the first person to sign a license agreement with Robert in his new role as CEO of Jimmy Choo. Jimmy was granted a seven-year license on his own name in exchange for royalties of one pound per year and a number of conditions: Jimmy was free to continue making shoes for his private clients provided that he branded them Jimmy Choo Couture, that he never operated outside of London, that he made sure his shoes would always cost more than the ready-to-wear collection, and, crucially, that he would never speak to the press about anything without the explicit permission of someone in charge at Jimmy Choo.

Sandra Choi was given a small amount of the sweet equity (shares set aside as an additional incentive for management), as had been agreed between Jimmy and Tom some years back. No Phoenix money was put into the actual operations of the company, but a £2 million ($2.8 million) line of credit was arranged with Barclays Bank.

On November 20, 2001, the day after the deal was finally signed, Robert and Stuart Chalfen went to celebrate in London. Chalfen said to Robert that there were still a few details to tidy in the setting up of Equinox, but that Robert and Phoenix's partnership agreement would have to wait. He was off to Jamaica with his wife for a vacation the next day. The following week Robert got a call from a managing partner at Dechert LLC, the law firm that had represented Robert, but it had nothing to do with his deal. He called to say that Chalfen was dead. He had died of a heart attack in Jamaica at the age of sixty-two. "It was a very sad day for me," Robert said.

Eleven

BLOOMING MARVELOUS

AFTER THE DEAL, David Burns said, "When we looked at Jimmy Choo it was a strong brand but not yet a strong company." Robert knew it was his job to change that. By late November 2001 he had plunged into work. The company was about to move into new offices that Tom had found on Ixworth Place, in the midst of London's swanky South Kensington district. Robert's top goals for Jimmy Choo were clear: open twenty-five new stores worldwide in the following five years; double the size of the company's wholesale business by developing and strengthening its ties with major department stores worldwide; and start the development of accessories and handbags, product categories that promised even higher growth and margins than shoes. Growth in the U.S. market was a priority, as America's love affair with luxury goods brands was really starting to blossom. Also needed were a review of manufacturing arrangements and an overhaul of the financial and control functions. Robert thought that the only thing that did not need changing at Jimmy Choo was the creative partnership between Tamara and Sandra.

The arrival of Robert and Phoenix did not mean the spending taps were wide open. The new offices were furnished mostly with inexpensive Ikea furniture. A dispute about the feasibility of a light-colored carpet favored by Tamara led to a compromise—lighter up front by reception, darker and more industrial in the offices in back. It was part of the deal that Tom would have an office in the new Jimmy Choo space. He was given a small one, symbolically between those of Tamara and Robert. But he rarely used it. It was Robert's ship now. Tom preferred to give his input to Tamara on the phone, and to Robert over lunch at the nearby Lowndes Hotel.

Despite the lack of systems, the business of Jimmy Choo was in good shape when Robert became CEO. Over the previous four years Tom had been running a tight operation. Sales at the company had grown significantly, and as the books closed in 2001 the company was booking £11.7 million ($16.8 million) from the sales of some 74,000 pairs of shoes, mainly through its four stand-alone boutiques in London, New York, Los Angeles, and Las Vegas. It also had a respectable wholesale business that included prestige retailers such as Saks Fifth Avenue and Bergdorf Goodman. Operating profits, or earnings before interest, taxes, depreciation, and amortization (EBITDA) had reached £2 million ($2.9 million)—finally a company for Robert to run with no losses—and a level of profitability (17 percent over sales) that, while remarkable for a company of its size, had plenty of room to improve to reach the 20 percent–plus level of other luxury brands such as Gucci, Tod's, or Hermès.

It was, Robert speculated to friends, "like a vintage car discovered in a garage: beautiful to look at, but lacking an engine." A key priority was the company's accounting and financial systems. Company accounts were being kept by a part-time accountant with an off-the-shelf program from Sage Software that was designed for small, growing companies. It was not suitable for a global brand like the one Robert envisioned. Understanding the power of having the right information easily accessible when making business decisions, Robert immediately contacted Deloitte & Touche, one of the Big Five accounting firms, who had done the standard accounting work necessary on the Jimmy Choo–Equinox deal, and asked them to send someone from their retail division to work with him to set up the appropriate systems for financial reporting. Deloitte sent in the head of the retail practice,

Alison Egan, on a three-month secondment contract. After just one month Robert decided she was exceptionally good. Impressed with her ability to grasp what needed to be done at the company and the speed with which she could execute, Robert offered Alison the job of CFO. This was his first hire at Jimmy Choo. Bringing new people into the tight Jimmy Choo team was not something Robert took lightly. He later explained, "One of the key reasons for success today is that we didn't take anyone on board, not one single person, without everyone's approval … If there was one partner who disagreed, we did not make the hire."

Next on the agenda was to eliminate the distribution agreement for international wholesale rights, which had been given to a German company called Body Lines. Body Lines had been one of the early retail customers of Jimmy Choo. The owner, Emmanuel Cusin, had approached Tom and asked for the rights to wholesale the brand in Europe. Without firsthand knowledge of the market or the means to hire additional personnel, Tom had agreed. It was a move that had taken much of the work off the shoulders of the small London staff, but it would stifle the potential for growth, as it prevented Jimmy Choo from taking control of its own wholesale destiny. Although these types of deals can be notoriously hard to get out of, at least it was the only deal Robert had to terminate. Executives coming into older companies often had to face a wide range of licenses for questionable products instead of just geographical distribution rights. Such was the case with YSL, for example, which had licenses for funeral mats in Japan and cigarettes in China when Gucci Group acquired it.

Robert renegotiated so that Emmanuel could keep Germany and Austria—for a while—and he got back the rest of Europe. "They weren't happy," remembers Lou Rodwell, who carried on working for Jimmy Choo as company secretary until he retired at the end of 2004. "They felt they had built up the market, and it was a difficult situation." Within a couple of years all the rights were brought back under Jimmy Choo control.

Robert also called a meeting with Natalie Massenet from Net-à-Porter. Although she claimed that Jimmy Choo was Net-à-Porter's most important supplier, the invoices from Jimmy Choo were not being paid promptly. Natalie remembers the meeting like this: "I got this call from Robert and he said, 'Okay, this contract doesn't exist anymore, because it wasn't executed in Jersey [the legal home of the company]. Now, tell me why we should be selling to you.' I was terrified." Robert says he told her, "If we're so important to your business, from now on you pay us first." In any case, the relationship continued—and prospered. Net-à-Porter managed the Jimmy Choo online store for many years.

Robert's first few weeks at Jimmy Choo were hectic as he introduced the new initiatives that would "start the engine" and allow the rapid development of the brand on a global scale. Many phone calls were traded back and forth with his contacts in the industry in a search for new architects. It was not his home or the new Jimmy Choo offices that Robert was concerned about—it was the boutiques. The development of the retail network (and of shop-in-shops in department stores) was critical to his strategy and would require an important investment in the stores, and the look of them needed to be just right. The initial design had been created by Association of Ideas, a London-based firm that Philip Rogers had used at Vidal Sassoon. It was not that the four stores Jimmy Choo had by the time Robert arrived were not attractive. The store in London and three boutiques in the U.S. (New York, Los Angeles, and Las Vegas) held their own among other brands the size of Jimmy Choo. But Robert knew that before he was prepared to invest a significant amount of money in new stores and, equally important, before he could ask people such as Phil Miller, then chairman of Saks Fifth Avenue, and Joseph Wan, CEO of Harvey Nichols, to devote substantial floor space to Jimmy Choo in-store boutiques, the design of Jimmy Choo boutiques had to be every bit as distinctive as that of Gucci, Chanel, or Prada. And he wanted a firm that specialized in this. He held a beauty contest and asked several design firms to submit their ideas. In the end he and Tamara chose an Italian firm instead of the English one led by Anouska Hempel, owner and designer of the Blakes and Hempel hotels in London.

Vudafieri Partners, a Milanese firm that in 2000 had created a whimsical yet luxurious store design for Pucci, was chosen to develop a new general design concept for Jimmy Choo boutiques and shop-in-shops. The firm went on to develop a certain expertise in the retail design for shoe brands, more recently developing global store concepts for Roger Vivier, Tod's, and other luxury brands such as Moschino and Loewe. A team from Vudafieri worked with Tamara at Jimmy Choo for months after completion of the initial design to make sure that the rollout for subsequent stores went off smoothly.

In came Swarovski crystal chandeliers, polished chrome fixtures, plush velvet sofas, and thick carpets, all in a soft beige and pale lavender palette. Out went the strong shade of purple and imitation Venetian chandeliers. Tamara said, "It's the opposite of masculine, minimalist black. It's very feminine ... The feeling is very Forties, with satin, velvet and mirrors."[45] It could also be done in three color schemes: aqua, lavender, or beige, depending on the location of the store. "We want to give the shopper a change of atmosphere, in a subtle way," said Tamara. "These changes ensure the customer has a slightly new, but then again familiar, experience in our store."[46] The first store to open with the new design was the concession in Harvey Nichols.

With the search for new architects under way, Robert packed his bags and went to Italy to visit the shoe factories near Venice and Florence that had been found by Jimmy Choo's production agents, Anna Suppig-Conti and her brother Mossimo. When he arrived at the factory he inevitably found a group of very scared people. One of the first things a new CEO usually does is to reevaluate, renegotiate, and, possibly, cancel contracts with manufacturers—a fact these longtime players in the shoe business knew all too well.

While Robert's time at a textile company in Brazil taught him simple tricks—like knowing if a fabric was turned in a different direction, more pieces could be cut from it—that had helped him negotiate with ready-to-wear factory owners, he had no real knowledge of the intricate details of the shoemaking business. Nevertheless, he knew one thing: costs had to come down without sacrificing quality.

This was all the more difficult given the rising value of the euro. Robert knew he would have to start hedging by buying euros a year or two ahead to anticipate the fall of the dollar. But there was a limit to how much he could squeeze his suppliers. Instead he began to raise prices. "We preferred to do it [raise prices] first, knowing that everybody would have to do it one day," he later said. "Even the people who had hedged their euros versus their dollars quite well could not take that for a long time. By raising prices first our customers have got used to it."

Robert kept all of the four factories that had been found by Anna and Mossimo. They were, so far, working with the brand on a nonexclusive basis, but he started to treat them like true partners, negotiating hard and promising to improve volumes in exchange for lower costs. In the wake of September 11, owners of those factories had started to complain that other brands had cut back on their orders, so Robert confidently picked up the slack. But in a bid to win the loyalty of his suppliers, he insisted that the factory must reject offers from brands wanting to get back on the production schedule when things got better.

With stronger confidence in the company's production capabilities, and with a new store concept ready to leap off the drawing board, Robert set up his first big department store appointment. He began by going back to the store where he had first discovered the brand—Harvey Nichols.

Following its stock market debut in 1996, Harvey Nichols was the epicenter of the London fashion scene, from its designer floors to its posh penthouse supermarket to the fashionable Fifth Floor café and bar. Of added interest for Robert was that it was also the only major luxury department store in London to run its own shoe department. Shoe selling in the UK operates differently from most other markets. Rather than take on the responsibility for ordering and storing inventory, most major department stores lease their floor space to a third party to manage. In the UK a company called Kurt Geiger (in the past a division of Harrods) had more or less a monopoly on the shoe business among London's department stores. But at Harvey Nichols it was all done in-house.

Harvey Nichols's majority shareholder was Dickson Poon, the wildly successful Asian retail mogul. He had brought in a trusted colleague from Hong Kong, Joseph Wan, to run the company and oversee its ambitious expansion plans. Wan, a trained accountant, ran the Harvey Nichols business with a keen eye on the bottom line: "We look at how we spend every penny. If there is no benefit, then we save the penny."[47] At the time of Wan's arrival at the helm of Harvey Nichols, the retailer's experience with running its own shoe floor had not been all that successful. For one thing, at the time there were a limited number of exciting, design-driven shoe brands. Manolo Blahnik was stubbornly refusing to sell to any London retailers, and Christian Louboutin was just a tiny brand with its own franchised store, coincidentally on Motcomb Street. Much of the floor space at Harvey Nichols was dedicated to the U.S. shoe brand Joan & David. In the U.S. Joan & David's primary distributor had been Ann Taylor, but in the mid-1990s Ann Taylor launched its own shoe line and stopped carrying Joan & David shoes. Rather than cut back on the number of shoes in production, the owners of the company embarked on an aggressive distribution push. In the UK they opened a huge flagship store on Bond Street in addition to two concessions at Harvey Nichols. The plans turned out to be too aggressive; the company could not replace the lost sales quickly enough, and by 2000 Joan & David had filed for bankruptcy.

This left the shoe department at Harvey Nichols with a large void, one they were trying to fill when Robert came knocking.

"I knew Robert from his days at Lacroix," said Wan. "I knew he was a very sharp businessman with creative ideas." Wan's team had been highlighting shoes as a likely area of exponential growth in the future, and he was pleased that Robert had come to see him before any of his competitors. "Many brands use Harvey Nichols as a launchpad into the high end of the market," Wan explained. "If they only open their own stores, they will only attract people who already know about their brand. At Harvey Nichols they know we can drive the right kind of traffic." Wan was so impressed by the brand, the working relationship of Tamara and Robert, and the new plans for the shop design that he gave Jimmy Choo a preferential seven-hundred-square-foot space at the front of the Harvey Nichols shoe department. With his ideal spot at London's most fashionable department store secured, Robert went off to conquer America. He knew there was just one logical place for Jimmy Choo—Saks Fifth Avenue.

Saks Fifth Avenue and Neiman Marcus are the last two survivors in the luxury department store game in the United States. Some, like the much-loved San Francisco–based chain I. Magnin, have gone out of business, while others, like New York's Barneys, have been acquired by foreign owners. Bloomingdale's and Nordstrom operate on a slightly lower tier in the market. Neiman Marcus, the country's most prestigious chain, had long been the domain of king shoemaker Manolo Blahnik. It was an exclusive position that George Malkemus, Blahnik's long-term U.S. licensing partner, guarded jealously. Under no circumstances would the buyers at Neiman take on Jimmy Choo, a brand Manolo had come to despise. But by the same token, Manolo Blahnik was forbidden by Neiman Marcus to sell his shoes to Saks Fifth Avenue in those cities where Neiman had a store.

The chairman of Saks, Phil Miller, was another old friend of Robert's. Jimmy Choo had been selling shoes to Saks since 1997, but they had never had the kind of pull that Robert had with top management. At a meeting with Miller, Robert laid out his plan:

He wanted to make Jimmy Choo to Saks what Manolo Blahnik was to Neiman. He wanted more Jimmy Choo presence in more stores and more floor space devoted to the brand in those stores. And he wanted to work hand in hand with Saks every step of the way. Miller recalls that it did not take much for him to sign on to Robert's vision. In fact, he was practically on board before Robert even crossed his threshold. "I was backing the jockey as much as the horse," he said. "He gave us a leg to stand on since we didn't have Manolo." Pre-Robert, a store like Saks would have been cautious about placing large orders with a small company like Jimmy Choo no matter how much they liked the shoes. More than one designer company had taken on large orders and gone bankrupt trying to fulfill them, leaving the store with gaps in inventory. Without an experienced luxury executive at the helm, the risk of this happening was high. But with Robert at the helm, Miller had no such fears. The Jimmy Choo business at Saks Fifth Avenue went from about $200,000 (£132,000) the year before Robert arrived to more than $2 million (£1.3 million) in 2002. By the end of 2004, Saks Fifth Avenue was selling Jimmy Choo shoes in thirty-nine of its stores.

Department stores are a great way to build brand image and to increase visibility, but when it comes to profits, a strong network of company-owned, freestanding stores was the way to go. In the U.S. that meant opening many of those stores in malls, as much of the shopping, luxury or otherwise, in the States takes place in them rather than in city centers, as is the case in Europe. The country's mall space is dominated by two key landlords—Taubman Centers and Simon Property Group. When it came to taking a risk on a new brand, it was a case of catch-22. One landlord did not want you unless the other had you.

Robert found a way to break the cycle in Orange County, California. The South Coast Plaza mall is one of the country's most prestigious, with nearly every major luxury brand from Armani to Chanel to Tiffany spread out over 2.8 million square feet. It is said that Hermès waited twenty years to get the space it wanted within its confines. But aside from prestige, it had an added advantage for Robert—it was privately held. It was not part of either the Taubman or the Simon group, so it was far easier for Robert to make a direct approach. Barney Page, a legendary figure in American retail, was in charge of the mall's real estate. Robert took his proposal directly to him. Page liked the idea—again, a good shoe brand was hard to find—but had to clear the addition of Jimmy Choo at South Coast Plaza with the other designers already there. Everyone agreed that the brand possessed significant stature to join them, and Jimmy Choo took its place next to the boutique of Giorgio Armani.

Precisely nine months after Robert's arrival at Jimmy Choo, the first batch of new Jimmy Choo stores were born. The new Harvey Nichols concession opened in August 2002, followed by South Coast Plaza, and two stores in Florida, one in Coral Gables (at the Village of Merrick Park mall), and one in Orlando (at the newly opened Mall at Millenia).

While Robert was busy striking deals for new points of sale and building up sales volumes as fast as possible, Tamara continued to take the lead on the creative and public relations front, making a fashionable appearance at every store-opening bash, charming the press, and wining and dining the celebrities in attendance. Every so often, they would clash—Robert would get more involved in design than Tamara thought appropriate or Tamara's irregular working habits would begin to annoy Robert—but when they did, Tom would step in to make the peace. "Tom would take Robert to lunch and he'd say, 'One thing I will tell you is do not tread on Tamara's toes. She's a fashion girl through and through,'" said Ann.

The launch party for the new Jimmy Choo space at Harvey Nichols was held in September 2002, a year after the whole deal with Phoenix had nearly collapsed along with the Twin Towers. If the mood was somber in New York, it was not in London. The night before the bash, London luminaries such as Crown Prince Pavlos of Greece and his wife, Princess Marie-Chantal, came to an exclusive dinner at the Knightsbridge restaurant San Lorenzo that was organized by Brower Lewis and hosted by Liz Hurley and Alexandra Schulman, the editor of British *Vogue*. For the opening party Tamara wrote a poem about an unfaithful shoe and had it printed on T-shirts.

> I think I'm in love with my shoe
> I was sure that it felt the same, too
> 'till it happened to mention
> with heartless intention
> "I'm dating a gold Jimmy Choo."[48]

"We wanted to do something quirky and fun and to make a T-shirt that women would actually wear out, rather than to bed or to the gym," Tamara said.[49] The shirts were delivered to Geri Halliwell, Mario Testino, Julien Macdonald, Jade Jagger, Jodie Kidd, and Jemma Kidd. Of the dinner, Lisa Armstrong, the fashion editor from the *Times*, wrote, "A relatively intimate dinner party with hand-picked guests and—excluding a handful of Voguettes—only two journalists, your reporter and the London correspondent of *Women's Wear Daily*, seemed just the ticket. The emphasis was on discretion and exclusivity. Most of the fashion posse at the party to launch Jimmy Choo's new space in Harvey Nichols … didn't even know about the dinner." Tracey Brower had explained to her: "Anyone with a big budget can get a celebrity on board. But the key now is getting the perfect fit. It has to look authentic." A month later, in October, Tamara, dressed in a skirt and lace-up blouse from the most recent Tom Ford collection for Yves Saint Laurent, celebrated the opening of the South Coast Plaza store in California with a dinner attended by the actress Debra Messing, among others.

As time went on, Robert found he had an unexpected advantage in shopping for space in the U.S. market—one that resulted from the financial doldrums of the downturn in the economy after the 9/11 disaster. Rents were relatively cheap and stayed cheap as many brands were still recovering from the slump in 2002 and 2003.

David Burns, the Phoenix partner on the board of Jimmy Choo, explained, "If we had bought Jimmy Choo four years ago, we would have found it difficult to find the same number of sites. There is availability now."[50] As a result, 2003 saw the opening of four stores in the U.S.: Dallas (March); Manhasset, Long Island (May); Short Hills, New Jersey (September); and a new flagship store in New York City at 716 Madison Avenue (August). All the while Robert continued to negotiate agreements with partners to open more Jimmy Choo stores in the fastest-growing of the developing markets. Moscow's opening in early 2003 was followed by stores in Dubai and Kuwait in 2004 and by the first outposts in South Korea and Hong Kong later that year. All the U.S. stores were between one thousand and fifteen hundred square feet, large enough to accommodate the rapidly growing collections that Tamara and Sandra had started to churn out. And many had the potential to accommodate the handbag collection that was well under way by mid-2003.

The most important item on the product side of Robert's to-do list was to build a strong second product line for the brand. Since the success of the Fendi Baguette in the late 1990s, which changed the fortunes of the company, the so-called It bag, the must-have bag of the season, became crucial to the fortunes of the luxury goods brands. The Baguette was followed by the Prada Bowling bag, the Chloé Paddington, and the YSL Mombassa, among others. By 2003 most brands hoped to create a bag that would have the moneymaking aura of an It bag each season.

Having more than one core product not only made sense from a sales standpoint, but it also made sense from a valuation standpoint. As a private equity company, Phoenix would want to own Jimmy Choo for only about three to five years before selling it again, at a profit. Being seen solely as a shoe brand would limit the price that the company could command when it was time to sell. It was much better to be regarded as a luxury accessories brand.

At the time of Robert's arrival at Jimmy Choo, handbags were little more than an afterthought. The company had sold only about six hundred handbags in 2001, mostly evening bags that complemented the shoes, and Robert promptly discountinued their production. Tamara and Sandra started to work instead on the development of a serious handbag business, one that would capture the feminine and sexy aesthetic of the brand and would eventually comprise a full range of bags, not just ones for evening. It would also have a strong design link to the shoes, but had to be a product line that could successfully stand alone on its own merits, so that the sales of the bags would not be necessarily linked to the sales of the shoes.

The role model for the development of accessories at Jimmy Choo was Tod's, the Italian shoe company that had successfully developed its own accessories line. Just as Diego Della Valle, Tod's owner, had linked its bags to the brand's iconic driving moccasin through the use of the pebble shoe sole that could now be found on the bottom of the bags, Robert wanted to find subtle ways to link Jimmy Choo bags to Jimmy Choo shoes. Given that Sandra and Tamara were busy with the expanding shoe collection, and given that handbags require technical expertise that is different from shoes, Robert and Tamara brought in freelance designers who possessed talent and experience specifically in handbag design. Those designers would work in parallel with Tamara and Sandra and their team of shoe designers, creating a line that shared elements similar to the shoes, like colors, jewels, or other adornments.

For the launch of its handbag line Jimmy Choo strategy focused around a single bag. They would bet on a well-designed, well-positioned bag rather than develop a full collection of various shapes and models. This would allow the company to put all of its efforts and resources behind the launch of just one bag and hopefully make it the It bag of the season.

As the first handbag prototypes started to arrive from Italy into the offices at Ixworth Place, the Jimmy Choo team organized impromptu focus groups with the girls from the office and their friends. They congregated in the showroom, passed on their views, and picked favorites. It was clear early on that the hands-down winner was the Tulita. Made with soft leather, it felt sensual, but embellishments like external pockets and gold buckle-type hardware gave it the utilitarian edge that was coming into vogue while still remaining feminine.

Public relations at Jimmy Choo was now being done in-house. In November Robert hired Tara ffrench-Mullen, with whom he had worked at Gianfranco Ferré. All her communications efforts around the bags, including PR, advertising, and celebrity placement, would convey the same message: The Tulita is the bag to own.

In March 2003 Tamara hosted a luncheon at the Plaza Athénée in New York. Most of the city's major socialites, including Serena Boardman, Cornelia Guest, Tory Burch, Marjorie Gubelmann, Alexandra Lind, Emilia Fanjul, Dori Cooperman, Marina Rust, Lillian von Stauffenberg, and Jennifer Creel, thought they had been invited so that they could be briefed on the new Jimmy Choo store opening on Madison Avenue in June. But at the end of the meal they got more than just a goody bag. They got the handbag. Although the Tulita would not be in stores until the following August, Tamara knew the best way to get the word out was to get the bags out on some of the most fashionable arms of the world. It worked. The Tulita—the style came in many shapes and sizes, from a small evening bag to a large sailor's duffle—became an instant It bag, and had long waiting lists.

By the end of 2003 it was clear that Robert would meet his business goals a year early. Jimmy Choo had gone from manufacturing 3,000 pairs of shoes a year in 1997 to 73,000 in 2001 to about 125,000 in 2003. Some 180,000 pairs were planned in 2004—more than even Manolo Blahnik was making. They also planned to achieve sales of 23,000 bags in 2004, up from fewer than 1,000 in 2001. In July 2003 Robert had joked, "Chanel has 200 stores worldwide, Dior has 250, Louis Vuitton 350. We have only 18. We are so far behind, we are already more exclusive."

Revenues at Jimmy Choo had almost doubled in two years, increasing from almost £12 million ($16.8 million) in 2001 to close to £22 million ($36 million) in 2003, with £34 million ($56 million) expected for 2004, a further increase in sales of close to 60 percent. Profitability was also on the rise, with operating profits doubling from the £2 million ($2.9 million) achieved in 2001 to almost £4 million ($6.5 million) in 2003, and they were expected to almost double again in 2004, reaching £7.5 million ($12.3 million). The accomplishments at the company were all the more laudable given what was going on in Tamara's personal life.

While Robert was growing the business, Tamara was growing impatient. The year 2002 had begun with the usual round of promises from Matthew. Only this time it was a business of his own that he said would save him. On a trip to a trade fair in Bologna, Matthew had seen a sort of classy sneaker sole and said he was going to place an order for ten pairs, and he would design the shoes himself. Those shoes became the basis of a shoe brand called Harrys of London, after his grandfather Harry Coxe Stokes, which would sell the £250 ($350) men's dress and casual shoes. The company logo was a heron, taken from the Mellon family crest. Tamara did not make the Oscars that year, as she was too pregnant to travel to Los Angeles. But Matthew did. He took along thirty prototypes for a new Harrys shoe line, took an adjoining suite to Jimmy Choo at the Peninsula Hotel, and retained Jimmy Choo's L.A. publicist, Marilyn Heston. Journalists who came through to look at the Jimmy Choo selection were then whisked next door to look at Harrys. Marilyn and Matthew invited not just the celebrities but each celebrity's agent, manager, PR person, and lawyer, and invited each to come by and get a pair of shoes for themselves in the hopes that the word would get back to the celebrities. In this way they managed to get them on the feet of Sting, Elton John, John Travolta, Denzel Washington, and Hugh Grant. Stories appeared in the press pointing out the connections between Harrys and Jimmy Choo. Robert was not amused. He told Matthew that it must be made clear that going forward Harrys of London had nothing to do with Jimmy Choo.

*   *   *

On her own at the Oscars without Tamara for the first time, Sandra Choi was afraid she wasn't holding up the company image. Dressed in a denim skirt and sparkly flats the day before the awards, she asked a reporter. "Do you think I look too scruffy? Tamara may tell me I'm not dressed smartly enough." Back in London, eight months pregnant, Tamara was still a role model on how to look stylish, telling a reporter that she only traded in her famous four-inch heels for the lower, one-inch-high "kitten heels" in the final weeks of her pregnancy. She had gone to great lengths to make sure she looked just as stylish as before. "I don't feel comfortable showing my stomach. I'm quite protective of it … A lot of the great pregnancy stuff isn't available in this country, so you have to order it on the net … The challenge is finding things that don't make you look big all over."[51]

In *Bright Young Things*, a 2002 book about London's "junior society set at home" by the New York socialite Brooke de Ocampo, who had recently relocated to London, Tamara declared, "Matthew still loves his Brooks Brothers boxer shorts. That I will never be able to change." Sadly, it seemed it was not the only thing she couldn't change. Even in the weeks preceding the birth of their daughter in April 2002, Matthew was seen partying hard in Los Angeles. He later said, "When your wife makes $100 million during the course of your marriage, it's quite a shocker. I felt my masculinity had been stripped from me. I was no longer the big man in the relationship. I feel like my balls are in a jar, like a Damien Hirst artwork on the mantelpiece. And here I am ball-less."[52]

Tamara was comforted by her old friends Emily Oppenheimer, of the famous diamond family, and *Tatler*'s feature editor, Vassi Chamberlain, who threw a baby shower for her and featured it in the magazine's pages. The guest list included model Claudia Schiffer; the founder of Coffee Republic, Sahar Hashemi; and heiresses Jessica de Rothschild and Daphne Guinness, who gave Tamara a baby trousseau from the Monogrammed Linen Shop.

After the birth of their daughter, Araminta, Tamara and Matthew tried again to reconcile. In July they went together to the Cartier

International Polo Tournament at the Guards Polo Club in Windsor, one of the key events of the London summer social season. Tamara said, "It is such a glamorous sport … We're even planning on taking lessons."[53]

In September 2002 the fall Jimmy Choo ad campaign appeared in fashion magazines throughout the U.S. and the UK. Conceptualizing and organizing the ad campaigns was one of Tamara's favorite roles and one of the best things about the sale to Equinox. Previously, some of the most strenuous arguments she had had with her father were about budgets for the expensive ads. But for the debut ad campaign under Equinox's ownership she decided to work with one of the world's most famous—and most expensive—photographers, Helmut Newton. Although Newton was a short, Jewish, happily married man, his lens captured images of powerful, sexy women. The Jimmy Choo ad was tamer than much of his work. It featured a woman wearing black stockings and black stilettos, sitting with her legs held to her chest leaning against a chain-link fence on a pier by the water. Her face turned up to the sun, she looked serene and oblivious to the fact that any passers-by could see straight up her skirt. If the ad was meant to reflect Tamara's peace of mind, it was misleading.

Tamara and Minty celebrated Christmas without Matthew. He went to Bermuda while Tamara stayed in London working and taking care of their daughter. Matthew was torn between his family, his addictions, and, increasingly, his own shoe business. In 2003 Harrys of London was officially launched. Matthew's friend and hedge fund manager, Max Gottschalk, became the nonexecutive chairman, and Jennifer Moores, the daughter of the owner of the San Diego Padres baseball team, invested £1.5 million ($2.2 million) for a 15 percent stake. Matthew hired away two of Patrick Cox's key employees. In the midst of the prelaunch publicity tour, Matthew had his publicist request that journalists stop referring to him as "the husband of" and take his brand on its own merits. It was a request that was pointedly ignored by all.

With Marilyn's help Matthew got his shoes on actors Jack Nicholson, Nicolas Cage, Denzel Washington, Jim Carrey, and Cuba Gooding Jr. at the 2003 Academy Awards. And he was already sounding like an old hand in the fashion game. He told *Footwear News*, "I'm not going for numbers, I'm going for quality. It's not how many people you dress, it's who you dress."

In the summer of 2003 in an attention-grabbing move, Jimmy Choo launched its cheapest-ever product—a £185 ($300) high-heeled flip-flop made from terry cloth. It was not well received by some of the fashion press. Kate Spicer of the London *Times* wrote: "This is a preposterous invention. It is a shoe made for no more than slipping on after your pedicure, or, at the very most, teaming with your Melissa Odabash bikini for the short trip from poolside lounger to the beach-club bar. Buy it at your peril, however—it's not exactly made for walking in." Tamara told the journalist, "When you buy our shoes, it is like buying a little piece of fantasy, a bit of escapism. It is the fantasy of my lifestyle—the helicopters, the holidays, the marriage, the cars my husband owns, the fantasy fairy-tale elements of my life."[54]

Fantasy indeed. In June of that year Matthew fell off the wagon—again. He and Tamara had rented a house from Jacqueline de Ribes, an aristocratic French socialite, on the Spanish island of Ibiza. Famed for its club scene and relaxed attitude to social mores, the island was an increasingly popular vacation spot among the European jet set. Tamara said they chose Ibiza because "we wanted a more hippy vibe." Staying at the house were Elle Macpherson, Simon and Yasmin LeBon, Oscar Humphries, as well as a few friends from Narcotics Anonymous and Alcoholics Anonymous. The idea was that their presence would help to keep Matthew on the rails. It did not work. Tamara used a concierge service to make sure the group got the best tables at Las Dos Lunas (one of Ibiza's chicest restaurant) and VIP tables at the most famous clubs, Pacha and Amnesia. The lure of the clubs was too much for Matthew. He went out clubbing one night and came back two days later. "I couldn't take it anymore," Tamara said. "It was the last straw. I had three little girls in the house, mine and those of friends of mine. I kicked him out of the house."[55] She phoned her father and asked him to find her a new house in London.

Back home and settled in her new house in trendy Chelsea, on Sydney Place, Tamara began an affair with one of the other guests from the Ibiza holiday. Twenty-two-year-old Oscar Humphries was a well-known figure on the social scene and the son of the Australian comedian Barry Humphries, who played the famous cross-dresser Dame Edna. Tamara said, "I think people behave in a lot of different ways when they've been in a lot of pain. And I think it was the whole thing of kicking Matthew out and wanting attention. Oscar is very smart and very good-looking."[56] She took no great pains to keep the affair private, even bringing him along to the opening of *Legally Blonde 2*.

In New York in early September Tamara was orchestrating the opening of the Madison Avenue store, which was done using the new design concept. "We have so many people asking to buy the furniture, I'm almost feeling like starting a home line," she said.[57] The party was so packed with socialites and celebrities, including Andie McDowell, Kim Cattrall, Claire Danes, Nina Griscom, Rena Sindi, Gigi Mortimer, Jennifer Creel, and Emilia Fanjul Pfeifler, that one of them, Ghislaine Maxwell, daughter of press baron Robert Maxwell, whined to *Women's Wear Daily*, "You could get in a fistfight in there or you could get felt up."

Back in London at the end of September Tamara found that Oscar, an aspiring writer, had published an article in the *Daily Telegraph* about his summer fling with an unnamed older woman. The streets of Chelsea, Mayfair, and Belgravia were buzzing with speculation about the identity of the woman in question, and Tamara's was the name most bandied about. After all, Humphries described his older woman as a successful businessperson and mother; plus he had told friends he was going to Milan at the end of the month, a visit that would coincide with the opening of the Jimmy Choo shop there. It did not take long for it to be confirmed that the mystery woman was

Tamara. When the news broke, a friend of Matthew's told the *New York Post*, "Matthew is in California now and he's pretty ticked off. She's been traveling in Europe with her boy toy and left her baby with her parents." Her parents had more practical concerns—Tom told her that now, with the affair in the newspapers, it was the time to divorce Matthew. The pressure of the press eventually took its toll. By November the affair was over and Oscar went to Australia to lick his wounds.

As for Matthew, he had allegedly spent much of the summer in a relationship with a Russian millionaire named Katia. But when his drug use got too much even for her, he finally went off to the Meadows Clinic in Arizona. Post–drug rehab, Matthew gave an interview to the London *Evening Standard* in December 2003, saying he was crying all the time: "Tears about what I had done." He also used the interview to beg Tamara to give him one last chance, promising her a significant amount of money if he relapsed again.

Tamara had been understanding of Matthew's problems and supportive of his attempts to recover, and since he was the father of her daughter, in this she continued. She attended a party with Matthew for Harrys in December 2003. He told a reporter, "We've sorted a lot of things out now … I'm pleased to say that our marriage is back on. Let's just see what happens over Christmas."[58] Tamara was less committal. "I'm here to support Matthew's business, I don't want to say more than that."[59] And with good reason—although she was not eager to divorce, despite the urging of her father, she knew she was not going to reconcile with Matthew either.

"It was too late," Tamara said later. "So much damage had been done at that point that it was irrevocable. I didn't want my daughter to be around him. For Minty, now that we are split up, that's just the way it is. She hasn't gone through a trauma of Mummy and Daddy breaking up or one moving out."[60]

The scandal of the separation and Oscar's indiscretion dominated the papers for much of December, overshadowing the opening of the first Jimmy Choo boutique on London's Bond Street. Cohosted by her friend Zoe Appleyard, a socialite and venture capitalist, Tamara threw a party at the store for women working in the investment banks of the City of London. They sold about one hundred pairs of shoes in two hours, at nearly £400 ($575) per pair. And although most City women did not want to brag about their wardrobes the way most of her friends did ("How many Jimmy Choos do I own? That's totally private," said one), Tamara realized it was time to start courting the City. It was a thought shared by David Burns and Robert—but for very different reasons.

Twelve

THE LION ROARS

"NOTHING GETS TAMARA EXCITED like talking about creating value," said one of her colleagues. One of the most exciting parts of the monthly board meetings at Jimmy Choo was the discussion about the potential value of the company on the open market. A key factor in determining the value of a company is how the rest of the sector is performing. After the turbulent couple of years for the luxury sector that followed September 11, the situation by January 2004 was decidedly less grim. LVMH, the bellwether stock for the luxury sector, had seen its share price recover from thirty-five euros in late 2002 to sixty-one euros, a 75 percent increase. Tiffany & Co. was up even more, some 95 percent, while Burberry had recovered from the lows that followed its IPO in the summer of 2002 and was up 116 percent. Bulgari shares had increased in value a staggering 130 percent. The usual valuation multiples (such as enterprise-value-to-EBITDA, price-to-earnings, or price-to-sales ratios) had all recovered alongside the stock prices. The companies were reporting better-than-expected results, and although management at the companies still maintained a note of caution when it came to expectations for 2004, Wall Street and City analysts had started to look positively upon the luxury sector again.

The stock prices of luxury companies were already anticipating what were expected to be golden years ahead. The U.S. economy was booming, Japan appeared on its way to recovery, and customers from the so-called emerging markets of Southeast Asia and Russia were beginning to exercise their wallets. Good news seemed to abound on all fronts.

So how much was Jimmy Choo worth? A back-of-the-envelope valuation using one of the most typical valuation metrics, multiples of sales and EBITDA, placed the value of Jimmy Choo in the realm of £100 million ($175 million). This implied a multiple of three times the sales and thirteen times the EBITDA that Jimmy Choo was expected to generate in 2004, which meant that Equinox's 51 percent stake would be worth roughly £50 million ($88 million)— and a similar amount for the stake of the Yeardyes. Not many private equity deals could boast those kinds of returns. Equinox would have multiplied its investment by more than five times in just three years.

When the board met again, Robert Bensoussan, Tom Yeardye, and David Burns discussed the idea of selling Jimmy Choo. Of the three, Robert was the most hesitant. He thought there was value left behind by exiting the investment early. Furthermore, he had a long and comfortable relationship with Phoenix, and it was he, as CEO, who would have to work most directly with any new owners, should he decide to stay on board. But he agreed there was no harm in testing the waters. Tamara, for her part, was happy to do what her father thought best. With the blessing of the board, David put in calls to a few London investment banks to try to figure out the best way forward.

An initial public offering was certainly almost out of the question at that time. True, the UK retail conglomerate Great Universal Stores (GUS) had recently spun off Burberry, floating it on the London Stock Exchange in the summer of 2002, and had seen its stock price skyrocket. But this was still unwise for a company of Jimmy Choo's size. Despite the growth of the last few years, which had driven sales to the roughly £22 million ($36 million) mark achieved in 2003, the company was still too small to compete for the attention of the institutional investors who managed the multibillion-dollar pension and hedge funds that drove the market. As a result, the value of Jimmy Choo shares was likely to suffer if traded on the stock market. More promising, they thought, was another private sale. Although the big luxury groups like LVMH and Gucci Group had not made acquisitions in a while, it was possible they would bite if something as tasty as Jimmy Choo were on offer. Tom, Robert, and David began scheduling meetings with the various advisory houses and investment banks. The bankers' beauty contest had begun.

No one could have predicted what happened next. On April 21, 2004, at the age of seventy-three, Tom Yeardye died of a brain aneurysm at the home he shared with Ann in London. The death of the affable and charismatic Tom came as a shock to everyone, but for Tamara it was a particularly powerful blow. Ever since she was a child, her father had been her guiding light. She had not gone a day without speaking to him—in fact, he regularly called her first thing in the morning to make sure she was out of bed. To make matters worse, the London *Evening Standard* leaped at the opportunity that had opened up—in the UK one can't libel the dead—and delved into Tom's past, declaring that he was "an associate of some of London's most infamous gangland names, including the Krays." The accusation was not as bad as it sounded. In his second book about the Krays, *The Cult of Violence*, author John Pearson noted that "every taxi driver in London knew someone who had known the Krays." But the accusation against Tom was very unlikely to be true. Pearson, who spent several years with the Krays while researching his book, said he was almost certain to have met Tom if he had been part of their circle—and he had not. More likely, the Krays may have been behind the tough tactics Tom had experienced when he was running nightclubs in the 1950s. It was devastating to Tamara and the rest of the family to see their beloved Tom's name dragged through the mud. And it was made more painful for Tamara by the fact that she was the reason why. Had she not been at the helm of Jimmy Choo, it was unlikely that anyone at the papers would have cared about, or remarked upon, the passing of a man once known as Mr. Muscles. Although Tom and Vidal Sassoon had not spoken in years, Tamara called Vidal in tears and asked him to please tell the truth about her father to anyone who asked.

While Tom's death slowed down the initial round of meetings with the various investment banks, it sped up the need for a sale. Tom's estate, which included his stake in Jimmy Choo, now had to be settled and divided between his surviving family members in accordance with his will. Tom's and Tamara's stakes in Jimmy Choo were held in an offshore holding company called Thistledown International Ltd. that Tom had set up years ago. Thistledown was now in turn owned in equal parts by two Jersey-based trusts of which Tamara and Ann were respectively principal beneficiaries.

In the late spring of 2004, the first official rounds of meetings with the investment banks that had been vying for the Jimmy Choo transaction were completed. Robert now led the negotiations on the Jimmy Choo side pretty much by himself. Rothschild and Goldman Sachs were the last two in the competition to win the mandate to sell the company. In a typical Goldman gesture—the American investment bank is known for going to great lengths to flatter potential clients—Goldman created an all-woman team and had the female bankers on the project show up to make the final presentation clad in Jimmy Choo stilettos. It was a cute touch. But the Rothschild team had a secret weapon of its own: Akeel Sachak, the global head of its consumer investment banking team. Born in Tanzania of Indian descent, Akeel was one of the British immigrants who, as they say, was more English than the queen. He had been sent to boarding school in England and went to college at Oxford. He was on his way to becoming a barrister when he passed the Inns of Court (where historically most English barristers have their offices) and thought, "I've spent too much time in rarefied places—time to get closer to the real world." Rothschild isn't everyone's idea of the real world; founded more than two hundred years ago, it is one of the country's oldest banks and is still regarded as a prestigious launching pad for gentlemen bankers from the best British families. Still Akeel joined right out of university and never left. He spent three of his twenty-two years at Rothschild in Milan, where he opened the bank's office. "My secret weapon is that I speak Italian," he says. His wardrobe was every bit as smooth as his manner. He wore custom-made suits by Huntsman of Savile Row, Ralph Lauren Purple Label shirts, Hermès ties, and handmade Berluti shoes, a fact that did not escape the notice of Robert, who himself always wore shoes by John Lobb.

To underplay the fact that Rothschild did not have as much experience in luxury goods as Goldman, Akeel focused instead on the personal connections Rothschild's advisers had with the Big Three luxury goods groups: LVMH, Richemont, and Pinault-Printemps-Redoute (PPR), the owner of Gucci Group. Rothschild had advisers on each of the boards of directors of those three companies. Felix Rohatyn, a famous American investment banker and the former U.S. ambassador to France, had a seat on LVMH's board. Another senior banker, Yves-Andre Istel, was on Richemont's board, and French businessman René Barbier de La Serre was on the board of PPR. Akeel maintained that financial sponsors like private equity companies were unlikely to pay above £70 million ($127 million), insinuating that the Rothschild's connections would land Jimmy Choo a big money deal from one of the three prestigious buyers. "Akeel is great at overpricing," said one Rothschild banker. "That's his special talent; he just can't help it." He not only promised that Jimmy Choo would get top dollar, but he also assured them that it would be from one of the Big Three luxury groups.

Selling the Jimmy Choo business to one of those top corporate buyers would be a major coup for the Jimmy Choo team, as well as for Rothschild. For one thing, strategic buyers tended to pay more for assets since they can highlight their ability to realize synergies or cost savings among brands. And none of these groups had made any significant acquisition since 2001. Getting them back in the game would be a feather in the cap of everyone involved. In comparison to

Rothschild, Goldman had extensive experience in luxury, including working closely with LVMH for years and advising Bernard Arnault during his takeover attempt of Gucci. But Goldman had proposed a very public auction and presented a huge list of potential buyers, many of whom—including Chanel or Armani—were highly unlikely to even want to take a look. Rothschild instead proposed a more discreet approach that was also preferred by the Jimmy Choo team. Connections, a more focused sale process, and an aggressive valuation of the business were the factors that pushed the mandate into the lap of Akeel and Rothschild. Project Jewel—the code name for the Jimmy Choo transaction—was born.

Although at the expected valuation of approximately £100 million ($185 million) the deal was smaller than the usual Rothschild transaction, the profile of the Jimmy Choo company was much larger than those they usually worked with. The team at Rothschild spent the early part of the summer of 2004 preparing a slick investment memorandum worthy of the Jimmy Choo image, a key feature of which was a DVD that, according to Akeel, had "high-octane music and legs everywhere," including clips from *Sex and the City*. The deal was hailed as a "unique opportunity to purchase an iconic British fashion brand, which has achieved global status and which has significant unrealised growth and brand extension potential." It went on to brag about Jimmy Choo's "proven ability to deliver profitable growth," its "sustainable margins and returns of a 'superbrand,'" its "successful and dedicated design team," and its "highly professional management team with significant depth."

But even before the selling information memorandum was completed, Akeel began speaking with his contacts at the Big Three groups. If a deal could be done with one of those strategic buyers—LVMH, Richemont, or PPR—why bother with the rest? And why couldn't it? The early months of 2004 had continued to deliver strong growth at Jimmy Choo. Like-for-like sales growth—a good measure of a brand's health, as it only included sales growth from stores that had been opened for one year or more as opposed to sales from new stores—was 30 percent. Revenues were forecasted to reach £34 million ($56 million) by year's end, a substantial increase from the £22 million ($36 million) achieved in 2003. Operating profit margins had increased from 16 percent in 2002 to 18 percent in 2003 and were expected to reach 22 percent in 2004, finally matching those of the other big brands in the sector.

Yet the Rothschild bankers did not get the warm response they were hoping for from the big luxury groups. The feedback was consistent—and tepid. Thanks to the launch of the handbag collection, it was true that they no longer saw Jimmy Choo as only a shoe brand; but they still saw it as a fashion brand, one that could fall out of favor just as easily as it fell in. So a key issue to address was the sustainability of Jimmy Choo's popularity and its growth prospects for the long term. How long could the company continue to grow at such a fast pace? How could potential buyers be certain that it wouldn't be just another of the once-hot brands, like Fiorucci or Thierry Mugler, that litter fashion history?

In addition, each of the groups had its own particular reasons for refusal. LVMH was Akeel's primary target. Although he had never done a deal in luxury with LVMH, he had advised the group in its acrimonious acquisitions of Guinness and Grand Metropolitan in 1996 and 1997, so he knew the company well. It also seemed the most logical target. After all, LVMH did not have a luxury women's shoe brand in its portfolio. Berluti, maker of the shoes that Akeel himself wore, was part of the group, but it made only men's shoes. Furthermore none of the many fashion or leather goods brands in its portfolio had a particularly strong women's shoe business. LVMH's chairman, Bernard Arnault, was intrigued by Jimmy Choo and its rapid ascent, but many of his trusted deputies, including Yves Carcelle, who at the time was the head of the fashion and leather goods division of LVMH, were much more hesitant. (Sidney Toledano, the CEO of Christian Dior, said that although he knew the proposal was making the rounds, Robert never spoke to him about it. "We want to protect our friendship more than anything," Sidney said.) Arnault's colleagues were particularly cautious at the time because LVMH shareholders and the equity analysts who followed the stock were demanding that the company focus on growing the brands it had already acquired and stop spending money on new ones. Recent moves by management to shed assets, including designer labels Christian Lacroix and Michael Kors, beauty brand Bliss, and makeup brand Hard Candy, were finally being reflected in the company's upward-moving stock price. The cost-saving synergies envisioned when LVMH bought many of those brands had never quite materialized. The new managing director hired from Procter & Gamble, Antonio Belloni, was being lauded in the press for keeping Arnault's shopaholic tendencies at bay. It was clear that what was working in the group were the old established names like Louis Vuitton and Christian Dior rather than the less successful, fashion-heavy Johnny-come-latelies like Kenzo or Donna Karan. A purchase of Jimmy Choo could send the wrong message to the market, indicating that the group may be contemplating making many acquisitions again. It was the wrong time for the €12 billion (£8.3 billion, $13.5 billion) LVMH group to risk reversing its stock market fortunes for a company as small and as young as Jimmy Choo.

From the outset Richemont was a less likely potential purchaser than LVMH. Its founder and chairman, Johann Rupert, was, for the most part, only interested in jewelry and watch brands. Chloé, the only Richemont fashion brand, was a booming success, having been transformed under the leadership of British designers Stella McCartney and Phoebe Philo, both graduates of Central Saint Martins, and Robert's old friend from Morocco, Ralph Toledano, its CEO. But Richemont had not yet managed to turn around the French luggage and accessories brand Lancel, which Sidney Toledano once ran before he became CEO of Dior. It languished in the group's portfolio along with Dunhill, the British brand of accessories for men, while Rupert lavished love and praise on his many watch and jewelry companies. The official excuse given to

Rothschild's bankers was a clear snub: Jimmy Choo was fashion, not luxury, and Richemont was only interested in luxury.

Gucci Group, now part of PPR and controlled by French billionaire François Pinault, had bigger issues to deal with than worrying about Jimmy Choo. The group was still reeling from the abrupt departure of its leaders, creative director Tom Ford and CEO Domenico De Sole, in April 2004. Tom and Dom had left disenchanted with François Pinault after his dramatic, white-knight takeover of Gucci in 2000. They were followed out the door by several key executives, including Bob Singer, the CFO; Brian Blake, head of the watch and jewelry division; Tom Mendenhall, the number two at the Gucci brand; Tomaso Galli, the head of financial public relations; and Lisa Schiek, the company's longtime head of fashion public relations; among others. A new CEO, Robert Polet, previously a high-ranking executive at Unilever, had been appointed in July and was busy getting to know the company, its brands, and the luxury landscape in general. In addition to the management turmoil, Gucci Group, like the other strategic buyers, was still recovering from the 2000 and 2001 acquisition spree that had swelled its portfolio from just one brand, Gucci, to ten, including Bottega Veneta, Yves Saint Laurent, Alexander McQueen, Boucheron, Stella McCartney, and, problematically for Rothschild, a competing luxury women's shoe brand that was not doing particularly well—Sergio Rossi. Gucci also passed.

The unenthusiastic reaction from the top three potential buyers prompted an abrupt move to widen the list of prospective acquirers to just about everyone else in the fashion universe that might be able to come up with the money—just as Goldman had initially proposed. Akeel circulated a new list of possible buyers. On it was everyone from Ralph Lauren and Chanel to Jones Apparel Group, owner of Anne Klein and the midmarket shoe brand Nine West. But still no bites.

That July another Rothschild banker, Justin Abbott, was sunning himself on a beach on the Côte d'Azur, blissfully unaware of what was going on, when he got a phone call telling him to come home. Because of internal changes at Rothschild, he had to join Akeel's team in orchestrating the Jimmy Choo sale. He arrived back in London to find a situation filled with stress and growing animosity. Robert, encouraged by Rothschild, had his hopes set on selling to one of the Big Three groups and was not at all pleased that no offers were forthcoming. And while the initial plan had been to keep the sale very quiet until they had a blue-chip buyer on board, going to the wider group of fashion targets increased the likelihood of word of the sale leaking. This, he feared, could hurt the Jimmy Choo image, as well as the business. But the really big problem was that even though feelers had been put out to the widened group of candidates, there were still no offers. Tensions between the Jimmy Choo contingent and the bankers at Rothschild were rising. "There were a couple of difficult weeks," admits Justin. Other bankers at Rothschild were impressed—with the size of the failure. "People [at Rothschild] were saying, 'You're meant to be on this iconic transaction. The rest of us are selling industrial companies in the North of England and we get bids. You haven't got one? You've got NO bids? That's incredible!'"

Finally it was time to resort to plan B: financial sponsors. Selling to a strategic buyer would mean that the brand was likely to have a long-term home. Selling to another financial player meant that a future sale or IPO was inevitable. Financial investors generally earn their money by selling the company again, not by pocketing the dividends earned by the company. It also meant that the new owners might not understand the idiosyncrasies of the luxury market—and therefore might be less willing to pay up for the asset. On the plus side they were less likely to care if a brand was "fashion" or "luxury," since it was unlikely they would be around long enough for the gloss to dull. Robert made an introduction to Swiss private bank Pictet, which had recently formed a private equity division and supposedly had a large, secret investor. But all of the leads led nowhere. A daily e-mail was sent detailing who was still in the running and who had dropped out.

Jimmy Choo. (GETTY IMAGES)

Tamara Mellon at the "4 Inches" celebration, a photographic auction to benefit the Elton John AIDS Foundation, hosted by Jimmy Choo and Cartier. (GETTY IMAGES)

Tom Yeardye (right) and
friend in the 1950s.

Tommy Yeardye

PRESENTS

Le Condor

LONDON'S NEWEST NIGHT CLUB

OPENING TUESDAY, SEPT. I

LE CONDOR, 17 WARDOUR STREET, W.I. (GER 7905)
DANCING AND DINING NIGHTLY 9.30 p.m. to 3 a.m.
(Licensed 3 p.m. to 2 a.m.)

Cabaret stars glamorous
KATHY KIRBY

Do you know that Europe's most unique restaurant

TOMMY YEARDYE'S
PAINT BOX

has been

- Televised by the B.B.C.
- Filmed by Pathe Pictorial.
- Networked across the U.S.A. by N.B.C.
- Broadcast about by radio to Australia.
- Written about by *The Telegraph, Daily Mirror, Daily Sketch, Empire News, Star, Evening Standard,* and in Italy—*Il Gornia.*
- Visited by Royalty.

The Paint Box is the rendezvous of England's Film and Television Stars.
World wide interest has been aroused in this excitingly different Restaurant.
Have you visited it yet? We welcome everyone.

29 Foley Street (off Gt. Portland St.), W.I.   **Reservations: LAN 5771 & 3249**

Two minutes from B.B.C.

An advertisement for
Tommy Yeardye's
Le Condor night club and
Paint Box restaurant.

Young Tamara Mellon with her parents, Tom and Ann Yeardye.
(WITH KIND PERMISSION FROM ANN YEARDYE)

Tamara and her mother, Ann, in Gstaad, Switzerland, in 1986
while Tamara was a student at the Institut Alpin Videmanette
finishing school. (WITH KIND PERMISSION FROM ANN YEARDYE)

Ann Yeardye in the
basement office of the
Motcomb Street Jimmy
Choo store. (WITH KIND
PERMISSION FROM
ANN YEARDYE)

Jimmy Choo's first boutique in Los Angeles. (GETTY IMAGES)

The interior of the first boutique in Los Angeles. (GETTY IMAGES)

Robert Bensoussan, CEO of
Jimmy Choo from 2001 to 2007.

Tamara Mellon and Sandra Choi at
Jimmy Choo's tenth-anniversary party.

Sandra Choi at the Jimmy Choo suite before
the Academy Awards, fitting Angela Bassett.

Matthew and Tamara Mellon at the launch party for Harrys of London, Matthew's new line of men's shoes. (GETTY IMAGES)

Tom Yeardye with his sons. (WITH KIND PERMISSION FROM ANN YEARDYE)

Lyndon Lea, founder of Lion Capital.
(DAVID LOMINSKA)

Christian Slater, Tamara Mellon, and Joshua Schulman (CEO of Jimmy Choo) at the launch party for Amanda Goldberg and Ruthanna Khalighi Hopper's book *Celebutantes*, hosted by Tamara Mellon at Saks Fifth Avenue. (GETTY IMAGES)

On October 31, 2004, the *Mail on Sunday* broke the news that Jimmy Choo was for sale, but although the paper got the £100 million ($182 million) price right, they got the buyer wrong. In the article, Burberry was reported to be the likely buyer. In fact, talks with Burberry never went far, despite Robert's relationship with CEO Rose Marie Bravo. Burberry was very focused on developing its own brand and was not really looking to diversify with other acquisitions. True, they would look from time to time at various opportunities but few passed the "first test" of synergies that the team at Burberry would systematically subject them to when evaluating them. With Jimmy Choo, the synergies were potentially there, as Burberry was looking to aggressively grow its women's shoe business and Jimmy Choo's experience and leadership in that product category could be invaluable. But in the final analysis, the business would demand too many internal resources and the price tag was too high to be a bolt-on acquisition for Burberry. They passed.

Nevertheless, the story that Burberry was in the game was picked up by all the major newspapers the next day. The word was out. To take control of the situation, Jimmy Choo issued a statement confirming that the company was indeed for sale. Robert told *Women's Wear Daily*, "We received unsolicited approaches this summer, and gave the mandate to NM Rothschild. But we're at the very, very early stages, so there is no timetable as such." There was no timetable, of course, because so far there were no offers, unsolicited or otherwise. But then the smooth-talking Akeel came through. Behind the scenes he had been quietly grooming one of his most likely candidates—Lyndon Lea.

Known in the City as "the boy banker," Lyndon, at thirty-four, was the head of the European operations of Hicks, Muse, Tate & Furst, a Texas-based private equity firm known in Europe for buying mega consumer brands like Weetabix cereal and Typhoo Tea. Lyndon and Akeel had already done several deals together, including Premier Foods and Weetabix. The two went back to 1995 when Lyndon was at Glenisla, the European affiliate of the famous U.S. buyout firm

Kohlberg Kravis Roberts (KKR). Akeel knew Lyndon could move fast on the deal, and not only because he had included him when he sent out the second round of proposals to the luxury brands, giving Lyndon an almost two-month lead on other financial buyers. Akeel later said that he did not expect Lyndon to buy either Kettle Crisps, a deal he brought to him a couple of years later, or Jimmy Choo. "One of the things that set Lyndon apart from other private equity guys is that he is interested in growth, willing to buy it and to pay for it," Akeel said. "Hicks Muse thought about deals more like a strategic buyer than a financial sponsor ... Lyndon has more strategic vision than many other private equity investors that are too focused in the easy part of private equity—leveraging and financial engineering."

Lyndon was at an airport in the U.S. that fall when Akeel phoned him about the Jimmy Choo sale. He explained some of its complications. Namely, there were some questions about how the Yeardye shares would be divided and the fact that, although Robert and Phoenix jointly controlled 51 percent of the company, they were not quite in agreement about the sale. "Robert did not think it was the right time to exit, but Phoenix did," Lyndon said. To complicate matters even more, Alison Egan, the CFO of Jimmy Choo and the person with the best grasp of the numbers, was about to go on maternity leave. But all of this only gave Lyndon an advantage over other buyers. "What Akeel saw was that there was lots of complexity and uncertainty. He knew we could say yes and deliver on a rapid timetable at auction," said Lyndon.

Back in London, Lyndon was afraid Hicks Muse's investment committee would not share his enthusiasm. As Robert had done with Phoenix, Lyndon asked his business partners to go home and talk it over with their domestic partners. "Every wife and girlfriend was very excited about it," he said. Lyndon and his partner at Lion Capital, Robert Darwent, ran through the numbers quickly, aided in the process by the top-notch management information systems Robert Bensoussan had put in place. "It had one of the best systems

I had ever seen," said Lyndon. "It was exceptional in terms of what we've had to wade through in other due diligence processes. You could see sales and profits store by store, product by product, down to the point where if I give the cleaning staff at the store in Coral Gables, Florida, a fifty-cent raise, I can immediately tell what that is going to do to the profits."

Akeel and Justin introduced Robert and Tamara to Lyndon and Darwent at a presentation in the Phoenix offices. Tamara was very impressive when it came to presenting to bankers. She arrived in what Akeel described as "South Kensington business attire"— chic suit and sky-high Jimmy Choo shoes. "Although she was not financially sophisticated, she invariably displayed a native cunning that allowed her to come out on top in most situations. She came alive on the spot. She did not come across as a flighty It girl or of the sort that some might imagine her to be," Akeel noticed. For example, she could convincingly explain her role in the company. "I lead the design process," she would say to a potential buyer. "I decide if this season people are feeling in a hippie chic or in a sexy, glamorous mood." Robert focused on the business side, going in detail through the strategy for growth. Lyndon listened intently and left the meeting feeling that "Robert and Tamara truly knew how to inspire buyers with their enthusiasm for the brand and its potential." Lyndon, too, struck the right chord with the Choo team. "He came across as genuinely interested," Akeel said. "He was not aggressive and seemed a civil person and not someone who was going to stomp on their plans." Left out of the initial process was Tamara's mother, Ann. Although since Tom had died she now owned nearly a quarter of Jimmy Choo's shares, no one thought to keep her in the loop.

Afterward Lyndon and Darwent pushed forward on the homework of due diligence. "The guy is incredibly hardworking," Justin said of Lyndon. Indeed, Akeel's big concern was not the ability of Lyndon to get through the due diligence fast, it was that he knew Lyndon was in the midst of splitting off the European arm of Hicks Muse, which he ran, from its underperforming counterpart in the United

States and establishing his own private equity fund, Lion Capital. The performance of Hicks Muse funds in the U.S. had been badly damaged by a number of poor investments in the technology and telecom sectors in the U.S. and Latin America. Lyndon's European investors were urging him to split before they would commit money to a new fund. Although Lion Capital, the company to which Lyndon would move the Hicks Muse team, had already been formed when he was evaluating the Jimmy Choo transaction, for legal reasons it couldn't be used yet. Lyndon reassured Akeel that it would not be a major issue. Jimmy Choo could be held in a temporary investment vehicle and then be transferred into the core fund. When the creation of Lion Capital was finally announced in April 2005, every article in the press mentioned Jimmy Choo. "It was our way of sending a signal," Lyndon said.

In October 2004, as Lyndon was finishing the due diligence on the company, he asked Akeel to arrange a dinner with the two Roberts (Bensoussan and Darwent) and Tamara at the glamorous private club Harry's Bar in Mayfair to talk about their future together. A key subject of the dinner was the working relationship between Robert Bensoussan and Tamara. Would it continue to thrive without Tom around? The pair swore that it would. Once convinced, the mood turned jovial and they began to discuss their plans for the company and the ways they would work together. But unbeknownst to them Rothschild had started to receive other nonbinding offers from interested parties in the open auction process that Akeel had decided to run in parallel, "just in case."

However, bids from these other parties were either far from the target price or too far behind to catch up with Lyndon's lead. "What surprised everyone was that by the time it went to auction, our due diligence had been done. The auction came down to what the contracts looked like," said Lyndon. And since Lyndon had more than a month's head start, no one else was able to come up with a contract that looked as good. One of those interested parties was another fund, Soros Private Equity. Although Soros's offer was as high as Lion's, they had not enjoyed the head start Akeel had given Lyndon. So theirs was a nonbinding offer, while Lion's was firm. "We were dining at Harry's talking about how we were going to do business before the auction started," Lyndon said. The only real contender was a small public company called the Lambert Howarth Group. The group's main business was to supply midpriced shoes to the likes of Marks & Spencer. The company was being advised by the New York–based independent advisory boutique Financo.

Financo's founder, Gilbert Harrison, couldn't be more different from Lyndon. In 1971, a couple of years after Lyndon was born, Gilbert had set up Financo in New York and was focusing exclusively on deals in what was then known as the apparel sector. By 1985, when Lehman Brothers acquired Financo, he had completed more than 140 transactions. But in 1989 Gilbert became convinced the partnership was not working, and he reacquired the name and reestablished the firm as an independent company. He had since done deals with a wide swath of fashion industry companies ranging from American shoe brand Stuart Weitzman to Chinese production giant Li & Fung.

Lambert Howarth's key reason for wanting to acquire Jimmy Choo was to try to rebrand itself on the stock market. It was thought that with the acquisition—and subsequent name change— the company could go from being valued as a lowly supplier with equally lowly trading multiples to a blue-chip brand with the hefty multiples of a luxury goods stock. (At the time this company was trading at a 0.5 times multiple of sales while the luxury sector was at 1.5–2 times sales. Jimmy Choo was being marketed at 3 times sales.) However, part of the money for the purchase of Jimmy Choo hinged on this expected increase in the value of its shares, making it a very complicated deal. Essentially, Equinox and the Yeardyes would be given stock in the combined company instead of cash. On paper the deal with Lambert Howarth seemed potentially more attractive than the offer from Lion Capital, possibly generating up to 20 percent more money—making it a price tag of £120 million

($220 million)—but to take the money off the table they would have to take shares in the quoted company and then sell them on the stock market after the transaction was completed. And the value that Lambert Howarth was putting on its future stock was debatable—very debatable as it turned out. The company went bankrupt at the end of 2007 after Marks & Spencer cut off most of its business with them. "We thought we had a deal," said Gilbert. "But Lyndon was offering cash and our stock deal would have taken three months to close." Although tempted by the extra money they could earn, Robert and Tamara were not keen to see their luxury baby associated with a down-market manufacturer. When Robert finally came to Ann with the two alternatives, she tried to "channel Tom." "I thought [with the Lambert deal] we can't get out if this goes the wrong way." Ann agreed to sign off on the deal to sell to Lion Capital. On November 4, 2004, Gilbert got a call saying that Jimmy Choo was to be sold to another buyer.

A few days later, on November 14, Lion was also ready to commit. Rothschild distributed a memo among Jimmy Choo's shareholders that highlighted the terms of the Lion proposal. The final agreed price gave Jimmy Choo a total value of £101 million ($183 million), close to three times the sales expected for the year 2004 and thirteen times its operating profits. After subtracting all the large transaction fees and the small amount of debt the company had, the owners of Jimmy Choo would be left with a total of £95.7 million ($174 million). Lion Capital was to buy 78 percent of the company, comprising the stakes of Phoenix and the Yeardyes. Tamara and Robert were expected to stay on board and reinvest in the company at the new valuation.

The following day, on November 15, all the shareholders attended a meeting at the Jimmy Choo offices to discuss the offer from Lion Capital. In addition to Tamara, Robert, and David, the meeting was also attended by various trustees of the Jersey funds that held the Jimmy Choo shares, and by Tamara's mother, who was accompanied by her son Greg and by her financial adviser. The shareholders reviewed the structure of the offer from Lion

Capital outlined in the memo. The 49 percent Yeardyes' stake, including Tamara's, was worth £42.8 million ($77.8 million), and the 51 percent Phoenix/Equinox stake was worth £48.8 million ($88.7 million). But how the Yeardyes' stake would be realized has become the subject of much debate and two lawsuits. Tamara believes that at the meeting it was agreed that the amount to be received by the trust of which Ann was principal beneficiary (some £21.4 million [$39 million]) would be in cash, while the amount to be received by the trust of which Tamara was beneficiary (the same headline figure of £21.4 million) should be a combination of upfront cash (roughly £12 million [$22 million]) plus securities— namely, deep discount bonds (i.e., issued at a lower nominal value than their face value) that would be effectively stapled to the equity that Tamara would maintain in the company (roughly 12 percent). This is a fairly commonplace way to structure the stakes of management teams in private equity transactions. In this case, the stapled bonds issued to Tamara at £8.2 million ($15 million) had a face value of £18.2 million ($33 million).

Robert, like Tamara, was allowed to cash out of part of his investment (roughly 50 percent), but both were required to reinvest the rest of it in the business. Lyndon was insistent that the deal would go ahead only if all the shareholders not involved in the running of the business, which included Tamara's mother, were bought out. But he was equally insistent that the shareholders crucial to the brand's development should stay on board and stay committed.

The point of having both Tamara's and Robert's stakes take the form of deep discount bonds or loan notes was to minimize the tax bill of the company. Robert told Lyndon that because he was more involved in the day-to-day running of the company, he and Tamara had agreed that he should be given 5 percent of the sweet equity and Tamara would have 3 percent. After the deal Lion would be the majority shareholder, followed by Tamara and then Robert.

As part of the deal, Robert also managed to negotiate small stakes for a few key members of the team who had not had equity before.

Among others, Alison Egan, the CFO and Robert's first hire, and the former sales assistant Hannah Colman, who was now the European director of retail, and who, according to Robert, was "part of the soul of Jimmy Choo and one of its biggest assets."

With the price and the structure of the transaction agreed upon, the lawyers set to work on drafting the contracts—Travers Smith, advising Equinox, Tamara, and the Yeardye estate, and SJ Berwin advising Lion Capital. The lawyers at Travers Smith were very familiar with the Jimmy Choo dossier; the firm had advised Phoenix Equity Partners on its acquisition of Jimmy Choo back in 2001. Philip Sanderson was the partner at Travers Smith in charge of this new transaction. Even given the time pressure, the usual closing details seemed to be progressing with minimum fuss. Despite the middle-of-the-night conference calls held to discuss things like the size of Tamara's clothing allowance and the complexities of Robert's own compensation, which allegedly required its own spreadsheet, Lyndon recalls that negotiations over Tamara's and Robert's contracts were straightforward: "Robert rang and said this is what we make now and this is what we want to make. I said fine." But getting the deal done in such a short amount of time was still taking its toll. Justin had to arrange a conference call line to be open twenty-four hours a day to field the many emergencies, and his new girlfriend was beginning to complain about hearing the fax machine that he'd installed in his bedroom ring at eight A.M. on Sunday mornings.

On Thursday, November 18, everything appeared in order. It was time to sign the deal. Due to the corporate and fiscal structure of the company at the time, part of the deal had to be approved and signed in Jersey. The company's structure was typical of many UK-based companies where the brand name has significant value. The brand name was held in a company located in Jersey, and the operations of the business were held in other companies located in England and the United States. Both companies were owned by the same shareholders. The brand-holding entity, J. C. Jersey Ltd., licensed the Jimmy Choo brand to the UK-based company, J. Choo Limited, which ran the operations. In exchange, the brand entity received royalties from the operating company. Because the brand was in the offshore tax jurisdiction of Jersey, income taxes on the royalties received from the operational company were avoided as long as they were not repatriated into the UK.

Arrangements for the twenty-minute flights to and from Jersey had been made for the afternoon. Robert and David Burns were on their way to London's Gatwick Airport when Robert got a call from Akeel at Rothschild with some surprising news about how Lyndon planned to come up with the £101 million ($183 million) to buy Jimmy Choo. One of the key ways private equity works is by borrowing money to finance part of an acquisition, with the amount of the loans based on the cash flow of the companies to be purchased. That debt is the responsibility of the company, not the private equity firm, and the company must factor the debt payments into their profit and loss statements. The Jimmy Choo business was closing its 2004 books with almost no debt and with roughly £7.5 million ($13.6 million) in EBITDA, and if all went according to plan, the company would generate more than £10 million ($18 million) the following year. That was enough cash flow not only to finance the future expansion of the company but also for Lion Capital to borrow a significant amount of money, roughly £45 to £50 million ($80–90 million)—or half of what they were going to pay for Jimmy Choo. At the time of the transaction, a leverage multiple of five times EBITDA was considered aggressive; however, in the years to come, those high-leverage multiples became standard due to the overabundance of money being loaned by banks. Although it added risk, the amount of debt showed that Lyndon had confidence in the potential of the business to generate profits to make the repayments.

Robert didn't see it that way. When he realized that the company was going to be loaded with £45–50 million in debt—the payments on which would be ultimately his responsibility—he was not happy. About to board the Gatwick Express, he said, "Fuck it, I'm not going to go." The pressure to repay the debt with the profits generated by the company could hamper the development of Jimmy Choo, and therefore its value. Furthermore, it would leave very little room for error, and responsibility for it would fall on Robert's shoulders as CEO of Jimmy Choo as much as on Lyndon's as a main shareholder. While the rest of the deal team was aghast at the thought that all their work had been wasted, Lyndon calmly called Robert and said, "Come to my office." In his luxurious offices on Grosvenor Place, overlooking the gardens of Buckingham Palace, Lyndon and Darwent explained the exact details of the debt structure to Robert, who was joined by Alison. It was not nearly as bad as Robert had feared. For one thing, the debt was structured as a bullet loan, meaning that the principal did not have to be repaid for a very long time, and the interest payments were not onerous. And importantly, the structure allowed Robert to leverage his own equity stake in the company. He, too, would enjoy the same enhanced returns on the cash he was about to commit to the new deal. Robert was back on board.

But now there was another problem. They had missed the last flight to Jersey that day. "Don't worry," said Lyndon. "You can take my plane." And his NetJet was commandeered to fly Robert and David Burns to Jersey.

Tamara, Lyndon, and the rest of the team met again at the offices of Travers Smith to sign the documents. Lyndon had been waiting around the offices of the law firm hoping they would sign by five P.M. But some nitty-gritty details were still being sorted out. "Usually a deal like this would take a month," Justin said. "This took ten days, so some of the moving parts were still moving." The biggest issue was how Tamara was due to receive her portion of the proceeds. The trustee of the trusts of both Tamara and her mother told Tamara that there were "extra" shares in the deal and that since they were "extra," half should go into Ann's trust. In the weeks after the deal was signed, Tamara came to believe that the shares actually belonged to her and that the accountant and trustees had made a mistake. But by this point Ann felt just as strongly that those shares belonged to her.

Lyndon's patience was wearing thin. As the clock ticked on, he became convinced that the lawyers were taking longer than was necessary. He began threatening to leave in the hopes that it would spur them into action. Finally he retreated into a conference room with Tamara and Darwent to pass the time by discussing the nominations for the Academy Awards.

Things were equally annoying in Jersey. To get there Robert and David had to fly on the small plane through a terrible storm. Once they landed they went straight to the offices of the lawyers who were representing Jimmy Choo. At eight fifteen P.M. the pilot called to remind them that the airport in Jersey closed at nine. There was no way they would make it out on time. They would have to stay the night. After the contracts were signed at ten P.M. Robert and David listened to the champagne corks popping in London over speakerphone, and they began to make their way to one of the many forgettable hotels in Jersey. With no taxis to be found, they walked in the rain, with briefcases in hand. They arrived at the hotel soaking wet with nothing but papers—no clean clothes, no toiletry kits. At least they had some entertainment. While they ate some sandwiches and drank a beer in the bar of the hotel lobby, they watched the antics of a group of girls having a Bond Girl–themed party. The girls invited them to join, but they were too tired. The next morning, at six A.M. theirs was the first plane to leave Jersey. They arrived at London Luton Airport in the city's far north suburbs to find no one had thought to book them a car. They boarded the commuter train and stood holding the rails for the duration of the thirty-minute journey to London. There was very little glamorous or luxurious about it. Never mind, the deal had been done and in record time.

"Bidders are constantly looking for ways to get an edge in the auction process," said Lyndon later. "Speed of execution has become increasingly important. And we were fast." This feeling was echoed on the side of the sellers: Hugh Lenon, the managing partner of Phoenix Equity Partners, said, "If someone can write you a check in a week instead of a month, that has to be attractive, and Hicks Muse

[Lion Capital] moved fast. A speedy exit allows the management of the company to focus on running the business without the distraction of a lengthy sale process. This is of particular importance on the run-up to Christmas."[61] And what a Christmas it was. Phoenix walked away with net proceeds of roughly £35 million ($64 million), or almost four times its initial investment made just three years earlier—a hefty 55 percent return.

The transaction was announced on Friday, November 19, 2004. For a relatively small deal, the sale struck it rich on the publicity front. Articles about the acquisition appeared on the AP and Reuters news wires and in the *New York Times*, *Wall Street Journal*, *Financial Times*, and on the business pages of every major British daily. Some in the private equity business grumbled among themselves that the hefty price tag was setting a bad precedent in the luxury goods sector. Lyndon dismissed those criticisms, saying, "Of course we overpaid. We overpay for everything or we wouldn't get anything." He pointed out, "There was another bidder that was offering even more."

Indeed there was. Within days of signing the deal, Financo's Gilbert Harrison phoned Lyndon and put forward an offer from Lambert Howarth to buy the company from him, with a £20 million ($36 million) profit. But Lyndon said no. Now Jimmy Choo was part of his portfolio, and he planned to make a lot more than £20 million from it. His first task as owner was not a difficult one: Brushing aside Robert's comment that he should pay the company a licensing fee, Lyndon named his new Santa Barbara–based polo team Jimmy Choo and had polo jerseys made in the brand's lavender and white colors.

Thirteen

TROUBLE IN PARADISE

THE REVERBERATIONS OF TOM'S death were felt far beyond the boardroom. Even though Robert Bensoussan had been at the helm since 2001, the company still felt like a family one, with Ann and Tom acting if not as Mom and Dad, then definitely as Grandma and Grandpa. On the day he died Tom and Ann dropped into the Jimmy Choo office with a handwritten copy of Tom's memoirs to have them typed. As they were leaving, Tom remembered that there were some new faces in the company. "I haven't done the rounds in a while," he said to Ann. "Let's go say hello to everyone." On his way out, Alison Egan called him back, "Mr. Yeardye, Tamara is sixty thousand pounds [one hundred thousand dollars] over her budget for clothes." "What else is new," said Tom. "This time, try asking her what *she* is going to do about it."

Robert's method of managing was more professional, but colder and alienating to one of the longtime employees. Lou Rodwell said, "I'm not a fan of Robert's, but I recognize he did a good job. I had chemistry with Tom, but there was none with Robert. With Tom you felt part of it."

Without Tom to help manage Tamara's extravagant impulses, and to help keep Robert's "I-can-do-it-all-myself" impulses in check, the relationship between the two key members of the management team deteriorated quickly and fatally. After the deal with Phoenix, David

Burns had said, "When Tamara first embarked on Jimmy Choo she had genuinely identified an underserved marketplace and then went about the business in a way which many entrepreneurs do so well, by making the most of minimum investment. She was initially explosive, and joining with Robert has added fuel to the fire. Robert brought experience of a corporate environment, and we could see the potential for him and Tamara to form a potent partnership, which they have." With Tom gone there was more emphasis on explosive than on potent. Buried with Tom was a key piece of the communication structure of the company. And Robert found he was far less adept at curbing Tamara's more grandiose tendencies. While Tom could make Tamara understand that an expensive shop on Rodeo Drive was not yet necessary, Robert could not convince her that there was little value to the company in sponsoring a flashy event like the annual Serpentine Gallery Summer Party, one of London's early summer social events. Each year a company, usually a fashion company such as Cavalli or YSL, sponsors an architect to design and build a special pavilion in the middle of Hyde Park to hold the party. In 2005 she went over Robert, directly to the board, and got the approximately £100,000 ($180,000) she needed to do it. A huge sum of money for the company. Robert refused to attend.

Although the company had grown significantly, it was still relatively small and Robert kept a careful eye on costs. Rather than pay big salaries, Robert promoted from within. "A lot of people had no prior experience," said a former employee. That strategy may have its downsides, but it built loyalty and, for most, Robert was a good leader. "What came through from the people at the company was a love of the brand and an amazing level of dedication. Robert got people to work incredibly hard because they felt they were part of something unique," said Muriel Zingraff, who joined Jimmy Choo to work with Robert on business development in March 2006.

Now almost everyone in the office suffered as the result of the strife between Robert and Tamara, although they tried to stay focused on getting the job done. Of most concern for the company was the conflict between Tamara and Sandra. Until then, they had enjoyed a great creative relationship. "Sandra is like the architect of the shoe and I am more like the interior designer," Tamara liked to point out. But Sandra, perhaps encouraged by Robert, began to recognize the importance of her own role in the company. And she thought that some comments Tamara made to the press had diminished her role. Sandra began interviewing for new jobs, nearly taking a position at Bally until Robert convinced her that Jimmy Choo was her home. "Part of Sandra wanted to be publicly recognized, but she also liked to be in the background. It was more comfortable there," said a coworker.

Complicating the situation for Tamara was the fact that things were not yet resolved with Matthew. Tom's death did not send her back into Matthew's arms, but she tried to remain on good terms with him and told friends that she saw no point in divorce. She said she hoped they could remain married but live separately for the sake of their daughter, Minty. But her father had convinced her that such an idea was not practical, particularly since she had been outed in the newspapers as reportedly having had an affair while still married to Matthew. Before he died, Tom had made an appointment for Tamara with Sandra Davis, the head of family law at Mishcon de Reya, which handled divorces for Princess Diana and Jerry Hall. Tamara still hoped the process would go smoothly. "My idea was because we have got to be friends for the rest of our lives and we have a child together," she said, "I wanted a very easy break. I don't need the money so I let him have what he has and I'll have what I have."[62] Instead she would get an agonizing and public spat. Matthew hired Raymond Tooth, the London divorce lawyer nicknamed "Jaws" because he is known for being particularly tough on rich spouses. He has handled the divorces of Sadie Frost, the ex-wife of Jude Law, and Irina Abramovich, the former wife of Russian billionaire Roman Abramovich. Tamara would soon learn the nickname was fitting—Matthew was claiming to have helped his wife build her business, if only through lending his name. In early

2005 she received a letter from Tooth saying that the reason Jimmy Choo was a success was because of Matthew's name and money. "I was floored by that," Tamara later told *Vanity Fair*. "He believes the Mellon name made Jimmy Choo … People buy the shoes because of his name? It's quite polluted."[63]

But not nearly as floored as she would be by what happened next. On February 4, 2005, at about five A.M., Matthew was arrested and charged with "conspiracy to cause unauthorized modification of computer material," or in layman's terms, hacking into the Jimmy Choo computers. The talk of the sale of Jimmy Choo to Lion Capital at the end of 2004 had sent Matthew into overdrive. He felt he had a claim to some of Tamara's Jimmy Choo stake and to the proceeds from any sale. He hired Active Investigation Services (AIS), a firm of private investigators. Unbeknownst to him the associates at AIS figured that the best way to find out what Matthew wanted to know was to infiltrate the computers of Jimmy Choo with a program that would record keystrokes, enabling them to read the e-mails Tamara was sending and receiving. Unfortunately for Matthew, the private investigators turned out to be former Scotland Yard officers who were being closely watched by London's Metropolitan Police in what was known as Operation Barbatus. In Tamara's case she noticed something was fishy when she received an e-mail with an attachment offering information integral to her divorce proceedings. The attachment was empty but she soon began to notice that Matthew had a lot of information about the Jimmy Choo business. She quickly reported it to the IT department and experts were brought in to check the system. They detected the AIS-installed virus. When months later the police busted the offices of AIS, they collected Matthew's file along with those of the rest of the firm's clients. The arrest of the scion of one of the world's richest families attracted all the press one might expect. Some articles wrongly claimed Matthew was part of a criminal ring, tapping phones on behalf of rich clients. He retained the hard-hitting London law firm

Schillings, which specializes in media law, and they demanded, and got, some corrections. But that did not erase the fact that Matthew was in big trouble. A conviction could come with a five-year jail sentence.

Throughout the spring and summer, as her divorce from Matthew was fought out in the courts, Tamara was beginning to recognize her new currency on the dating market. No longer was she just another It girl, now she was a glamorous almost-divorcee and multimillionairess. In the last half of 2005 she was linked with an array of celebrities, including Joe Francis, the founder of the *Girls Gone Wild* empire; singers Kid Rock and Robbie Williams; several rap stars; and Formula One boss Flavio Briatore. Instead of store openings, sightings of Tamara in the press centered on her love life—who was in, who was out, and who was waiting in the wings. "I just have to go within five feet of a man and I'm dating him," she said.[64] Courting celebrities no longer interested her—becoming one did. In sync with her growing celebrity status she began using film director Brett Ratner to shoot Jimmy Choo ads that starred other celebrities, such as Nicole Ritchie, often with dead men floating in the background or left in the trunk of a car. She also began to tell friends that she was going to move to Los Angeles to be near her mother so that Minty could stay with family, not hired help, when Tamara was working.

In August 2005 Tamara achieved that pinnacle of celebrity, the *Vanity Fair* profile. The article, titled "The Lady and the Heel," focused almost entirely on the details of her troubled marriage to Matthew and read like one of the magazine's investigative reporting features, making the highly styled glossy photos of Tamara and her daughter running in front of their Chelsea home and Tamara getting out of her chauffeur-driven car seem all the more odd.[65]

The feature was the talk of the summer in London. Some in her circle were jealous, others perplexed as to why she would announce to the world that she was divorcing one of the world's richest men and then pose with her daughter by their home. Wasn't she concerned about security? To the staff at Jimmy Choo it was more than perplexing. It was disrupting. Sandra told executives at the companies she was interviewing with that she was very upset about the *Vanity Fair* article.

Matthew's criminal trial was also dominated by the appearance of Celebrity Tamara. When she waltzed into the courtroom in the spring of 2007 to testify as a witness for the prosecution, she did so wearing a Roland Mouret pencil skirt and Jimmy Choo heels. The paparazzi photographers had been given the fashion credits and the pictures and the plugs appeared in all the major papers.

Her supportive testimony was important in securing Matthew's acquittal. Nick Purnell, Matthew's Queen's Counsel (or lawyer), essentially argued that Matthew lacked the sense to know what the detectives he hired were doing. Tamara's testimony perfectly supported the defense case. "Matthew can not even read a comic, let alone a legal document," she said. "Being married to Matthew was like having another child … When I was married to him I had to take responsibility for his bank accounts and bills. He is totally incapable." And, she added, he "missed planes like other people miss busses."[66] Her colorful commentary, like the details of her outfit, was picked up by all of the major newspapers. Matthew later said, "I had an epiphany sitting in the glass box with the jury to my left. I'd had this fantasy of an American coming over to marry a British girl, and this is what it's come to: a fucking circus."[67]

All of this was irritating for Robert, particularly as he felt Tamara refused to recognize that she could not be both the day-to-day president of Jimmy Choo and a celebrity. "Depending on her love life, she was more or less involved in the business," sniped a former employee. The problem was that to Tamara, that was no problem. She would travel regularly for professional and personal reasons and would often return to the office upset that decisions had been made without her. Robert would respond that if she really cared, she should be around more often.

*   *   *

When Lion Capital bought the company in 2004 it had nineteen stores—a big achievement given that it had only three when Robert and Phoenix bought it in 2001, but still far fewer than its luxury peers. It was perceived, Lyndon said, "as a cult brand, known only to those in the know." In the two years under Lion ownership, the brand went from cult to mainstream. Robert continued his all-out assault on the world's top luxury locations, focusing strongly on the United States and Europe. New stores were opened on Bond Street and Sloane Street in London and on Via San Pietro all'Orto in the center of Milan. Opening stores in Europe is no mean feat. Because of the limited supply of top retail property, rents had started to skyrocket. Key money (or premiums) was a major hurdle for brands trying to access the top properties, and the amount required could be in the millions of dollars. Key money was essentially a lump sum paid by new tenants to buy out old tenants' lease contracts. This enabled them to take over desirable retail premises while enjoying the same favorable low rents as the original tenants. There was no way that a company like Jimmy Choo could compete with the likes of LVMH, Gucci, and other major groups that had deep pockets when it came to being able to fork out huge amounts of cash to secure a space. Without cash Robert had to be creative. One of his greatest successes was what the staff at Jimmy Choo began to call the "miracle store."

Robert, with his connections to Paris, was desperate for a space in the world's most famous fashion city, but he could find nothing within his means, particularly on avenue Montaigne, Paris's unrivaled luxury shopping street. A friend of his father suggested he take a look at a space in the apartment building where he lived on avenue Montaigne. The apartment building sat in a courtyard just off the famous avenue, but on the avenue itself was an empty space. It had once been used as the apartment for the building's porter, or superintendent, but it had been empty for years. It sat next to an unused alley. Robert was able to lease this ideal spot with no key money, almost certainly the only such deal on avenue

Montaigne in years. All he had to do was spend two years fighting with the office of the mayor of Paris for permission to convert the structure and the alley next to it into a shop. And although the rent was cheap by retail standards, Jimmy Choo paid more each year than all the residential tenants of the building combined. The store was barely fifty square meters (538 square feet) but it had fourteen feet of windows along avenue Montaigne. The miracle store opened in November 2005. "He had to be smart. He had to be profitable right away, so he started with these very small shops. Only Robert could open a store out of a concierge apartment," Sidney Toledano said. The Paris store was small, but Robert had big ambitions for it. He told *Women's Wear Daily* he expected it to do €2 million (£1.4 million, $2.4 million) in business the first year, paving the way for even more Paris outlets. In fact, that tiny miracle store did close to €3 million (£2 million, $3.7 million) in sales that first year.

Robert was also keen to get a Jimmy Choo store in India, home of the five-day wedding party. He believed that it was the perfect market for an accessories brand. Indian ladies may not be ready to give up the sari, but they would certainly be happy to match their traditional clothes with the sparkly Jimmy Choo shoes. Robert was introduced to the Murjanis, an Indian family that was bringing Western brands to India, by Marvin Traub, who was their consultant. Over lunch in London they signed the deal. Later, he sent his deputy Bonnie Takhar, an executive he had hired from Earl Jeans to help him with developing the business with franchise partners, to visit the market and open the Mumbai store in 2006. Because of the lack of a luxury shopping street like avenue Montaigne, or a luxury shopping mall like South Coast Plaza, in Mumbai, the Murjanis were having to build their own mall.

Robert had also been flirting with a fragrance license. Since early 2005 he had been having preliminary conversations about a perfume deal with some of the key players in the industry, although so far the project had not enticed any of them. Clarins, which owns the fragrances for the iconic French brands Loris Azzaro and Thierry

Mugler, could not envision how a shoe brand would translate into a fragrance despite the dossier Robert and Tamara prepared on the world of Jimmy Choo. Procter & Gamble was refocusing on its core brands, Valentino and Hugo Boss, and also was not interested. In March 2006 Muriel Zingraff joined the company to take over the venture. Muriel had worked at L'Oréal and Harrods, and had been the CEO of Paco Rabanne for three years. She had just moved to London and took on the role of heading the licensing activities solely to work with Robert. Before she could develop a fragrance she felt she had to do an internal brand audit. "The company had grown so organically no one had taken the time to write it down," she said. The brand analysis she did focused on defining the brand attributes that made Jimmy Choo unique. A key one was that the company made products *for* women *by* women (it was a source of amusement in the office that Robert seemed to prefer hiring women). Also its products were sexy as *women* defined sexy, not as men did; and it had a heritage as a shoemaker, thanks to Jimmy, rather than being a designer brand extending into shoes. Jimmy Choo was a brand that would never compromise elegance or glamour for the sake of a fashion trend. Once the brief was ready, she approached a few additional candidates—the most promising turned out to be Selective Beauty.

In 2000 Corrado Brondi, a former Goldman Sachs mergers and acquisitions banker who had also run the fragrance business for Kenzo, founded a fragrance distribution company called Selective Beauty. Although it was primarily a distribution company, in 2005 Selective Beauty had successfully staged the fragrance launch in the UK for the British naughty-chic lingerie brand Agent Provocateur—a brand that had been started by the son of designer Vivienne Westwood. It also launched the fragrance of John Galliano, which was too small for LVMH. Revenues at Selective Beauty were growing fast and had reached €152 million (£82 million, $190 million) in 2006; it was becoming one of the leading independent players in the competitive fragrance sector, and they were looking for another British brand to work with. "They were very enthusiastic," Muriel said. "They really wanted it."

Selective Beauty seemed the ideal partner for a company like Jimmy Choo; the brand would have gotten lost in the large cosmetics companies such as L'Oréal, Procter & Gamble, or Estée Lauder. Not that they were particularly interested anyway. With Selective Beauty Jimmy Choo would have more control over the final product, which was crucial. And the distribution legacy of the company gave an added advantage. "We cover two-thirds of the global market," said Marc-Antoine Breuil, head of business development at Selective Beauty. "Only U.S. companies with sales over $1 billion [£550 million] can say that." Jimmy Choo gained the flexibility, creativity, and quick reflexes of a small company and the efficiency and reach of a multinational one. Selective Beauty had nine international subsidiaries. "Jimmy Choo realized that we understood the brand. The product will be very luxurious [it would sell at over one hundred dollars], exceptional, with narrow but meaningful distribution." The launch was so important for Jimmy Choo that Robert told the company to take their time. The top priority was to get it right, not to hurry into the crowded fragrance market.

The other license that Muriel worked on was eyewear. The Italian company Safilo was the opposite of Selective Beauty—it is one of the largest players in the game. It makes and distributes eyewear (both prescription glasses and sunglasses) for a wide range of brands, including Armani, all the Gucci Group brands (Gucci, YSL, Bottega Veneta, Alexander McQueen, Balenciaga, Boucheron, and Stella McCartney), as well as Dior, Valentino, Hugo Boss, Diesel, and Marc Jacobs, among others. Muriel liked Safilo because they had the technical expertise to mix plastic with metal hardware, part of the look that was crucial to the Jimmy Choo aesthetic.

Robert was also looking into other possible acquisitions. Ever since he partnered with Phoenix to set up Equinox he had hoped one day to build and manage a stable of brands, not just a single one. In that he was joined by Jim Sharp, a former Schroders and Citigroup banker who joined Equinox in 2003. Jim and Robert worked well together. At Equinox they looked at new investment opportunities outside Jimmy Choo (such as Italian leather company a.testoni and Holland & Holland, the British hunting brand), but in the end all Robert acquired was a friend and confidant—Jim. He became a consultant for Jimmy Choo, where he negotiated with their Japanese distributor, Bluebell, and covered for Alison, the CFO, during her maternity leave. Jim had also assisted during the sale process of the company to Lion Capital.

When the French shoe company Stephane Kélian was in trouble some years back, Robert took Sandra to see it and get her impressions. They were both impressed with the company's wide-ranging production facilities in France and the number of stores they owned. But the price the owners were asking was too high. Even after it went bankrupt the legal quagmire of saving a French brand was too daunting. Robert had also considered some iconic American brands. His short list included Geoffrey Beene, Bill Blass, and Halston.

Roy Halston had gained fame in the 1970s for dressing the Studio 54 disco crowd, including Liza Minelli, Bianca Jagger, and Diane von Furstenberg, in simple, sexy jersey dresses. The brand and its associations held a special place in the hearts of people, like Robert, who had come of age in that era and had spent many a happy 1970s night in a disco. But even before Halston's death in 1990 the company had been left in turmoil after being bought and sold several times. The various owners had brought along a string of new designers, including Randolph Duke, Kevan Hall, Craig Natiello, and Bradley Bayou, none of whom managed to revive the excitement around the brand.

But that didn't stop people from trying. Halston was still mentioned regularly as a potential target for acquisition. Robert found the same problem that all others who had looked at buying Halston in recent years had found. The price. The owner, James

Ammeen, who was a Halston license holder when he acquired the brand in 1999, had letters from mass-market retailers Wal-Mart and JCPenney saying that they wanted to license the name, and they were willing to pay a lot. Although Ammeen didn't want to see the name taken down-market, he was not willing to sell for less than they were offering—an astronomical $20 million (roughly £10 million). Robert worked on various scenarios to finance the deal, but in the end the numbers all said the same thing: It was just too expensive for a brand with almost no sales. There would not be any returns on investment for a very long time unless he milked the brand through aggressive licensing, which was not Robert's idea of how to develop a label.

Vintage Halston had been a long-standing favorite brand of Rachel Zoe, the stylist who had worked on the Jimmy Choo campaigns and was a friend of Tamara's. Together they, too, had begun to talk about Halston and ponder if it was possible to bring the brand back. Tamara mentioned the project to one of her new celebrity friends, Harvey Weinstein. Weinstein, with his brother, had launched Miramax, a film production company that had produced hits like *The English Patient* and *Pulp Fiction* before it was sold to Disney. Their new company, the Weinstein Company, was now the producer of the hit TV show *Project Runway*. Weinstein was dating, and is now married to, one of Tamara's old London friends, Georgina Chapman. Tamara often offered her advice on Chapman's fashion line, Marchesa. Weinstein had been very helpful when Tamara was putting together the *4 Inches* coffee-table book and auction in 2005. Not everyone leaped at the chance to pose naked, save for the Cartier jewels and the Jimmy Choo heels. "He made a couple of calls," Tamara said. "And suddenly everyone was talking to me." Weinstein was impressed with the success of Jimmy Choo and often would ask Tamara what else she would be interested in doing. She said, "I think the biggest missed opportunity in the luxury market is Halston. I've always bought a lot of vintage Halston pieces and worn them."[68] Weinstein was keen to hear more. Tamara went to Robert and told him the news. In early 2007 Robert agreed to have a conference call with Weinstein and tried to explain the depressing reality of the situation. But Weinstein would not listen. At a meeting with the owner, James Ammeen, Weinstein said, "I'll give you four million dollars. Take it or I walk out the door." Ammeen responded with what he had been saying for years—twenty million dollars or no deal. Tamara and Weinstein got in touch with Marvin Traub, the former president of Bloomingdale's, who had his own brand and retail consulting company and he matched them up with a Toronto-based private equity company, Hilco Consumer Capital. If interested, Hilco would finance the bulk of the transaction. Hilco was interested, and the presence and involvement of Weinstein and Tamara sealed the deal in April 2007. When the sale was announced it was revealed that Tamara would sign on as a member of the advisory board, and, though it was not part of the official deal, Harvey would make a film about Halston's life. Robert would just shake his head.

Tamara's first move was to help the company find a new CEO and a designer. For CEO Tamara knew just the person—Bonnie Takhar. Although it was Robert who had brought Bonnie into Jimmy Choo, she had quickly formed an allegiance with Tamara. The appointment of the designer soon followed. By mid-July 2007 Marco Zanini, the head designer at Versace, was appointed as creative director. His first collection was presented in New York in February 2008 for fall/winter '08. Just in time for the February debut, London's *Daily Mail* reported that Jude Law would be playing the role of Halston in the movie to be produced by Weinstein. But as Cathy Horyn reported in the *New York Times* on July 16, 2008, "It seems to be a recurring theme at Halston: another collection, another designer."[69] Zanini left Halston less than a year after he took the job.

At Lion Capital, Lyndon had been used to acquiring companies and then allowing the managers to run their businesses independently with little interference from him. But the Jimmy Choo executive team wanted more feedback—and praise—from their owner. One executive who made a presentation to Lyndon said, "They did not ask a lot of questions. They seemed a bit indifferent." When Robert came looking for more than just praise, for help managing Tamara, the response was not what he was seeking. "As an investor, you can't let yourself get drawn into the internal conflicts," Lyndon said. "All companies are filled with intrigue and politics, but who cares, if it is working?" Although he talked a good game, Lyndon knew that if the situation got worse, it could affect his ability to sell the company. He asked Robert to find a solution before he had to find one for him, because that would not necessarily be one that Robert would like.

Fourteen

MARRYING TOWERBROOK

IN APRIL 2005 Ramez Sousou walked into his new offices at
83 Pall Mall, at the heart of St. James's in Mayfair, the London
neighborhood where the who's who of the private equity and hedge
fund world had congregated during the boom of the early years of
the twenty-first century. A Harvard MBA of Palestinian origin, Ramez
had spent most of his career at the U.S. investment bank Goldman
Sachs in New York and London, where he was a member of Goldman's
prestigious principal investment group—the team that invested
Goldman's own capital and the partners' own money—before heading
the Goldman Mezzanine Partners fund. In 1998 Ramez and his
Goldman colleague Neal Moszkowski had left the bank to launch the
private equity arm of Soros Fund Management, the investment empire
of billionaire financier George Soros, one of the world's most legendary
investors. Soros was well known for "breaking the Bank of England"
on Black Wednesday (September 16, 1992), when his Quantum Fund's
bet against the UK pound forced the Bank of England to devalue the
UK currency. His private equity division was conceived to limit his
exposure to the stock market and its inherent risks by investing instead
directly in companies, not just publicly traded securities.

At the end of 2004, Soros decided to retire. Ramez and his
partners at Soros Private Equity proposed to buy the business. Soros
agreed and TowerBrook Capital Partners was born. By April 2005

the amicable split was completed—Soros himself was their first and one of the largest investors—and fund-raising for their new maiden fund was under way.

They took over most of the companies that had been owned by Soros Private Equity and put them under the TowerBrook umbrella. Soros was joined in his investment by almost fifty other investors, including wealthy family funds, institutional investors, and funds of funds. The additional capital that these investors committed by the time the fund-raising period ended one year later was $2.5 billion (£1.4 billion), all to be dedicated to acquiring new companies. With offices in both London and New York, TowerBrook's Web site says the fund focuses on "leveraged buyouts, leveraged buildups and distressed situations."

Distressed was almost certainly the way Robert felt in late 2006. The internal tensions with Tamara at Jimmy Choo were becoming unbearable and were increasingly difficult to conceal. Robert was frustrated with Lyndon for his hands-off approach. Lyndon had made it clear that he did not see it as his role to mend fences between managers.

Robert decided the best way out of the situation was to find a new buyer for Jimmy Choo, one that ideally would not only purchase Lion's stake in the company but—at a minimum—would give him the support he needed to manage the situation by scaling down Tamara's official duties at the company.

When Robert phoned Lyndon in September 2006 and asked him what he thought of a sale as a way out of the issues with Tamara, he had his arguments at the ready: The financial markets continued to be buoyant, with luxury goods stock prices and valuations climbing higher and higher. The share prices of most luxury stocks had increased exponentially since December 2004—LVMH was up 50 percent, Richemont was up 64 percent, and Italian shoemaker Tod's increased by 100 percent—but so had the sales and profits expectations. Thus, by late 2006, trading at multiples of two to three times sales and ten to thirteen times EBITDA, the luxury goods sector did not look particularly expensive relative to its forecast growth potential.

Inside Lion Capital, the investment in Jimmy Choo had already exceeded Lion's goals, so why not exit early and avoid any risks of a potential downturn in the stock market that would hurt the value of the company? Also, the first goals of the development of the brand, growing the business in the U.S. and launching accessories, had been successfully achieved. Jimmy Choo was now sold in almost forty locations of Saks Fifth Avenue, and since it had a slim chance of getting into Saks's main competitor, Neiman Marcus, where Manolo Blahnik still reigned supreme, the U.S. wholesale market for shoes was pretty well penetrated. (Since Manolo Blahnik doesn't make bags, Neiman had been carrying Jimmy Choo bags since the early part of the year.) The next challenge globally would be to make Jimmy Choo a success in Asia, a market with which Lion Capital was less familiar. Most important, an exit would mean Lyndon would not have to deal with the potential nightmare of a management team falling apart. With Tamara's high profile in the public eye, such a schism could hurt the brand image with consumers, but, much more important from Lion's point of view, it would also make it a toxic asset—one that would be much more difficult to sell.

Lyndon didn't need much persuading. He was more amenable to the idea of selling than Robert anticipated. Lyndon had already been talking to potential buyers. One by one, feelers were put out to the usual suspects. UBS tried to convince Gucci managers that buying Jimmy Choo could be a boon to the Gucci Group, but after some exploratory talks, dialogue suddenly stopped. Gucci explained that, in their view, there was nothing that Jimmy Choo had that could not be replicated with Sergio Rossi, the shoe brand they had owned since 2000. Bankers at Goldman Sachs reached out to managers at several levels of LVMH. But the message back from the top was clear: Bernard Arnault was just not interested.

Bankers at Rothchild got back in touch with Burberry to gauge their level of interest this time around. Although John Peace,

Burberry's chairman, and Angela Ahrendts, the new CEO, thought that Jimmy Choo was a great brand that could contribute to the development of Burberry's own women's shoe business, it was still just too demanding a purchase for them to take on. Lyndon knew an easy sell to a strategic partner was not going to happen. So when Robert asked Lyndon if he would sell—and at what price— he responded with a quick yes. "Get me 185 million pounds [340 million dollars] and it's yours," he said.

Robert had met Ramez Sousou, the cohead of TowerBrook, two years earlier during the sale to Lion Capital in 2004, through the Paris-based mergers and acquisitions firm Aforge Finance. At that time, while he was still with Soros Private Equity, Ramez had been a contender to buy Jimmy Choo. Ramez had made a £100 million ($185 million) offer, but lost out because his offer was nonbinding, unlike Lion's, who had a head start in due diligence. Since then, Ramez had kept in touch with Robert, inviting him to the yearly CEO dinners that TowerBrook, like other private equity firms, hosted to maintain an ongoing dialogue with the CEOs of the companies they would like to work with one day. When Robert phoned him, Ramez was already very familiar with the Jimmy Choo story. The new news Robert had to tell him was all good: Revenues were on track to reach £65 million ($120 million) in the fiscal year 2006, tripling the almost £22 million ($36 million) levels reported in 2003 and running almost £15 million ($27 million) ahead of the forecasts presented to buyers in the investment memo circulated by Rothschild to Ramez in late 2004. That meant the business had been growing at 45 percent per year since 2001. Jimmy Choo was also on its way to reaching the sixty-store mark by the end of 2006. New store openings were delivering growth above expectations, driven by successful product launches. The Tulita's successor was the equally successful 2006 Tahula range of handbags, the round handles of which were based on the hula hoop. "I don't pick the names," said Robert. Handbags now accounted for 40 percent of the company sales, particularly good news since profit margins on bags are about 10 percent higher than those on shoes. And there was still plenty of room for growth. Jimmy Choo was still behind other big brands in terms of number of stores. Gucci had close to two hundred stores, and Louis Vuitton was nearing four hundred. Even relatively young brands like Bottega Veneta had one hundred stores. Plus, Asia represented only 10 to 15 percent of the Jimmy Choo sales at the time, which was a tiny percentage compared with the average 40 to 50 percent boasted by most well-established luxury goods brands.

The year was a good one for the luxury goods industry at large. The global economic climate was sunny thanks to low interest rates, rising incomes, low unemployment, and ever-increasing house values. These factors all contributed to buoyant levels of consumer confidence, unseen since the dot-com bubble of 2000. On the fashion runways, which some say capture the zeitgeist of the times, hemlines were rising and heels were skyrocketing to levels beyond the iconic Jimmy Choo four inches.

Things had been going well for TowerBrook, too. In October 2005 they had pocketed more than $300 million (£165 million) from the sale to Liberty Media of Cablecom, the Swiss telecom company. The deal had been awarded the prestigious "European Large Deal of the Year" award and TowerBrook had also been selected as the "European Fund of the Year" at the European Private Equity Awards, sponsored by the European Private Equity and Venture Capital Association. The fund was recognized for being "one of very few firms in the market with a highly differentiated strategy" of focusing on unusual or complex transactions. In addition to the successful exits and awards TowerBrook had also added a few new investments to the European portfolio: Odlo, a small Swiss-based maker of sports underwear and apparel, GSE, a provider of facilities for large logistics and distribution companies, and Archimica, a manufacturer of pharmaceutical components. All were investments that had barely been reported in the financial press, which suited TowerBrook partners' discreet approach to business.

Robert told Ramez of the problems he was having with Tamara at Jimmy Choo, trouble that was compounded when in early November 2006 Tamara appeared on the cover of the European edition of *Newsweek*, which hailed her as one of the most powerful women in business. The feature focused on her leadership skills. This was a slap in the face to Robert, since he had been the business brain behind the growth of the company since 2001. Far from being dissuaded by Robert's complaints, Ramez was enthused. This was exactly the kind of "distressed situation" he prided himself on specializing in. He realized Jimmy Choo was a phenomenal business but that the management issues would scare off other potential purchasers. It was likely to be an exclusive sale, and this time around he had the advantage.

On November 17 Ramez and Robert met Lyndon with a preliminary offer to discuss the key points of the deal. Lyndon was firm on two things: that the price should be at least £185 million ($340 million), and that although it was Robert who had brought the deal to TowerBrook, Tamara had to be happy with the deal before it could go through. Although he did not explain his reasoning at the time, Lyndon had to ensure that Lion Capital would not be publicly perceived as a firm that sold companies out from under their founders. Unofficially, Lyndon did not care much whether Tamara remained involved in Jimmy Choo or not. As a majority shareholder, Lion Capital had drag-along rights that impeded any minority shareholder from blocking a sale. But if she were to complain publicly about the sale, it could have negative consequences for Lion Capital when they tried to buy other companies. Who would want to sell to someone who had pushed out the face of the brand? Lyndon and Ramez agreed that until December 22, TowerBrook would have exclusive access to Jimmy Choo data and key staff and that Lyndon would not solicit any other offers or share company figures and information with any other parties.

Lyndon then encouraged Ramez to meet with Tamara as soon as possible to get her on board. She was as yet unaware of the potential sale, and the longer that situation lasted, the more alienated she would feel. But when the two met at TowerBrook offices, Ramez failed to win her over. Not that he cared much, winning her over was not his main objective at this time. He was quite happy to do the deal without her. His "this deal is going to happen with you or without you" approach made Tamara furious—and distraught. She called Lyndon and begged him not to sell the company to TowerBrook. She threatened to go to the media, as Lyndon had feared. Then she set about finding her own buyer.

Using her links with Riccardo Pavoncelli, a banker at Lazard and the husband of one of the women in her social circle, Tamara made contact with a Saudi Arabian company that she believed was interested in acquiring Jimmy Choo. Tamara was flown to several meetings abroad where she explained all about the Jimmy Choo company.

Although Lyndon knew about Tamara's conversations with the company, he could not entertain even nonbinding offers until after December 22, when TowerBrook's exclusivity expired. With that deadline approaching, TowerBrook was plowing ahead on its due diligence—analyzing figures, interviewing members of the team, and evaluating employment contracts such as Tamara's. To remain a part of Jimmy Choo, she was demanding £1 million ($2 million) a year in total compensation, half for her personal expenses and half for her salary. Something Ramez thought was completely out of the question.

Which was not to say he didn't value her at all. Having had the chance to speak to most of the staff at Jimmy Choo, Ramez had begun to reconsider the importance of Tamara's role in the company. The more he came to understand the business, the more it became clear that she was crucial to the running of the company. While some might have thought she didn't deserve to be on a magazine cover as one of the fifteen most powerful women in the world, that did not mean she should be let go easily. Far from it. She was, he decided, important to maintaining the brand's image. Not because she was the public face of the brand, but because everyone at Jimmy Choo said she was the brand's visionary—at least where product was concerned.

On December 19, with the end of exclusivity looming and knowledge that there was another potential buyer waiting in the wings, Ramez began to push to complete the sale. Lyndon refused, saying that Tamara was still not happy and her approval had always been one of the conditions of the sale. As far as Ramez was concerned, it was not part of the agreement. He started to think that the situation was becoming too complicated for such a pricey deal. Seemingly endless phone calls from Tamara's powerful friends, including Harvey Weinstein, urging him to keep her on board only encouraged his reticence.

Later that week, on December 23, the day after TowerBrook's exclusivity expired, Lyndon received a nonbinding offer from the Saudi Arabian company for £200 million ($363 million). On Christmas Eve, he received a message saying, "Patience is required, the Chairman is away but when he returns [we] will move faster than any buyer Lion had ever seen." Lyndon had his doubts. A few days later an embarrassed Riccardo Pavoncelli told Lyndon that the deal was off but that he had no idea why. Suddenly TowerBrook was again the only game in town.

Keen to keep the deal alive, Lyndon left his ski vacation in Whistler, Canada, to meet a distraught Tamara at Soho House, the member's club in New York's Meatpacking District. He talked her through the best way to deal with the TowerBrook team. Back in London, Ramez was also eager for a fresh start and arranged another meeting with Tamara. Ahead of that meeting, Tamara sat down and, with help from her adviser Mark Bolland, the former deputy private secretary to the Prince of Wales, set out to Ramez what she saw as her strengths, and Robert's weaknesses. She compared herself to designers Helmut Lang and Jil Sander, both of whom were removed from the houses that bear their names and whose brands suffered from the loss. She also compared herself to both Tom Ford and

Ralph Lauren, who, although they do little actual designing, are regarded as the keepers of their brands' vision, as she saw herself. She urged Ramez to go back to the key members of the Jimmy Choo staff and conduct another round of interviews based on the subject of creative due diligence. If she were not to remain the creative lead of the business, she said, she would prefer to sell her stake in Jimmy Choo now. She compared acquiring a business without the creative stimulus at the heart, namely her, to buying a property without the title deeds.

If ever there were thoughts to strike fear into the heart of a private equity investor, these were those. "Private equity is scared by the creative side," said a former employee of the company, who was there at the time. "Particularly if they think it is going to disappear." The inexact science of creating desirable products is the one part of the business investors will never fully comprehend, and therefore cannot be sure they will be able to duplicate. Less worrying were some of Tamara's other arguments. She took much of the credit for many of the accomplishments of Robert and the rest of the team—including her father—over the last ten years, asserting that she had been responsible for the development of the business in the U.S., including picking all store locations, designing the stores, and deciding how they were to be managed and stocked. Likewise, she tried to take credit for establishing the way production worked in Italy, claiming that it ran exactly as she had set it up a decade earlier. She then accused Robert of managing through fear, unreasonable pressure, and anger, suggesting that if he ceased to be involved in the day-to-day management of the company productivity would significantly and immediately improve.

Ramez suspected that some of her arguments were born out of desperation, but he agreed with her larger point—that she should stay. He lowered her total compensation to £600,000 ($1,110,000)—£300,000 as salary and £300,000 in benefits, including a clothes allowance, a stylist, and a chauffeur. He rejected other of her requests, like a board seat for Kris Thykeir, a public relations executive who had worked with Matthew Freud.

By the end of January Robert began to understand that he was the one who could make this deal happen. Ramez, still loyal to Robert for bringing him the deal, said he would pull out altogether rather than betray Robert and do the deal without him, but … could he not make it work with Tamara? No way. Although they had been bickering frequently before, Robert was so put off by Tamara's tactics that the relationship between them had deteriorated fatally. Becoming a happy team again was not a realistic option. And Robert knew that if the deal went sour he would be stuck at Jimmy Choo, with Lion Capital and Tamara, which was the worst possible outcome. Beyond that, it could have disastrous consequences for his personal wealth—much of which was tied up in Jimmy Choo shares. After a few days of soul-searching and back-and-forth conversations with various advisers, Robert came to Ramez with a proposal. In exchange for being able to cash out most of his stake in Jimmy Choo, and for a generous portion of additional sweet equity and a seat on the board, he would back out gracefully and let the deal go through without him. He would even manage the company during the transition period until a new CEO could be named. Ramez agreed.

At the offices of TowerBrook's lawyers, located at the famous London building known as the Gherkin, the closing proceedings advanced at the usual slow pace. Every team had its own meeting room, six in total, in which to retreat as the last bits of negotiating the agreements proceeded. Finally they were finished, only this time there were no champagne corks popping at the signing. It had been a real struggle to get there.

The deal was signed and announced by the parties on Sunday, February 4, 2007. The news made the front page of the *Financial Times*, taking the market somewhat by surprise. Jimmy Choo was valued at £185 million ($336 million), of which £170 million ($309 million) was paid upfront and a performance fee of £15 million ($27 million) was to be paid a year later, if the company met its targets. This was a hefty multiple of 2.2 times the sales, and close to 10 times the operating profits of 2007. The Lion Capital investment had more than doubled in just over two years. TowerBrook brought another finance group into the deal with them. Gala Capital, the secretive Spanish private equity vehicle that invested the money of some of Spain's wealthiest individuals and family offices, including Alicia Koplowitz, one of Spain's wealthiest women and the former chairman of the construction group Dragados; and the del Pino family, owners of Ferrovial, a major Spanish construction company, and of the UK airport operator BAA. Gala Capital had been an adviser to George Soros Funds since 2005 and was among TowerBrook's "friends" in the Spanish market, with whom they often looked at and shared investment opportunities.

The transaction was over, and according to the press release jointly issued by Jimmy Choo, TowerBrook, and Lion Capital, Robert and Tamara would continue in their current roles as CEO and president of the company, in addition to remaining significant shareholders in the company and members of the board. An article that appeared in *Women's Wear Daily* said that Robert and TowerBrook would be looking to do more luxury deals together up to a value of $500 million (£275 million), something that had been discussed earlier in the process but that would never materialize. Instead Robert's future ventures were done with Jimmy Choo's first private equity owner, Phoenix.

When all the paperwork was done, Tamara was the second-largest shareholder, with a stake in the low teens. Gala Capital ended up with a stake in Jimmy Choo close to 10 percent, making it the third-largest shareholder. Thanks to his sweet equity deal with Ramez, Robert still remained the fourth-largest shareholder, despite the fact he would no longer be actively involved in the day-to-day running of the business. The remaining 65 to 70 percent stake was TowerBrook's.

As is usual in a private equity deal, part of the acquisition price

would be financed with debt. Swiss bank UBS was the underwriter
of the roughly £90 million ($163 million) in debt that TowerBrook
would add to Jimmy Choo's balance sheet. The 5 times leverage
ratio on 2007 EBITDA was as steep as that which was put on the
company after the Lion Capital purchase, which was about 5 times
EBITDA. The debt was mostly senior, meaning that should the
company go into bankruptcy, it would be paid off first. And it had
collateral privileges, meaning it was guaranteed by the assets of the
company. As is often the case, some of the debt was subsequently
syndicated, or sold, to other banks and financial institutions. Robert
and Alison Egan embarked on the traditional road show across
the City of London in late February and early March 2007. They
successfully drummed up demand for that debt among various
interested institutions. The debt offering was oversubscribed two
times.

When the post-deal euphoria evaporated, the reality about
Robert's role at Jimmy Choo became clear. The news of Robert's
departure was first reported by *Women's Wear Daily* in May 2007,
but no one was particularly surprised. The rumor had been making
the rounds in the luxury goods circles since TowerBrook had arrived.
It had even appeared in the unlikely pages of British *Vogue*, which
had done a feature on Tamara. And indeed, by the time the *WWD*
story appeared, the farewell party for Robert was well over. It had
already taken place in April, two months before his departure from
the company in June, to make it coincide with a week of pricing
meetings, for which many of the Jimmy Choo staffers from around
the world flew in. Robert had specifically told Alison that she was
not to authorize the spending of any Jimmy Choo money for a
party. But after seven years she had her first opportunity to directly
disregard his instructions. Alison phoned TowerBrook, who told her
to spend as much as she wanted to. When Robert entered Home
House, the private member's club on Portland Square, he thought
he was simply going to dinner. Instead he was greeted with hundreds
of images of his own face. Hannah and Maggie, Robert's former

assistant, who had risen through the ranks to become head of store development, had organized a unique twist for the party. All guests wore masks with Robert's face. Employees who could not make it to London joined via streaming video from various offices and stores of Jimmy Choo around the world. Robert was given a red leather scrapbook from Asprey filled with photos of the best moments from his career at Jimmy Choo, and last but not least, he was given a giant pair of red patent leather Jimmy Choo stilettos in size 43 (a U.S. 9.5), manufactured specially for him. As the evening's finale, he put them on and modeled them without shame for all the guests—the guys from TowerBrook, the guys from Phoenix, and the entire office staff. Everyone except Tamara, who did not attend.

Fifteen

THE BIG GUNS MOVE IN

IN LATE JANUARY 2007, while the executives at TowerBrook were going over the details of their deal, they were also beginning to look for someone to fill Robert's shoes. In this they had some help. One of the partners at TowerBrook was Andrew Rolfe, the man who had run the wildly successful Pret A Manger sandwich chain in the UK before moving to U.S. clothing retailer Gap to run its international division. His specialty at TowerBrook was in branding and retail. He was the best person at TowerBrook to identify a new CEO for Jimmy Choo.

They needed to search for a candidate that was both a strong and experienced manager to lead the brand into the future, but that also had the soft side needed to repair some of the fractures in the staff caused by the tensions between Robert and Tamara. Andrew knew just the person. He had met Joshua Schulman while working at Gap. Andrew had been in charge of the $1.7 billion (£1 billion) international division at Gap for two years, and Joshua had reported to him. Although Andrew had left Gap in February 2006 to join TowerBrook, he and Joshua stayed in close touch. Andrew's previous experience was primarily in food, not fashion—and certainly not luxury. He found that Joshua, a fashion insider, was able to explain clearly to him the strengths and weaknesess of the various brands that were looking for funding. He had spoken with Joshua earlier during the due diligence process to ask for his thoughts on Jimmy Choo. At the time no change in management was envisioned. But then in January he called back to say there would be a shake-up after all and TowerBrook would be looking for a new CEO.

Joshua's managerial experience couldn't have been more different from Robert's. While Robert was by nature an entrepreneur, who had already been CEO at Lacroix and Ferré before Jimmy Choo, Joshua had spent eight years at Gucci Group working in a strictly structured environment.

Gucci Group was known as one of the best training grounds for talented luxury goods managers. Executives felt stifled at LVMH, which had a highly political atmosphere, due to the formal French nature of Bernard Arnault, while at Gucci Group they were allowed more freedom under the American-style leadership of Domenico De Sole. Domenico, an Italian by birth, had become an American citizen, and was proud of the American management style of the Gucci Group. Many of his top hires and deputies, including Brian Blake, one of the longest-serving senior managers, who had held various posts; Mark Lee, who was given the challenge of building YSL; and Gucci Group's CFO Robert Singer were American born and trained. The language of Gucci Group was that of Seventh Avenue, and divisions in the company mirrored those at brands like Ralph Lauren. Everyone had a title (unlike at the European brands, where managers frequently mocked the American practice of bestowing lavish titles on every executive no matter how inconsequential), everyone had set responsibilities, and everyone was able to act autonomously. "We had the greatest talent in the world," said Domenico. "Everyone wanted to work for us because I wasn't making all the decisions myself. I told them, 'No bullshit, no politics, let's just go out there and make money.'" It also helped that the company was public, no longer controlled by a family or a patron who made all the decisions. "There was no single owner," said Domenico. "It had to have a very professional structure."

Joshua Schulman's title when he was at Gucci Group was a long one—executive vice president of worldwide merchandising and distribution for Yves Saint Laurent. He was one of the managers who left Gucci after the departure of Tom Ford and Domenico. He then joined Gap, where he was hired as the senior vice president of international strategic alliances and was quickly given more responsibilities as the vice president of merchandising for Gap in Japan. Josh left Gap to become president of the Kenneth Cole brand in October 2006, but before he had a chance to do much work, he got a phone call from Andrew with an offer he couldn't refuse. It was a chance to lead another major brand, but this one, Jimmy Choo, had the same luxury heritage he had been schooled in while at Gucci Group. Kenneth Cole's brand was much more mainstream and more like a designer version of Gap. Aside from its luxury positioning, Jimmy Choo had another key advantage for Josh: It was neither too big nor too small. He thought it was just the right size for a manager with his experience going into his first role as CEO. Three days after the press release announcing the sale of Jimmy Choo to TowerBrook was issued, on February 7, Josh was in London to interview with Ramez, who had become chairman of the board of Jimmy Choo after the acquisition, as well as with Robert and Tamara.

It is easy to see why Tamara felt comfortable with Josh. For one thing they had similar childhoods. They both had grown up in Beverly Hills and even attended the same elementary school, El Rodeo, although not at the same time (Josh is several years younger than Tamara). But more important, it was readily apparent that Josh was a very different leader from Robert. Where Robert was exciting, albeit fiery and demanding, Josh was serene, measured, and calm. It was almost impossible to imagine him in a screaming rage, no matter what the circumstances. Not everyone thought it would be a change for the better. Some on staff claimed that part of the success at Jimmy Choo was actually because of the tension between Tamara and Robert, which can lead people to push themselves to do their best work. Would a softer style make people complacent?

Meanwhile Andrew did some additional checks to make sure that

Josh was indeed the right candidate. Andrew also knew Domenico De Sole, who he met when Domenico was a member of the board at Gap. Andrew called Domenico to ask his opinion of Josh. "He asked me, 'Do you think he can run a company?'" Domenico said. "And I said, 'Yes, I think he's terrific.'" Aside from calls to personal contacts, one of the top executive search firms in the world, Egon Zehnder, was hired not to find new candidates, but solely to help check Josh's references and conduct a thorough leadership assessment and evaluation of him. They said if they had been asked to find a candidate, Josh would have been the one.

The announcement of Josh's new job took place on April 18. Kenneth Cole, the man, was not too pleased to find he would be losing his new star less than one year after he had joined the company. Josh felt guilty about it, too, and told friends that leaving Kenneth Cole so quickly after having joined was his only regret about the move.

By the time Josh began work in early June, he was well versed in the challenges facing the company. Fortunately, his first public task within weeks of his arrival was not at all unpleasant. On June 25 he and Tamara unveiled the largest Jimmy Choo store in the world, the revamped location on Madison Avenue, which was three thousand square feet. As was the case in 1998 when the first New York store opened, it was quickly followed by the opening of a new Jimmy Choo store in Los Angeles, this time on Rodeo Drive. Tamara said, "The brand should be on Rodeo now. That's where it belongs, with the right neighbors." The original location next to Vidal Sassoon that had been found by Philip Rogers was closed. Celebrities like Debra Messing, Angie Harmon, Lisa Kudrow, and Tamara's new Halston colleague Harvey Weinstein were all there, but two of the key players in the company's history were left out. Although she was instrumental in making Jimmy Choo into a household name in celebrity homes, Marilyn Heston, the company's first PR rep in L.A., wasn't invited to the party. Neither was Tamara's mother, Ann. Nevertheless, hundreds of people were, and eventually the Beverly Hills police arrived to shut the party down. It then continued at the home of Wendi Murdoch, wife of media mogul Rupert Murdoch.

The party was an important one for Tamara. A new store in L.A. should have been a homecoming of sorts. After all, her mom and two brothers lived there. But now it seemed more an outward and very public expression of the way her life had changed. She was a full-fledged celebrity now. She had perfected her own red-carpet smile. Her new boyfriend, actor Christian Slater, was a reformed Hollywood bad-boy actor, and together they made a perfect couple—for the paparazzi. Photos of Tamara frolicking topless on the beach while on vacation in the Caribbean island of Saint Barths with Christian had been recently published in the UK papers. At the store opening she posed with celebrity after celebrity for the cameras—it was part of the job. But Ann was not there to witness her daughter's success and ever-growing public profile. Unable to come to an agreement on the disputed wayward Jimmy Choo shares that had come to light in the sale to Lion Capital (which are worth roughly $8 million [£4 million]), Tamara and her mother were no longer speaking to each other.

On Robert's way out in June 2007, the first two licensing agreements since Jimmy had licensed his own name, eyewear with Safilo and fragrances with Selective Beauty, were announced. Although the deals had been orchestrated by Robert, the launches would be overseen by Josh. Soon to follow Robert out of the company were some of Jimmy Choo's senior managers: Alison Egan, Licensing Director Muriel Zingraff, and the head of PR, Tara ffrench-Mullen, left in his wake.

On his side, Ramez was taking a significantly more interventionist approach at Jimmy Choo than its previous owner, Lyndon. Not only was he an active chairman of the board, but also he had four members of TowerBrook spending most of their time minding the Jimmy Choo investment, one of them on full-time assignment to help Josh.

When the hangover of the store openings subsided, Josh, like Robert before him, began to reconsider the various strategic moves at Jimmy Choo. Josh's strategy was not dramatically different from Robert's. He wanted to do many of the same things that Robert had done, but now that the company was larger and more successful, he wanted to do them bigger and better. His main focus would be on improving branding; enhancing the product in terms of design, merchandising, and deliveries; and continuing the fast pace of store openings. It wasn't just that some of the systems in place could be revamped; it was that the entire industry had changed dramatically. No longer were shoes a second thought. They were now the new It item, quickly replacing handbags in importance and costing almost as much.

Whereas in the early days of Jimmy Choo the only competition on the luxury shoe market front came from Manolo Blahnik, now there were new and serious competitors everywhere. Besides the shoe ranges launched by nearly every fashion designer, from Dior to Dolce & Gabbana, the famous Italian luxury leather goods houses like Prada and Gucci continued to develop their shoe offerings. Ferragamo, once the shoe brand of choice for Hollywood and royalty, was beginning to shake the dust off of the conservative image it had developed since the 1980s. Bally, once synonymous with sensible Swiss shoes, had hired Brian Atwood, an American shoe designer with a cult celebrity following, and charged him with the seemingly impossible task of making the brand sexy. The French were not going to sit quietly on the sidelines either. Rebounding from the early 1990s, years that witnessed the decline of brands like Stephane Kélian and Charles Jourdan, the French were getting back in the shoe game—and winning. Chanel, which had initially started to push shoes in 2000 as an entry-price product to entice new customers to the brand, was tweaking its designs to appeal to younger and more fashion-conscious customers. Pierre Hardy, the women's shoe designer for Hermès, had started his own line, which was becoming much better known thanks to a collaboration with Gap, and the 1960s brand Roger Vivier had been revived by Diego Della Valle, the major shareholder and chairman of Tod's.

Its collections by the French designer Bruno Frisoni were getting raves from fashion editors and customers alike. But bigger and more threatening than them all was the Red Menace.

The red soles of Christian Louboutin shoes are one of the most powerful icons of luxury today. They are the perfect way to show off, just to the people who are in the know, what kind of shoes one is wearing. The very sight of them brings despair to shoe designers and CEOs of shoe companies everywhere, some of whom resorted to copying them, prompting Louboutin to file for trademark protection in 2007. But it is not the red soles that make Louboutin creations appealing. His designs have a light and elegant, modern and sexy touch that has captured the imagination of the fashion zeitgeist. Louboutin had worked with Roger Vivier before starting his own collection. In 1992 he opened his first store, in Paris's bohemian-chic Saint-Germain neighborhood. By the end of 2008, Louboutin had thirteen boutiques worldwide, including, most upsettingly for Jimmy Choo, a shop-in-shop concession in Harvey Nichols, which had long been their sole domain. Harvey Nichols stocked an array of shoe brands, but only Jimmy Choo had a shop-in-shop until they opened one with Louboutin. Although the company is still privately held by its founder like Manolo Blahnik, it has none of Manolo's fear of wholesale distribution. Louboutin was selling approximately £132 million ($260 million) at retail by the end of 2007, compared with Jimmy Choo's £250 million ($500 million).[70]

With all these new shoe brands on the market, more floor space to sell them was needed. Department stores like Saks Fifth Avenue and Bloomingdale's devoted entire floors to shoes. The shoe department at Saks in New York is a block long and has its own zip code, 10022-SHOE. Browns, the famous London fashion boutique where Tamara started her career, decided an all-shoe store was in order and was planning to dedicate what once had been Browns bridal boutique on Davies Street entirely to shoes. Just as Zara and TopShop became adept at taking the best and most wearable of high-fashion trends and reproducing them at bargain basement prices, lower-tier footwear brands like Nine West and the online store Piperlime (owned by Gap) started to hire designers and consultants (including Rachel Zoe, Tamara's friend from Halston) to turn out collections that were the fast-fashion equal in shoes.

But just as things were looking up in the world of shoes, the world economy tripped. Within weeks of Josh's arrival at Jimmy Choo, in the summer of 2007, the financial markets started to tumble, a consequence of the subprime mortgage crisis in the United States. The U.S. economy was under threat, and given the slide in home prices, it was impossible to imagine that the consumer—even the luxury consumer—would not suffer in the months to come.

Luxury brands, Jimmy Choo among them, did not seem to notice any dramatic slowdown at first. If anything, they continued to enjoy reassuring and, in most cases, surprisingly high growth rates, even in the beleaguered U.S. market, which was still the largest for Jimmy Choo. Even as the crisis worsened, Jimmy Choo held its own. It had reached revenues of over £85 million ($170 million) in 2007, and was expected to achieve £110 million ($220 million) by 2008, an increase of close to 30 percent over 2007.

In order to hold his own against Robert's daunting legacy, Josh was going to have to succeed in these ferociously competitive times. He began in his own backyard—the United States. The business in the U.S.—twenty-two stores plus the important wholesale business—needed someone to run it. Robert had already identified Brian Henke, a ten-year Prada veteran who would become the president of the U.S. subsidiary, but it was Josh who, after conducting his own search, signed his contract. Josh also organized the buying by region, under the control of Lisa Bonfante, who was hired away from Chanel to become head of merchandise planning.

From now on, at the start of each selling season, all of the regional heads would meet at the Jimmy Choo showroom in Milan and be briefed on the collection and given guidance on how to buy it for their specific stores. In the past the buying process was more freewheeling with less central direction, which was appropriate for a smaller company. From Burberry Josh also hired Michelle Ryan as senior vice president of merchandising and commerical development. She would oversee three critical areas: merchandising, commercial development, and licensing. She would provide commercial feedback to the creative teams and ensure that the collections were structured with a balance of fashion, price, and function. In addition she would manage the relationship with franchising and licensing partners (Safilo, Selective Beauty, and any others to come) and with wholesale accounts outside of the U.S.

Without Robert around Tamara and Sandra were working happily together again. Josh also worked with them on the product to make sure that the right balance between basic styles and fashion styles (or icons and innovations, as they are known internally) was achieved. When Robert was at the helm, he would push for a large collection of basics that were sure to sell every season. Tamara would always push for more of the glamorous and fashion-forward shoes she loved, and finally Robert suggested they should be grouped in a different collection, the Catwalk Collection. Josh understood the separation between design and commerce, but he had a knack for bringing them together. His former colleagues at YSL credited him with being instrumental in the launch of the successful YSL accessories collections. One of the first things the design team had to address at Jimmy Choo was the current trend in shoes. No sooner did Josh take his seat at the desk, than shoe designers decided to rethink even the most basic elements of the shoe, often turning out creations that were more oddities than footwear. Shoes without heels, shoes with seven-inch heels, or with huge platforms, made the pages of many fashion magazines. But Josh knew that Jimmy Choo should watch the crazy shoe trend from the sidelines. Instead he wanted to ensure that the big fashion trends were represented, but in subtle ways. Choo shoes took on a more aggressive edge, but this was seen in touches, like a zipper down the front of a shoe or metal grommets as a decorative feature.

But even as Josh and Tamara were flirting with the big fashion trends, they were wholeheartedly embracing the way fashion houses did business. They decided that deliveries to the stores should mimic the fashion calendar, which was undergoing a major upheaval. The old days of two major collections—fall/winter and spring/summer—were fast fading into history. Now, almost as important were the so-called pre-collections: cruise or resort, which arrive in the stores in November, and the pre-fall, which arrives in stores in June. Fashion houses like Chanel and Gucci had started to host massive parties and fashion shows to promote those additional collections, and in January 2008 the city of Florence began hosting a formal week of catwalk shows to present them. "In the future we are sure that all companies will start presenting collections four times a year," said Raffaello Napoleone, the CEO of Pitti Imagine, which organizes the Florence trade shows. For shoes and accessories, those pre-collections were becoming even more important than the collections themselves, and in many cases accounted for close to 60 to 70 percent of the total season's orders. Although Jimmy Choo had been offering four collections since Robert's days, Josh started to emphasize the pre-collections (which had more basics than the more trend-driven main collections), and officially launched the most fashion-driven Catwalk Collection to the press and retailers during the fashion shows. By late 2008, Jimmy Choo was offering six collections a year.

To show off its improved wares, the company devoted more money to advertising and promotion than ever before, including producing an oversized forty-eight-page bound catalog that would be mailed to the best customers twice a year. And for the first time there was an online advertising campaign to support their booming e-commerce business. No longer would Tamara solely decide what the campaigns would look like. Art director Raul Martinez, who had worked with the famously demanding editor Anna Wintour at *House & Garden* and at *Vogue* before forming AR, the New York agency, was also brought on board. He had previous experience with clients such as Valentino, Brooks Brothers, and Banana Republic. Forget about

film directors shooting minor celebrities—the first campaign under
AR was shot by famous fashion photographer Terry Richardson and
featured top-model Angela Lindvall lounging around another AR
client, the Plaza Hotel, surrounded by Jimmy Choo accessories and
strutting out its doors in electric blue Jimmy Choo shoes. The hard-
to-please members of the Fashion Spot Internet forum were almost
unanimous in their praise. One member said, "Flawless, I love it.
This is the first time that I like a Jimmy Choo ad."

Josh also wanted to improve the coordination between product,
public relations, and advertising and marketing. For the first time
since Robert brought the public relations function in-house, Josh
decided to seek outside input. Ed Filipowski is an old hand in the
fashion game, having managed one of the industry's most respected
PR companies, KCD, for twenty-five years. Ed is also the partner of
Mark Lee, the former CEO of YSL and Gucci, under whom Josh
first worked. KCD was founded in 1984 as Keeble Cavaco & Duka,
after the company's founders, Kezia Keeble, Paul Cavaco, and John
Duka. Kezia and Paul had been stylists working together when Kezia
left Paul for their friend John. In a modern take on the love triangle,
the three decided to go into business together. Tragically John died
of AIDS in 1989 and Kezia died of breast cancer the following year.
Ed had been hired in 1985 after sending Kezia a large bouquet of
flowers and asking for an interview. He and one of their first hires,
Julie Mannion, took over, and in 1992 Paul sold them his share of the
company. They changed the name to KCD in 1996. Whereas Kezia
had become famous for launching new talent, including designer
Anna Sui, artist Stephen Sprouse, and photographers Bruce Weber
and Steven Meisel, Ed and Julie decided to focus on their strengths.
Ed would do long-term PR strategy for designers and brands, and
Julie would produce parties and events, including fashion shows.
It was such an unusual move at the time that it warranted a major
feature in the *New York Times*. Over the years KCD has worked with
just about every major fashion label, including Gucci, Marc Jacobs,
Chanel, and Versace. Agencies like Ed's tend to be the most active

on the two ends of a brand's life cycle—in the beginning, when a company is so small it cannot afford to have staff people in all the key cities and later, as the brand reaches such a size that it needs an experienced leader to coordinate all of the PR efforts around the globe. With Jimmy Choo stores opening in places as far as Kuala Lumpur, São Paulo, and Phoenix, it would be part of the job of KCD to help manage priorities.

A strategic priority at Jimmy Choo continued to be expanding retail distribution. The relentless march of store openings at Jimmy Choo continued throughout 2008, with twenty-two new locations scheduled to open. With the United States pretty well penetrated, the focus was now on Europe, and boutiques opened on La Croisette in Cannes, Paseo de Gracia in Barcelona, Via Condotti in Rome, as well as the opening of the Gaza flagship in Tokyo, their first freestanding location in Japan. The increased Jimmy Choo turnover meant the stores founded under Josh's reign were able to sit right next to the most established brands in the world, brands like Hermès and Louis Vuitton. He did not have to rely on cunning as Robert did in the founding of the miracle store on avenue Montaigne in Paris.

As the business at Jimmy Choo continued to grow so did Tamara's image as a top businesswoman. In August 2008 she was appointed a director of the board of U.S. cosmetics giant Revlon, making her one of the few British women on the board of a U.S. publicly listed corporation.

What didn't improve was her relationship with her mother. In January 2008 Tamara decided to file a very public civil lawsuit in California against her mother. In a statement issued to the press she stated, "It is with great sadness that I take this action, but I see no other way to protect my daughter's interests, which are my paramount concern. The property in question was to help secure my daughter's future, and I am baffled by my mother's refusal to return assets which rightfully do not belong to her. The action I have initiated today seems the only course available to me."

Much as they tried over the past few years since the sale to Lion

Capital had taken place in November 2004, Tamara and her mother had not been able to agree how the proceeds of the sale were to be divided. In the lawsuit documents Tamara alleges that her mother agreed that she, Ann, would receive through her trust her share of the proceeds of the sale in cash and, in return, Tamara would receive through her trust, 100 percent of the stock and the unsecured bonds, plus a lesser amount of cash. Tamara contends that her mother breached that agreement because she has failed to transfer the shares that ended up in her trust and has denied that any such agreement was ever reached. Ann, for her part, has claimed that the agreement was for a division of the sale proceeds in equal value between hers and her daughter's trusts and that this involved a division of the extra shares between the two trusts. This dispute will hopefully be resolved when the case is scheduled to come to trial sometime in 2009.

But parallel litigation continues in Jersey between the various trust's trustees, focused on mistakes apparently made by the professional advisers in giving effect to the agreed division of proceeds. The Jersey case is expected to be heard in April 2009, but it is not clear if that decision will affect the L.A. case. What is clear is that courts in California and Jersey will ultimately decide how the sale proceeds should be divided, with a real possibility that different results will be reached in each case, leading to potentially further bitterly fought litigation between mother and daughter.

At the end of September 2008, as the stock market took the greatest hit since 1929, and as thousands of bankers were laid off and the highly anticipated IPOs of Ferragamo and Prada were postponed, Josh and Tamara sat giving interviews from the plush surroundings of another gleaming new store, this time in Paris's rue Saint-Honoré. Their message was clear and consistent—that everything at Jimmy Choo was just fine. More than fine. Sales were on track to reach the target of £110 million ($203 million) in 2008 and EBITDA should almost double from the levels achieved in 2006 to over £22 million ($44 million).

Beyond the figures, the company was also getting global recognition, and the nominations and awards the company received were piling up. Jimmy Choo shoes were often featured on the red carpet at various awards shows, but now the company was the star of the red carpet. In addition to receiving the British Glamour Women of the Year award for Accessories Designer in May, and the British Accessories Council Excellence (ACE) Brand of the Year award, the company was one of the five nominees to receive the Walpole Award for British Luxury Brand. Most important, it had also been shortlisted for the coveted British Designer Brand of the Year award, granted by the British Fashion Council, that in the past had been received by Stella McCartney, Burberry, and on four separate occasions each, Alexander McQueen and John Galliano.

But observers would wonder whether a brand founded on the ethos of glamour and decadence would be able to flourish in the tough times that lay ahead. At least one part of the brand was already suffering, but for different reasons. Back in London, Mr. Jimmy Choo was considering closing his couture business. An assistant said it was getting impossible to find companies willing to supply the components he needed in such small numbers. The sample shoes on the shelves were evidence of this—pointy toes, kitten heels— they hadn't changed since he opened the boutique, some ten years earlier. Without Tamara, it seemed Jimmy was unable to keep up with the times. But now the times were tougher than they had been in Tamara's lifetime. Fashion marches on, and at least for now, the Jimmy Choo company marches with it.

AFTERWORD

TAMARA MELLON continues to be the president of Jimmy Choo, a shareholder, and a member of the board of the company. In addition, she was appointed a member of the board at Halston and at Revlon, Inc.

SANDRA CHOI remains the creative director of Jimmy Choo.

JIMMY CHOO continues to operate his couture business from his shop in Bayswater, but was considering shuttering the business at the end of 2008 because of difficulty in obtaining components needed to stay abreast of fashion trends.

In June 2007 after leaving his post as CEO of Jimmy Choo, ROBERT BENSOUSSAN made a personal investment in Bremont, a small British luxury watch brand in September 2007, along with Jim Sharp, John Ayton (cofounder of Links of London), and Jaime Bergel (from Gala Capital, one of the investors at Jimmy Choo). In early 2008 Robert launched Sirius Equity, an investment company focusing on brands, with Jim Sharp. Jointly with another private equity fund, Stirling Square, Sirius acquired Jeckerson, an Italian premium apparel brand in May 2008. In July 2008 Sirius acquired LK Bennett, the UK shoe brand, in partnership with Phoenix Private

Equity. Robert remains a shareholder in Jimmy Choo and a member of the board of the company. He is also a member of the board at the cosmetics company Inter Parfums, French retailer Celio, and Aurenis Eaglemoss, a Franco-British publishing group.

Following the divorce from Tamara and a brief affair with the late fashion icon Isabella Blow, MATTHEW MELLON launched a new clothing line of luxury cashmere casual wear, Degrees of Freedom, with his then girlfriend, model and aspiring actress Noelle Reno, in February 2007. They broke up and Noelle left the company in May 2008 and filed a suit against Matthew in Manhattan Superior Court. Matthew has gone on to launch another fashion brand, Hanley Mellon, with another girlfriend, Nicole Hanley, a former Ralph Lauren designer and Palm Beach society girl.

Since exiting the investment in Jimmy Choo in November 2004 the team at PHOENIX EQUITY PARTNERS has made numerous investments, many of them in the consumer area, including Filofax (the stationary company, in March 2006); Radley & Co. (a UK accessories company, in February 2006); Gaucho Grill (a chain of Argentinean eateries in the UK, in August 2006, subsequently sold in December 2007); Abel & Cole (a leading retailer of organic produce, in October 2007); and Musto (the sailing gear brand, in August 2007). In July 2008, teaming up with Robert Bensoussan, they completed the acquisition of another UK shoe brand, LK Bennett. In the middle, Phoenix also completed the fund-raising for their fourth fund of £375 million in April 2006, and was named House of the Year at the BVCA Private Equity Awards in 2006.

Following the sale of Jimmy Choo in February 2007, Lyndon Lea, the founder of LION CAPITAL, started to focus his sights on a decidedly less glamorous but ultimately more stable sector—frozen foods. In a push to consolidate Europe's frozen-foods industry, Lion Capital made investments in three companies in the area (Hiestand,

Mora, and FoodVest, the owner of Findus pancakes and Young's Admiral's Pie, the UK's bestselling frozen meal). In addition, Lion purchased Vaasan & Vaasan, a Scandinavian bakery products maker, and Nidan, the leading brand of juice in Russia, in August 2007. They also completed investments in HEMA, the general retailer and the Dutch equivalent to Kmart; and in A.S. Adventure, a Belgian retailer of outdoor equipment and clothing, in November 2007. Lyndon also changed the name of his polo team from Jimmy Choo to Zacara, after his children, Zachary and Chiara.

Throughout 2007 and 2008, in the midst of the worst fund-raising environment in memory for private equity, the TOWERBROOK team successfully raised $2.8 billion (£1.5 billion) for their second fund, bringing their assets under management to close to $5 billion (£2.7 billion). TowerBrook also completed other notable investments in 2007–08: BevMo!, a California-based retailer of wine, spirits, and beer, in March 2007; pack2pack, a producer of industrial packaging, in February 2008; and Broadlane, a provider of supply-chain management to the U.S. health-care industry; as well as the sale of InfoPro Communications, a French professional information services group.

ACKNOWLEDGMENTS

O N JANUARY 11, 2005, on a cold wet London afternoon the authors met at Sagra's house near St. James's Park to talk about what we had done after leaving our respective jobs. We had met three years earlier when Lauren was a senior writer covering fashion and luxury for *Time* magazine and Sagra was the head of luxury goods equity research at J.P. Morgan. But as tea and cookies made way for wine and chips, a larger purpose for the meeting began to emerge. What if we teamed up to write books about the business of luxury? Various subjects were discussed, among them Jimmy Choo. While putting together a plan, Lauren began working with Sagra at the offices of Hemisphere One, a private equity company she was starting at the time. Some of the partners at Hemisphere One made a small personal investment in Harrys of London, the shoe company started by Matthew Mellon. The company is now part of Atelier, a private equity fund financed by Compagnie Financière Richemont, and the partners still retain a small share. For several months the British newspapers had been writing about Jimmy Choo and the people involved in it almost daily. First Jimmy Choo was sold to Hicks Muse Europe. Then the founders of Hicks Muse separated themselves (and Jimmy Choo) from their partners in the U.S. and set up Lion Capital in London. A mantra began to be heard in the office: This Would Make a Great Book. This sentiment was echoed by friends and prospective agents. The other possible subjects were shelved. On the last day of March, Lauren met with Tara ffrench-Mullen, the public relations director of Jimmy Choo, to broach the idea of an independent book. Over the next two months the authors met with then CEO of Jimmy Choo Robert Bensoussan, president Tamara Mellon, and Lyndon Lea, the majority shareholder at the time. All three could see the advantages in a high-profile book but were wary about the prospect of a project that would be outside their control. But with their knowledge and tacit permission the authors put together a proposal. Our agents, Kim Witherspoon and David Forrer at Inkwell in New York and Elizabeth Sheinkman at Curtis Brown in London, then brokered the sale to Bloomsbury.

As we were to learn later, while we were writing and marketing the proposal, internal relations between the top managers at Jimmy Choo were under great strain. Eventually the company officially decided that it would not participate. Due to this restriction, in order to bring the scenes to life, quotes from some of the key players have been taken from previously published articles. But to reconstruct the events, most of which have never been reported before, the authors have relied largely on firsthand reporting with sources in and around the company, both on and off the record. Off-the-record emissaries were received from nearly all camps. They cannot be thanked for obvious reasons. What follows is a list of people who can be thanked: A small but crucial minority.

Following the sale of Jimmy Choo to TowerBrook, Lyndon Lea had several conversations with the authors over the objections of some of his more cautious advisers because, as he said with his typical candor, "I told you I would." For this we would like to thank him. We would also like to thank Justin Abbott, the banker who had us in stitches when he told us his version of the sale to Lion Capital and provided a critical introduction to Akeel Sachak, his former colleague at Rothschild, who worked on two of the Jimmy Choo sales. Philip Rogers and Lou Rodwell, two of Tom Yeardye's oldest colleagues, both of whom worked for the company, helped fill in not only details about the earliest days of its operations, but about Tom himself. They also helped make an introduction to Ann Yeardye, Tom's widow and Tamara's mother. Despite the fact that the lawsuit her daughter filed against her was still pending, Ann, over the course of nearly twenty hours, had no qualms about speaking openly about her life with Tom and their involvement in Jimmy Choo, an almost unheard-of occurrence where lawyers and lawsuits are involved. Marilyn Heston, the woman most responsible for the now instinctual connections between Jimmy Choo shoes and celebrities, was also happy to tell us her side of the story. Cameron Silver of L.A.'s premier vintage shop, Decades, and Mark Holgate and Harriet Quick of American and British *Vogue*, respectively, all helped provide historical context and offered up suggestions for further sources. Marius Brinkhorst, a former colleague of Sagra's at J.P. Morgan and a great friend, vouched for us to Lyndon Lea and provided comments on the proposal. Tom Walker, a partner at the private equity firm CCMP Capital and also an alumnus of J.P. Morgan, provided both insights into the workings of private equity and valuable introductions. Lisa Rachal, the luxury goods analyst at Redburn Partners, was always ready to help with valuations and other tricky calculations. Ben Valentin, a barrister at 3–4 South Square, read through stacks of court filings to make sure that the few hundred words we included on the complex litigating taking place in Jersey and in Los Angeles were accurate.

We were fortunate to land the most overqualified researcher of all time, Melanie Warner, a seasoned journalist and alumna of both *Fortune* and the *New York Times*.

Many pages were written in the lavish confines of Andy and Blanche Sibbald's house in Studland, and Andy also provided an introduction to the team at Phoenix Equity Partners.

We would also like to thank Patrick McCarthy, the guardian of the Fairchild Publications legacy. Although he in no way participated in this book, every fashion journalist owes a great debt to the staff of *WWD* and *Footwear News*, which have fulfilled the mission of the founder to be the papers of record of fashion. Without the diligent work of their reporters many of the details of this—and every fashion story—would have been lost to time. The people still on staff who helped out off the record know who they are.

Most of our friends were more than willing to serve as an impromptu focus group. Silje Augustson, Miriam Shea, Tereska Buzek, Francesca Tondi, Iain Johnston, Dan and Dominique Goldstein, and Rory Tobin all kept our spirits up even as the inevitable rejections came in.

Sagra's colleagues at Reig Capital provided the flexibility needed to squeeze in more than a few interviews during her working hours.

Most important, we would like to thank our families. In addition to taking on more than his fair share of childcare—no small thing when the children in question are twins under the age of four—Dan Crowe also helped guide us through the mysterious waters of agents and publishers. Ian Rosen was our cheerleader, our taskmaster, and our landlord—taking the transformation of his house to office in stride. Isabel Rosen, Sagra's seven-year-old daughter, was an avid contributor to the title selection process (*Top Choo* was her favorite choice). Sandy Rosen, Sagra's father-in-law and an attorney in San Francisco, and his assistant Rosemary, kept us posted on the developments of the *Mellon vs. Yeardye* suit in Los Angeles Superior Court. Marcia Goldstein, Lauren's mother, proofread every page before the initial submission to Bloomsbury so that we wouldn't be embarrassed by dangling participles or spelling mistakes. Any remaining faults are ours and ours alone.

NOTES

1. Fashion Scoops: "Hey Big Spender," *Women's Wear Daily*, May 27, 2005.
2. Amanda Lynch, "Schools for Scandal," *Sunday Times* (London), July 23, 2006.
3. Barry Egan, "A Slice of Mellon," *Sunday Independent* (Ireland), October 30, 2005.
4. Liz Jones, "The Truth About My Marriage and My Toy Boy Affair With Dame Edna's Son; the Society Beauty Behind the Rise of Jimmy Choo Shoes Talks Frankly About the Affair That Made Headlines Around the World," *Evening Standard*, December 15, 2003.
5. Phoebe Eaton, "Who Is Jimmy Choo?" *New York Times*, December 1, 2002.
6. Chloé McEnery Beacham, "How We Met: Tamara Beckwith & Tamara Mellon," *Independent on Sunday* (London), August 26, 2001.
7. Egan, "Slice of Mellon."
8. Jessica Brown, "Jimmy Choo, Designer," *Draper's Record*, August 11, 2001.
9. Lizzie Enfield, "My Hols: Jimmy Choo," *Sunday Times* (London), August 12, 2001.
10. Kee Hua Chee, "How Jimmy Choo 'Lost' His Name," *Star* (UK), January 14, 2007.
11. *New Straits Times* (Malaysia), "Choo's Shoes," June 7, 1999.
12. Cat Ong, "If the Choo Fits," *Straits Times* (Singapore), June 4, 1998.
13. *New Straits Times* (Malaysia), "Royal Shoemaker Loses a Friend," September 11, 1997.
14. Stuart Husband, "No Business Like Choo Business," *Independent on Sunday* (London), February 20, 2005.
15. Eaton, "Who Is Jimmy Choo?"
16. Ibid.
17. *Sunday Times* (UK), "Head Over Heels," November 21, 1999.
18. Cassandra Jardine, "No Loafers In Tamara's World: Chief Executive Tamara Mellon Has Taken Jimmy Choo to Dizzy Heights and Made a Fortune from Spike-Heeled Boots," *Daily Telegraph*, November 23, 2001.
19. Chee, "How Jimmy Choo 'Lost' His Name."
20. Jess Cartner-Morley, "Choose Choos: High Heels, Big Bucks," *Guardian*, June 15, 2001.
21. Constance Haisma-Kwok, "Crafting an Image: At a Media Junket in Hong Kong, Jimmy Choo Designer Sandra Choi Talks Shop with FN," *Footwear News*, August 19, 2002.

22. Kee Hua Chee, "Sandra's Choice," *Star* (Malaysia), January 14, 2007.

23. Chee, "How Jimmy Choo 'Lost' His Name."

24. William Cash, "Swanky Doodle Dandy," *Tatler*, 2003

25. Ibid.

26. Ibid.

27. Ibid.

28. Samantha Conti, "Heir Conditioning," *W* magazine, December 2007.

29. Cash, "Swanky Doodle Dandy.

30. Ibid.

31. Ibid.

32. Ibid.

33. Ibid.

34. Andrea Billups, "Bush Twins Dress to Weather Publicity: High Visibility Forecast for Festivities," *Washington Times*, January 16, 2001.

35. Natasha Mann, "Choo Fetish," *Scotsman*, February 16, 1999.

36. *Sun* (London), "Heal Your Sole," November 5, 2000.

37. Vassi Chamberlain, "Oh Such a Perfect Day," *Tatler*, 2000.

38. Shane Watson, "Why All the Girls Love Valentino," *Evening Standard*, May 27, 2000.

39. Chamberlain, "Oh Such a Perfect Day."

40. Shane Watson, "The Woman Whose Shoes Are Worth £35 Million," *Evening Standard*, January 8, 2001.

41. Syrie Johnson and Emily Sheffield, "Get the Ultimate London Lifestyle and You Can Win It for Free," *Evening Standard*, April 23, 2001.

42. Evgenia Peretz, "The Lady and the Heel," *Vanity Fair*, August 2005.

43. Watson, "The Woman Whose Shoes Are Worth £ 35 Million."

44. Jardine, "No Loafers In Tamara's World."

45. Samantha Conti, "Equinox Charts Jimmy Choo Expansion," *Women's Wear Daily*, September 18, 2002.

46. Natalie Zmuda, "On Location—In the High-Stakes Battle for Customer Loyalty, Some Vendor-Operated Stores Are Now Custom-Tailoring the Shopping Experience to the Region," *Footwear News*, January 31, 2005.

47. Susan Berfield and Alexandra A. Seno, "How Dickson Poon Made Fashion Pay," *Asiaweek*, March 17, 1997.

48. *Women's Wear Daily*, "Fashion Scoops: Choo Love," September 16, 2002.

49. Ibid.

50. Carlos Grande, "Women of the World Go Choo Shopping," *Financial Times*, July 29, 2003.

51. Jess Cartner-Morley, "Bump It Up," *Guardian*, March 27, 2002.

52. Conti, "Heir Conditioning."

53. *Women's Wear Daily*, "Good Sports," August 2, 2002.

54. Kate Spicer, "Living in Hell Heaven," *Sunday Times* (London), July 13, 2003.

55. Egan, "Slice of Mellon."

56. Ibid.

57. Natalie Zmuda, "New Jimmy Choo Store Posting Strong Sales in Opening Weeks," *Footwear News*, September 8, 2003.

58. *Daily Telegraph*, "The Mellons—Back in Business?" December 3, 2003.

59. Ibid.

60. Egan, "Slice of Mellon."

61. Guy Paisner, "Speed Central to Jimmy Choo Success," Financial News Online, November 22, 2004.

62. Egan, "Slice of Mellon."

63. Peretz, "Lady and the Heel."

64. Lottie Moggach, " 'I'm Pretty Low Maintenance'—The Driving Force of Jimmy Choo Tells Lottie Moggach About Her Work Ethic, Life as a Single Mum and Where She Keeps All Those Shoes," *Financial Times*, July 9, 2005.

65. Peretz, "Lady and the Heel."

66. *Daily Mail*, "Marriage to My Playboy Billionaire Was Like Having Another Child," May 3, 2007.

67. Conti, "Heir Conditioning."

68. Katie Abel, "Empire Builders," *Footwear News*, January 7, 2008.

69. Cathy Horyn, "Halston Retreats, Again," *New York Times*, July 16, 2008.

70. Nina Jones, Christian Louboutin: "The Sole Man." *Telegraph* (London), August 10, 2008.

INDEX

A NOTE ON THE AUTHORS

Lauren Goldstein Crowe has written about the fashion industry for more than a decade. She is currently the writer of Fashion Inc., a daily online column about the fashion and luxury goods industries for *Condé Nast Portfolio*. Previously she was a senior writer at *Time* magazine, where she wrote cover stories on Gucci and Ralph Lauren. She also conceived and launched *Time*'s first ever fashion supplement, *Time Style + Design*. In June 2003, Lauren won Time Inc.'s highest honor, the President's Award. Prior to *Time*, Lauren was a writer at *Fortune* magazine in New York, where she covered fashion and luxury goods. Lauren has written freelance articles in a wide variety of newspapers and magazines, including Paris *Vogue*, *Harper's Bazaar*, the *New York Times*, British *Vogue*, the *Financial Times*, and the London *Times*. She has appeared as a fashion expert on CNN and Bloomberg Television and has been interviewed for numerous radio programs, including the BBC World Service. Lauren has a master's degree in journalism from Northwestern University, and undergraduate degrees in English and history from the University of Wisconsin-Madison.

Sagra Maceira de Rosen is the managing director of the Retail and Luxury division of Reig Capital Group, an investment company. Prior to Reig Capital, she was a highly ranked equity analyst at U.S. investment bank J.P. Morgan in London, and the head of its Global Luxury Goods Equity Research team and cohead of its European General Retail team. Sagra's career in luxury goods equity research started at Morgan Stanley, where she worked as an equity analyst in its number-one-ranked luxury goods team. Sagra has been a speaker at several luxury goods conferences and has an MBA from Columbia Business School in New York and a university degree in business administration from the Universidad de Santiago de Compostela in Spain.

A NOTE ON THE TYPE

The text of this book is set Adobe Garamond. It is one of several versions of Garamond based on the designs of Claude Garamond. It is thought that Garamond based his font on Bembo, cut in 1495 by Francesco Griffo in collaboration with the Italian printer Aldus Manutius. Garamond types were first used in books printed in Paris around 1532. Many of the present-day versions of this type are based on the *Typi Academiae* of Jean Jannon cut in Sedan in 1615. Claude Garamond was born in Paris in 1480. He learned how to cut type from his father and by the age of fifteen he was able to fashion steel punches the size of a pica with great precision. At the age of sixty he was commissioned by King Francis I to design a Greek alphabet, for this he was given the honourable title of royal type founder. He died in 1561.